The Exclusive Economic Zone

A Latin American Perspective

The "Foreign Relations of the Third World" Series

Editorial Advisory Board:

General Editor, Heraldo Muñoz, *I E I -Universidad de Chile and CERC-Academia de Humanismo Cristiano, Chile*

Carlos Fortín, *Institute of Development Studies, University of Sussex, England*

Wolf Grabendorff, *Stiftung Wissenschaft und Politik, West Germany*

Abraham Lowenthal, *Latin American Program, The Wilson Center, USA*

Luis Maira, *Instituto de Estudios de Estados Unidos, CIDE, Mexico*

Ali Mazrui, *University of Michigan, USA, and Department of Political Science, University of Jos, Nigeria*

R. Narayanan, *School of International Affairs, Jawaharlal Nehru University, India*

The Exclusive Economic Zone

A Latin American Perspective

edited by Francisco Orrego Vicuña

Westview Press • *Boulder, Colorado*

Foreign Relations of the Third World, No. 1

Westview softcover editions are manufactured on our own premises using the highest quality materials. They are printed on acid-free paper and bound into softcovers that carry the highest rating of NASTA in consultation with the AAP and the BMI.

All rights reserved. No part of this publication may be reproduced or transmitted in any form or by any means, electronic or mechanical, including photocopy, recording, or any information storage and retrieval system, without permission in writing from the publisher.

Copyright © 1984 by Westview Press, Inc.

Published in 1984 in the United States of America by
  Westview Press, Inc.
  5500 Central Avenue
  Boulder, Colorado 80301
  Frederick A. Praeger, President and Publisher

Library of Congress Catalog Card Number 83-50978
ISBN 0-86531-656-2

Composition for this book was provided by the authors.
Printed and bound in the United States of America.

5 4 3 2 1

Contents

1   THE EXCLUSIVE ECONOMIC ZONE IN A LATIN AMERICAN PERSPECTIVE: AN INTRODUCTION................. 1
Francisco Orrego Vicuña

2   THE ORIGINS OF THE CONCEPT OF AN EXCLUSIVE ECONOMIC ZONE: LATIN AMERICAN PRACTICE AND LEGISLATION.................................... 7
F. V. García-Amador

        Early Claims to Living Resources.............. 7
              The Claim to the So-called Sedentary Fisheries.................................. 7
              The Right of "Ownership and Protection" over the Seals of Bering Sea............. 8
              Claims to a zone in Moray Firth...... 10
        Proposals and Claims Relating to Conservation. 11
              Proposals Presented at the 1930 Hague Conference............................. 11
              The Truman Fisheries Proclamation (1945) 12
              The Nature of Claims Enunciated Subsequent to the Proclamation..................... 14
        Claims with Respect to Submarine Areas and Superjacent Waters........................... 15
              The Immediate Antecedents of Present-day Claims................................. 16
              The U.S. Proclamation of 1945 and other Similar Proclamations.................. 17
              The "Epicontinental Sea" and other Similar Claims.................................. 18
        The 200-Mile Maritime Zone................... 19
              The Chilean Claim of 1947 and the Four other Claims that Preceded the Santiago Declaration............................ 20
              The Santiago Declaration of 1952: Its True Legal Nature........................... 21

BNA 3/16/84

3	THE ECONOMIC INTEREST UNDERLYING THE FIRST DECLARATION ON A MARITIME ZONE................. 27
	Pilar Armanet

 Basic Principles................................ 27
 Origins of the Initiative...................... 28
 The Search for Precedents...................... 29
 Advancement of Maritime Interests.............. 30

4	THE EXCLUSIVE ECONOMIC ZONE IN THE LIGHT OF NEGOTIATIONS OF THE THIRD UNITED NATIONS CONFERENCE ON THE LAW OF THE SEA.............. 31
	Reynaldo Galindo Pohl

 The Historical Approach....................... 31
 The Process of Shaping the Exclusive Economic Zone
 33
 Interests Reconciled in the Economic Zone..... 38
 Specific Questions Relating to the Economic Zone
 43
  Delimitation........................... 43
  Coexistence of Competences............. 45
  The Sovereign Rights of Coastal States.. 47
  The Attribution of Exclusivity to the Economic Zone.......................... 48
  Scope of the "Pactum de Contrahendo".... 49
  The Economic Zone and the High Seas..... 51
  Maximum Sustainable Yield and Optimum Utilization............................ 53
  Military Uses.......................... 54
  Reservations and the Compatibility Clause
  55
  The Exclusive Economic Zone and International Custom................... 57
 The Economic Zone in the New International Economic Order................................ 58

5	THE ROLE OF INFORMAL NEGOTIATIONS IN THE SEARCH FOR A CONSENSUS ON THE LAW OF THE SEA......... 61
	Vicente Marotta Rangel

 The Expanding Scope of the Law of the Sea..... 61
 The Creation Process.......................... 62
 The Consensus Rule............................ 63
 Application of the Consensus Process in the law of the Sea...................................... 65
 Conflicting Interests......................... 67
 Importance of Informal Negotiations........... 69

6	THE LEGAL STATUS OF THE EXCLUSIVE ECONOMIC ZONE IN THE 1982 CONVENTION ON THE LAW OF THE SEA..... 75

Julio César Lupinacci

The Origins of the Exclusive Economic Zone.... 75
Basic Elements of the Latin American Position: The Montevideo and Lima Declarations.............. 80
The Concept of the Patrimonial Sea: The Santo Domingo Declaration............................ 84
African and Asian States and the Concept of an Exclusive Economic Zone: The Addis Ababa Declaration.................................... 88
The Concept of the Exclusive Economic Zone in the Negotiations of the Third United Nations Conference..................................... 91
The Concept of an Exclusive Economic Zone in the Convention, the Practice of States, and the Formation of a Customary Rule.................. 95
Current Trends Regarding the Legal Status of the Exclusive Economic Zone......................... 98
    The Exclusive Economic Zone as Part of the High Seas............................... 99
    The Exclusive Economic Zone as a Zone Sui Generis................................. 105
Basis of Application of the Sovereign Rights of the Coastal State............................... 111
Conclusions..................................... 112

7	THE EXCLUSIVE ECONOMIC ZONE: ITS LEGAL NATURE AND THE PROBLEM OF MILITARY USES................... 123

Alfonso Arias Schreiber

The Legal Nature of the Exclusive Economic Zone
.... 123
    First Thesis: The Exclusive Economic Zone is Part of the High Seas.................... 124
    Second Thesis: The Exclusive Economic Zone is a Zone Sui Generis.................... 127
    Third Thesis: The Exclusive Economic Zone is a Zone of National Jurisdiction...... 131
Military Uses in the Exclusive Economic Zone.. 139

8	THE REGIME OF FISHERIES IN THE EXCLUSIVE ECONOMIC ZONE.. 143

Hugo Caminos

Introduction.................................... 143
Basic Rules of the Regime on Fisheries in the Exclusive Economic Zone........................ 144
Special Fishing Regimes in the Exclusive Economic Zone.. 148
    Highly Migratory Species................ 148

        Marine Mammals............................ 149
        Anadromous Species........................ 150
        Catadromous Species....................... 150
        Sedentary Species......................... 151
Rights of Landlocked States and States with
Special Geographical Characteristics.......... 151
Application of the Coastal State's Laws and
Regulations in the Exclusive Economic Zone:
Controls and Supervision...................... 155

9   THE SETTLEMENT OF DISPUTES REGARDING THE LAW OF
     THE SEA AND ITS BEARING ON THE LEGAL NATURE OF THE
     EXCLUSIVE ECONOMIC ZONE....................... 159
     María Teresa Infante

     General Considerations........................ 159
     The General System of Dispute Settlement and its
     Exceptions.................................... 161
     The 1982 Convention........................... 162
     Resolution of Conflicts Regarding Fisheries and
     the Case of Scientific Research............... 164
     Summary....................................... 168

Contributors... 173
Index....:... 175
About the Book and Editor................................ 189

Francisco Orrego Vicuña

1. The Exclusive Economic Zone in a Latin American Perspective: An Introduction

One of the concepts most recently incorporated in the structure of international law is that of the Exclusive Economic Zone (EEZ). The foundation of this new institution, which has undergone a long evolutionary process, goes back as far as the earliest claims to national jurisdiction over marine resources of various types. But, the Exclusive Economic Zone is also partly the result of widespread contemporary national practices and of the diplomatic negotiations that have been conducted, concurrently, at the Third United Nations Conference on the Law of the Sea and other regional or global forums.

Precisely because it is a new concept and it springs from a variety of sources, the EEZ has not yet been the object of systematic analysis in the doctrine of international law. The studies published hitherto are few in number and are only just beginning to draw the attention of international academic organizations. Thus, for example, the first provisional report of the International Law Association's International Committee on the Exclusive Economic Zone came before the Montreal session of the conference in 1982.

Since the EEZ is indissolubly linked to Latin American practice, as reflected in national legislation and in existing regional instruments, the Institute of International Studies of the University of Chile deemed it opportune to convene a conference to discuss this topic. Held in October 1981, the conference was attended by distinguished scholars and diplomats from several countries in this region, many of whom had played a direct part in the negotiations of the United Nations Conference on the Law of the Sea. This book assembles the contributions made on that occasion and other studies that it has been thought important to include.

The first point that should be noted relates to the origins of the new concept. All Latin American writers agree that the Exclusive Economic Zone has its roots in the national claims asserted by countries of the region during the late 1940s; the first of these was the Chilean proclamation in 1947, which was followed by other similar instruments and by multilateral agreements dating from 1952. This early Latin American practice is carefully analyzed in the chapters by F. V. García-Amador and Julio César Lupinacci, which together cover more than forty years of Latin American legislation in this field. The subject is of considerable interest in the light of recent arguments suggesting different origins linked to initiatives on the part of other regions.

In addition to the historical approach, the process of creating the EEZ warrants special attention. Latin American writers, like many others throughout the world, are at one in holding that the widespread national practice already current in this respect is explicit enough to constitute a precedent on which an international customary rule can be based. In fact, the legislation of many countries, even though differing in specific approaches or modes of application, is essentially uniform as regards the basic characteristics and purposes of the exercise of national jurisdiction over the maritime space in question. Just as in the case of the continental shelf, this vast legislative movement is representative of an opinio juris in relation to the EEZ. Thus, irrespective of its expression through the Convention on the Law of the Sea, today the existence of a new consuetudinary rule can be affirmed.

At the same time, the evolution of the negotiations conducted through the Conference on the Law of the Sea is important. The analysis presented by Reynaldo Galindo Pohl, who was chairman of the Second Committee during the initial negotiations on the economic zone in the early years of the conference's work, bears valuable witness to the course of its deliberations. This type of contribution is of outstanding importance in view of the fact that almost the entire process of negotiation has been informal, with the result that there is a lack of official records that makes it extremely difficult to reconstitute the propositions and the bases that have paved the way for a compromise solution to each aspect of the problem. It is precisely to the importance of informal negotiations in the quest for a consensus on the law of the sea that Vicente Marotta Rangel refers in his study.

The Chapter by Galindo Pohl points out the basic problems that had to be examined in order to reach an understanding with respect to this new institution and the positions of the principal parties involved in the negotiation. He gives an accurate account of the nature and main characteristics of the compromise that was negotiated.

Similarly, Ambassador Galindo Pohl advances interpretations that are of special interest in view of the incipient discrepancies as to the scope of the provisions of the 1982 convention. These interpretations have the merit of being evolved in the light of the criteria that made the aforesaid compromise possible.

An essential part of this process of accommodation is that relating to the fishing regime within the EEZ and to kindred problems. The interests of the coastal states had to be reconciled with those of countries fishing in distant waters, as well as with the particular situation of the landlocked countries and of those with special geographical characteristics. At the same time, the most important of the different types of fish species needed a differentiated regime in keeping with their particular habits of life and migratory cycles, a necessity that gave rise to diverse regulations in this field. The study by Hugo Caminos, which focuses primarily on the fishing regime, offers an explanation of the different regimes referred to and of their essential components, facilitating understanding of the compromises that have intervened in the case of fishing.

The problem that has been of most lively concern to the Latin American countries in regard to the Exclusive Economic Zone has undubitably been that of its legal status. The long-standing discussions as to whether the jurisdiction exercised by a coastal state over its adjacent seas is (1) a type of specialized projection of its powers, or (2) a manifestation of its territorial sovereignty, identical with or similar to its sovereignty over the territorial sea, have continued to crop up in relation to the legal status of the EEZ. These differences arose at the outset among the members of the Permanent Commission of the South Pacific; Chile was decidedly in favor of the first approach; Ecuador leaned towards the second; while Peru adopted special modalities that revealed a preference for the latter.

The same situation recurred at a more universal level in the negotiations of the Conference on the Law of the Sea. Although the so-called territorialist group did not carry too much weight in these proceedings, it did prove influential enough to demand various accommodation formulas. The most serious source of conflict, however, was the discrepancy between the criterion of the coastal states and that of the maritime powers with regard to the specific provisions of the part of the convention on the Exclusive Economic Zone and to others of a kindred nature. This dispute accounts for the substantive compromise that was effected.

Imaginative as were the approaches adopted in the

convention to overcome the existing problems, they leave room for arguments on behalf of each of the two criteria, which in the near future will undoubtedly be reflected in conflicting interpretations. These have, in fact, already begun to rear their heads. The distinction drawn in this instrument between "sovereign rights," "jurisdiction", and "other rights and duties" obviously makes for gradation of the significance of the powers attributed to the coastal state in the maritime space under discussion, but it does not in itself settle the question of legal status. The position is much the same in respect to the subtle play of cross references with the articles relating to the high seas, which is another of the mechanisms designed for this purpose; for while it reaffirms some of the freedoms proper to the latter space, it makes no difference to the nature of the powers that the coastal state has authority to exercise.

The formula on residual rights contained in Article 59 of the convention is characterized by a balanced approach that aims at avoiding prejudgments on the question of the legal status of the EEZ and at the same time seeks to facilitate the settlement of any disputes that may arise. Perhaps one of the most important of the issues that have bearing on this matter of legal status is to be found in the sphere of the provisions for the peaceful settlement of disputes and the complicated set of exceptions and counter-exceptions appearing therein. From the study by María Teresa Infante, which looks at the problem from this angle, it can be seen that these provisions adequately safeguard the discretional powers of the coastal state.

A point of view that is shared by several authors is that the Exclusive Economic Zone can be described as a maritime space sui generis, different from the territorial sea and from the high seas although taking elements from both to combine them within a new institution. Similar efforts had been previously made in Latin America, particularly on the basis of the conceptual formulation referring to a patrimonial sea. These approaches are interesting in that they account for the modalities and characteristics of the Exclusive Economic Zone, but they too fail to solve the problem of the fundamental conflicts between one conception and the other, which are still in evidence. Probably this scenario will remain unchanged for a long time, until jurisprudence and other processes of refinement of international norms come to shed light on the real significance and scope of the provisions and concepts concerned.

This debate has been of particular importance in Latin America's case, both because of the role that this region has played in the negotiations of the Conference on the Law of the Sea and because of the characteristics of several countries' legislation. In many instances, these characteristics display contradictions or changes of direction. On other occasions different approaches have been tried out, such as that of describing the zone in terms of a territorial sea, subject, however, to regimes different from those traditionally applied. Be that as it may, the fact is that the controversy has not died down but, on the contrary, has been exacerbated in recent years, in some cases creating difficulties in connection with the signature and ratification of the new convention.

Several of the studies contained in this book take as their theme the question of the legal status of the Exclusive Economic Zone from a Latin American standpoint. Apart from the contribution by Galindo Pohl, which is concerned particularly with the process of forming a consensus, this subject is also dealt with in the chapters by Julio César Lupinacci and Alfonso Arias Schreiber. The former study is based mainly on an analysis of Latin American legislation and practice at the regional level, reviewing at the same time the negotiation of the Conference on the Law of the Sea, while the second pays particularly detailed attention to the arguments that have been adduced in this juridical and diplomatic debate. These approaches, together with other pertinent views existing in Latin America, constitute and adequate panorama of regional opinion.

The Exclusive Economic Zone involves many other questions, ranging from those of its delimitation to those of its relation with the regime of the continental shelf and including problems relating to installations of various types. These other angles have not been dealt with in the chapters in this book, whose object is rather to identify the concept of the Exclusive Economic Zone in the light of its significance in international law.

The material assembled in this book will serve to highlight, from one point of view, the wealth of intellectual discussion that has accumulated around this new institution. Perhaps the book's greatest merit lies in its testimony to the experience and farsightedness of many of those who are contributing to the birth of a new concept in contemporary international law.

_____ F. V. Garcia-Amador

2. The Origins of the Concept of an Exclusive Economic Zone: Latin American Practice and Legislation

In examining the Exclusive Economic Zone (EEZ) as provided for in Part V of the 1982 Convention on the Law of the Sea, one must bear in mind three fundamental aspects of this maritime area: the resources that are the object of exploration, conservation, and exploitation or development; the legal nature of the extended competences that are the zone's fundamental characteristic; and the area to be included in such a zone. It is of great importance to distinguish among these aspects in order to determine how the EEZ has been taking shape. Indeed, in distinguishing among the three aspects mentioned, the historical roots and antecedents of the zone do not always coincide. As this chapter will show, until the essential constituents of the EEZ came together in a new maritime space--and this is what happened in the case of the 200-mile "maritime zone" claimed by the Latin American countries bordering on the South Pacific-- the relevant historical roots and antecedents lay scattered in various claims and proposals that differed as to the aims and objects, the legal nature, and the size envisaged for the zone.

EARLY CLAIMS TO LIVING RESOURCES

The EEZ's earliest antecedents with regard to living resources are the claim to the so-called sedentary fisheries; the claim to the right of "ownership and protection" over the seals and other resources of the Bering Sea; and the claim to a certain area in Moray Firth.

The Claim to the So-called Sedentary Fisheries

Centuries before the appearance of the doctrine of the continental shelf, the area where these fisheries are based, a consensus already existed favoring the right of a coastal state to reserve unto itself the exploitation of the resources of the sea bed located beyond that state's territorial waters. Claims to the living resources of the sea bed date much earlier and are more numerous than those to mineral resources.[1] Some examples include the claims of Ceylon and Australia with regard to pearl fisheries, French and Italian claims with regard to Mediterranean coral, and the claim of the Bey of Tunis with regard to sponge banks.[2]

What is the essential nature of such claims to living resources? The answer is to be found in Emerich de Vattel's famous and oft-cited statement: "Who doubts that the pearl fisheries of Bahrein and Ceylon can legally be owned?" As R. Young has indicated, the prevailing view is that these are cases of the right of exclusive exploitation or utilization, since these resources are considered to be the fruit of the sea bed and are thus to be harvested, unlike free-swimming fish that can only be caught.[3] It is clear, then, that in these cases the claim relates to specific resources rather than to a maritime zone.

This, of course, does not provide grounds for underestimating the importance of the fact that, from the earliest times, coastal states have been acknowledged to "own" some of these living resources of the sea bed. Consequently, in studying the EEZ from an historical perspective, it is of special significance that the EEZ was the first claim to living resources to merit the acquiescence or consent of the international community, thus establishing the first exception to the principle of the freedom of the seas in relation to the right of fishing in the high seas.

The Right of "Ownership and Protection" over the Seals of Bering Sea

On the grounds that the species in question was commonly found on its territory or in its territorial waters, the United States unilaterally adopted strict conservation measures toward seals without fixing the extent of the territory over which these measures would apply. The application of these measures in 1886 and 1887 to several British Columbian schooners resulted in Great Britain's protesting against this action on the grounds that the ships in question had been seized outside the three-mile limit of the United States' territorial sea. Eventually, the two countries agreed to submit the matter to arbitration, by the treaty of February 29, 1892.

Of the five points submitted to the arbitration tribunal for its decision, the last has a direct bearing on the nature of the claim: "Does the United States have any right, and if so, what right of protection or ownership does it have over the fur seals which frequent the islands of the United States in the Bering Sea, when such fur seals are found outside the ordinary limit of three miles?"

Early in the proceedings, the United States stressed the importance of distinguishing

> between the exercise of the sovereign jurisdiction of a nation over the high seas --a sovereign jurisdiction the nature of which transforms the high seas over which it is exercised into part of the territory of the nation, giving that nation exclusive competence to legislate thereon-- and the claim of a right to perform acts of authority on the high seas for the purpose of protecting the property or industry of a population. The former constitutes a claim of sovereign jurisdiction, the latter in a way merely a claim to a right of self-preservation and legitimate defense, which every nation, like private persons, always may exercise.

Clearly, this second type of claim is in turn based on a right of a different kind: the right of "ownership" or "property," which was invoked with respect to the seals that frequented the terrritory then just recently acquired by the United States.

In arguing in favor of recognition of this right of "property" ad "protection," the United States cited as an analogous right the right that had traditionally been recognized with respect to sedentary fisheries. But above all it stressed the living habits or conditions of the fur seals as evidence of the existence of a vital link between these animals and the shore. The court of arbitration, however, not only refused to recognize a right of ownership but also refused to recognize a right to protect or conserve the fur seals. Indeed, the decision stated categorically that "the United States has no right of protection or of ownership over the fur seals which frequent the islands of the United States in the Bering Sea, when such seals are found outside the ordinary limit of three miles."[4]

Protection of the fur seals in the Bering Sea was a concern that led Russia also to take unilateral measures, the application of which sparked protests from the United States and Great Britain in 1891 and 1892. A new arbitration proceeding, convened this time between the United States and Russia in 1902, rejected the Russian proposition, which was essentially the same as the position the United States put before the court of arbitration in 1893. Russia insisted that this limit (i.e., the width of the territorial sea) was inadequate in the face of the greater destructive capability of the new firearms being used in the seal hunt and maintained also that freedom of the seas should not be jeopardized "to protect individuals guilty of attacks prejudicial to the rights of others." In reiterating the principles upon which the 1893 award had been pronounced, arbitrator Asser declared illegal the Russian seizures; in the absence of a treaty providing authority, the state had no special rights of jurisdiction for the protection of sea animals beyond the three-mile limit of its territorial waters.[5]

Claims to a Zone in Moray Firth

Unlike earlier claims, which were aimed at securing the exclusive exploitation or conservation of certain species, the unilateral measures adopted late in the nineteenth century with respect to Moray Firth, off the northeast coast of Scotland, related for the first time to a maritime zone, one that covered an area of approximately fifteen hundred square miles outside the three-mile limit. For a few years, the measures were applied only within the limits of the territorial sea, but in 1905 their application was extended beyond these limits.

The application of these measures outside territorial waters took the form of the seizure of fishing trawlers of Norwegian registry, some of which were owned by British subjects; the cases came before the court of justice. In an early case, on appeal, the court found that the legislation had made no distinction between British subjects and foreign nationals in regard to the applicability of the measures. Several cases that were subsequently decided also found the Norwegian captains guilty. The most famous case was Mortensen v. Peters, in which even the Convention on Policing of Fisheries of the North Sea of 6 May 1882 (which did not authorize the exercise of national jurisdiction outside the territorial sea) was invoked. Aside from other reasons of a more practical nature, the court found from the legal standpoint that "without reaching the point of holding that the Moray Firth is under territorial sovereignty for all purposes, obviously it can be said at least that one cannot hold, as does the petitioner, that it is inconceivable that the British Parliament would attempt to regulate fisheries with respect to everyone therein."[6] In any case, as one can well appreciate, the purpose of regulating fishing was to conserve fish stocks, not to secure any right of exclusive exploitation.

PROPOSALS AND CLAIMS RELATING TO CONSERVATION

Some of the more recent and direct antecedents of the EEZ as regards the right of a coastal state to take unilateral steps to conserve the living resources in waters adjacent to its shores but outside its territorial sea are the proposals made by some countries at the 1930 Codification Conference in the Hague, aimed at extending the scope of the so-called contiguous zone to include fishing interests. This zone, as defined by the conference, was an area of the sea extending beyond the territorial sea to a maximum of twelve miles from shore, over which a coastal state was given some powers of supervision in order to protect certain interests such as health and customs interests or the security of the state.[7] Other antecedents of the present-day EEZ include postwar claims such as President Truman's fisheries proclamation of 1945 and the subsequent claims by Mexico and Iceland, which also dealt with the conservation of living resources.

Proposals Presented at the 1930 Hague Conference

At the 1930 Hague Conference, only four delegations advocated extension of the scope of the contiguous zone to include fishing interests. In keeping with the comments that he had made regarding Schuecking's report on territorial waters, Barbosa de Magalhaes, the Portuguese delegate, proposed that the contiguous zone be extended for the purposes of "protection or supervision of fisheries." In one speech, he indicated that the three-mile limit was inadequate, as demonstrated by the claims of many other countries, some of which claimed a greater or even unlimited width for the adjacent zone. In his opinion, what a state would exercise in this zone would be "the right of jurisdiction," or "right to police fisheries," as he phrased it on another occasion.[8] In supporting the Portuguese delegate, Henri Rolin, the Belgian delegate, remarked that although a coastal state would not be able to restrict fishing in this adjacent zone to its own citizens, it ought indeed to be authorized to extend the application of conservation measures implicit in the regulation of fisheries to that zone, so as to prevent the damage that could result from uncontrolled fishing in its territorial sea. Specifically, he made the recommendation that "coastal states be assigned the protection of marine fauna in the adjacent sea."[9]

The other two delegations advocating such a step at the 1930 Hague Conference were those of Iceland and Denmark. Iceland simply stated that a sea four miles wide would be adequate "provided it were possible to protect fisheries in certain areas beyond the territorial waters" and put forward a proposal to this end.[10] For its part, the Danish delegation stressed the need to protect fry and young fish and suggested that an amendment to this effect be made to the text of Discussion Paper 5 that had been drawn up by the conference's Preparatory Commission.[11]

As a result of these positions and the initiatives and proposals put forward by Portugal and Belgium, the conference limited itself to adopting a resolution that, at least in some respects, is rather negative. Indeed, even though it admitted that the fishing industry was important to some countries and acknowledged moreover that the "protection of the various products of the sea should be considered not only in relation to the territorial sea but also to the waters contiguous thereto," the conference declared that it lacked the competence to deal with these issues or to do anything that might prejudice their solution and expressed its wish to affirm the importance of "the measures of protection and collaboration which may be considered necessary to safeguard the riches that constitute a common heritage."[12]

The claims discussed below are also exclusively concerned with the protection or conservation of living resources lying outside the territorial sea, but in an area of the sea other than the contiguous zone. The scope of these claims varies widely.[13]

The Truman Fisheries Proclamation (1945)

The proclamation of 28 September 1945 by President Truman claimed the right to take unilateral conservation measures in areas of the high seas, but only with respect to U.S. citizens; where fishing grounds were shared between U.S. nationals and the nationals of other countries, conservation measures would then be implemented by means of agreements involving all the countries concerned. Following is an extract from the proclamation in which the nature and scope of the claim are defined:

> In view of the pressing need for conservation and protection of fishery resources, the Government of the United States regards it as proper to establish conservation zones in those areas of the high seas contiguous to the coasts of the United States wherein fishing activities have been or in the future may be developed and maintained on a substantial scale. Where such activities have been or shall hereafter be developed and maintained by its nationals alone, the United States regards it as proper to establish explicitly bounded conservation zones in

which fishing activities shall be subject to the regulation and control of the United States. Where such activities have been or shall hereafter be legitimately developed and maintained jointly by nationals of the United States and nationals of other States, explicitly bounded conservation zones may be established under agreements between the United States and such other States; and all fishing activities in such zones shall be subject to regulation and control as provided in such agreements. The right of any State to establish conservation zones off its shores in accordance with the above principles is conceded, provided that corresponding recognition is given to any fishing interests of nationals of the United States which may exist in such areas. The character as high seas of the areas in which such conservation zones are established and the right to their free and unimpeded navigation are in no way thus affected.

On the same date, the president issued Executive Order 9634, instructing the secretary of state and the secretary of the interior to recommend jointly from time to time the establishment, by means of executive orders, of fishing conservation zones in areas of the high seas contiguous to the coasts of the United States in accordance with the proclamation. Such orders would contain provisions regarding the administration, regulation, and monitoring of fishery resources and fishing activities. The White House press release of the same date indicated that the new policy would enable the United States to give effective protection to fish species including its most valuable fish, the Alaska salmon. In regard to this fish, it was noted that since the salmon spends most of its life at sea, uncontrolled fishing in these waters, either by United States nationals or by nationals of other countries, had become a continuing threat to this resource. The press release also noted that the regulation of the salmon fishery within territorial waters could not prevent the overfishing or extermination of the resource taking place beyond the commonly accepted limits of territorial jurisdiction.[14]

President Truman's proclamation sparked a series of claims aimed at conserving the high seas' living resources, although not all such claims had the same legal characters or scope. As has been seen, this declaration simply claimed a right that coastal states had exercised from antiquity, and one that was frequently spelled out in national fisheries legislation; indeed, the right of a coastal state to regulate fishing activities by its nationals on the high seas has never been deemed incompatible with international law. What was regarded as contrary to international law was the extension of such regulations to the nationals of other states.

The Nature of Claims Enunciated Subsequent to the Proclamation

Most of the claims that followed the U.S. proclamation took its same approach, beginning with the Mexican claim of the same year. This can be seen clearly in the following passages from the statement of 29 October 1945 by the president of Mexico:[15]

> In the pre-war years the Western Hemisphere had to stand aside while permanent fishing fleets from other countries engaged in an excessive and exhaustive exploitation of these vast resources which, although they should of course contribute to international well-being, must belong above all to the country possessing them and to the continent of which it forms part. In view of its very nature, it is essential that this protection should consist in the extension of control and supervision by the State to the places and zones indicated by science for the development of high seas fisheries, irrespective of their distance from the coast.
> For these reasons the Government of the Republic lays claim to the whole of the continental platform or shelf adjoining its coast line and to each and all of the natural resources existing there, whether known or unknown, and is taking steps to supervise, utilize and control the closed fishing zones necessary for the conservation of this source of well-being.
> The foregoing does not mean that the Mexican Government seeks to disregard the lawful rights of third parties, based on reciprocity, or that the rights of free navigation on the high seas are affected, as the sole purpose is to conserve these resources for the well-being of the nation, the continent and the world.

These passages from the Mexican declaration are drafted so as to answer the key questions likely to arise as to the true nature and scope of the claim. Specifically, the first paragraph seems to declare exclusive or at least preferential rights over the fisheries resource wealth to which it refers. The second and third paragraphs seem to clarify the situation, however, stating that the only right being claimed is a right of conservation, as stated explicitly in the third paragraph.

Before the end of that decade, Iceland promulgated

its law 44 of 5 October 1948, relating to the "scientific conservation of the continental shelf fisheries." According to Article 1 of the law, the Ministry of Fisheries would issue regulations establishing conservation zones within the limits of the continental shelf, zones "wherein all fisheries shall be subject to Icelandic rules and control." The next article stated, though, that the regulations laid down would not apply insofar as they were incompatible with agreements signed with other countries. The first regulations were put into effect in 1952.[16]

The difference between the two kinds of claims -- the U.S. proclamation on the one hand and the Mexican and Icelandic claims on the other-- could not go by unnoticed since that difference was rooted in the key question of the extension of competence. Whereas the U.S. proclamation limited regulation by a coastal state to those fishing activities carried on by that country's own nationals on the high seas, the other two claims sought to bring all fishing activities, regardless of the nationality of those carrying on such activities, under the unilateral regulation of the coastal state. Although the two types of claim seem to coincide in their having one and only one aim --to establish regulations for the conservation or protection of fisheries-- they clearly differ as regards the nature or scope of the jurisdiction that would be exercised for this purpose outside the territorial sea.

After the United States, Mexico, and Iceland, other countries enunciated claims along the lines of the Mexican and Icelandic claims, although each claim had its own special features. By way of illustration, three such claims by Latin American countries were: the Dominican Republic's Law 3342 of 13 July 1952; Cuba's Law Decree 1948 of 25 January 1955; and Venezuela's law of 27 July 1956 respecting the territorial sea, the continental shelf, fisheries protection, and airspace. Since that time, other countries elsewhere in the world have enunciated claims of this kind, such as India (1956), Ceylon (1957), Ghana (1963), and Pakistan (1966), among many others.

CLAIMS WITH RESPECT TO SUBMARINE AREAS AND SUPERJACENT WATERS

Antecedents of the EEZ in regard to rights over submarine areas and superjacent waters claimed by coastal states also have a long history, although there are fewer of them from before World War II than there are antecedents of the other extensions of states' competence described in the preceding sections of this chapter. In fact, the only antecedents are (1) the

Cornwall Submarine Mines Act of 1858, which claimed mines and minerals located in submarine areas covered by the high seas as constituting part of the territorial possessions and sea bed of the British Crown,[17] and (2) the claims to sedentary fisheries insofar as such claims relate to a coastal state's sovereignty over or ownership of the sea bed; as indicated earlier, an exclusive right to sedentary fisheries "presumes" ownership of the sea bed in which the fishery is located.[18]

The Immediate Antecedents of Present-day Claims

In any event, the most direct antecedent of present-day claims to the continental shelf is the Anglo-Venezuelan treaty of 26 February 1942. By that treaty, Great Britain and Venezuela established the limits of their respective rights "to sovereignty or control" over the "submarine areas of the Gulf of Paria"; in other words, with respect to "the sea bed and the subsoil outside of the territorial waters of the High Contracting Parties to one or the other side of the lines A-B, B-Y and Y-X" (Article 1). The purpose of the treaty is not the direct and immediate claiming of these areas vis-a-vis third parties but rather the reciprocal recognition of rights of the sort mentioned that "have been or may hereafter be lawfully acquired" by the two countries (Article 2). In addition to the provisions of Article 1, the treaty refers expressly to the regime applicable to the superjacent waters. On this question, Article 6 states: "Nothing in this Treaty shall be held to affect in any way the status of the waters of the Gulf of Paria or any rights of passage or navigation on the surface of the seas outside the territorial waters of the Contracting Parties." It can be inferred from these provisions that the present and future claims that are the subject of the treaty relate only to the sea bed and the subsoil of the submarine areas located between the island of Trinidad and the coast of Venezuela; they do not in any way concern the waters covering those areas beyond the limit of the territorial sea of each of the contracting parties.[19]

One other antecedent of the U.S. proclamation of 1945 should be mentioned: the Argentine claim enunciated in Decree 1386 of 23 February 1944, which focused on the doctrine of the continental shelf -- that its to say, the question of the exploration and exploitation of submarine areas and the living resources of their superjacent waters. This decree established that "pending the enactment of special legislation, the zones at the international frontiers of the national territories and the zones on the ocean coasts, as well as the zones of the epicontinental sea of Argentina, shall be deemed to be temporary zones of mineral reserves" (emphasis in the original text). This claim, unlike the claim enunciated in the Anglo-Venezuelan treaty, does indeed affect the regime of the superjacent waters of the submarine areas with which the decree deals --that is, the waters of the Argentinian epicontinental sea. This is discussed in greater detail below.

The U.S. Proclamation of 1945 and Other Similar Proclamations

On 28 September 1945, Presient Truman issued with his fisheries proclamation a second proclamation concerning the continental shelf. The key part of this second proclamation reads as follows:

> Having concern for the urgency of conserving and prudently utilizing its natural resources, the Government of the United States regards the natural resources of the subsoil and sea bed of the continental shelf beneath the high seas but contiguous to the coasts cf the United States as appertaining to the United States, subject to its jurisdiction and control.

Quite apart from the domestic aspects and effects of this claim, its international purpose is clear and unmistakable: to declare an exclusive right of jurisdiction and control with respect to the conservation and utilization of the natural resources of the sea bed and subsoil of the submarine area in question. Like the Anglo-Venezuelan treaty, the proclamation did not affect superjacent waters, and said so in the following terms: "The character as high seas of the waters above the continental shelf and the right to their free and unimpeded navigation are in no way thus affected."[20]

Not all the claims respecting the continental shelf and other submarine areas enunciated since the Argentine decree of 1944 and the U.S. proclamation of 1945 have had the same effect on the superjacent waters. Most nations have chosen to follow the United States' example --that is to say, their treaties have had no effect whatsoever in this regard: beyond the outer limit of the respective territorial sea, these waters retain their status as waters of the high seas. This is the case of the claims enunciated by Iran, Saudi Arabia, and nine emirates of the Persian Gulf, among many other countries. All of these have proclaimed the coastal state's exclusive right to explore and exploit the natural resources of the sea bed and the subsoil of adjacent submarine areas, particularly mineral wealth, and in each such case it has been stated expressly that the proclamation of this right shall not affect or alter the status of the waters covering the areas claimed. The claims of the Philippines and of Pakistan also dealt only with the natural resources of the sea bed and the subsoil of those submarine areas adjacent to their respective territories. And the same has been true of the United Kingdom's Orders in Council relating to the Bahamas, Jamaica, and other British possessions and territories. A more recent proclamation of the government of Israel includes the sea bed and subsoil of submarine areas contiguous to the coasts of the state of Israel as part of the nation's territory beyond the territorial sea as far as the depth of the superjacent waters will permit the exploitation of the natural resources in these areas. The proclamation also contains a paragraph stating that this claim shall in no way "affect the status of the waters covering the submarine areas in question beyond the territorial sea as high seas."[21]

Some Latin American claims follow lines similar to those discussed above. The Brazilian decree of 8 November 1950 placed the continental and island shelf under the exclusive jurisdiction and domain of the Federal Union and reserved to the Federal Union the right to utilize and exploit the natural products or riches found in this part of the nation's territory. The decree also stated that rules respecting navigation in the waters covering the shelf would remain in full force, without prejudice to any other rules that might be established in that zone, particularly in regard to fishing. The legislation of other Latin American countries is not so explicit about the status of superjacent waters, but it is also less clear and precise in regard to the object of the claim. Guatemala's Petroleum Act of August 1949 only claimed the natural oil fields and petroleum reserves of the continental shelf. Nicaragua's Constitution of 1950, reiterating an earlier constitutional provision, simply refers to the continental shelf and the submerged lands. The Dominican Republic's Constitution of 1954 reserves unto the state the right of ownership and exploitation of the natural resources and riches found on the sea bed or in its subsoil.[22]

The "Epicontinental Sea" and Other Similar Claims

The orientation of other Latin American claims to the continental shelf or other submarine areas differs considerably from that of the claims discussed in the preceding paragraphs starting with the so-called epicontinental sea mentioned earlier, which Argentina first claimed in 1944. Two years later, Argentina reiterated its claim in Decree 14708 of 11 October 1946. This decree makes explicit reference to "the sovereignty of the nation in the Argentine epicontinental sea and continental shelf" (Article 1) and then adds that "for purposes of free navigation, the character of the waters situated in the Argentina epicontinental sea and above the Argentina continental shelf remains unaffected by the present declaration" (Article 2).

In rather different language, and in any case without using the terms "epicontinental sea," Mexico had in the previous year laid claim to submarine areas, with the same effects as regards the status of the superjacent waters. Certain constitutional amendments deriving from the Mexican president's declaration of 29 October 1945, discussed earlier, were submitted to the national Congress for its consideration and approval on 6 December of that year. The proposals sought to amend Article 27 of the constitution so that the waters of the seas covering the continental shelf and the submarine shelf would be considered "property of the nation." Despite the fact that these amendments were approved by the Congress and ratified by the requisite number of state legislatures, they were never promulgated by the executive branch.[23]

This group also includes a claim declared by Panama, as enunciated in that nation's Decree 449 of 17 December 1946. Honduras' claims of 1950 and 1951 are similar in that they affect the superjacent waters from the standpoint of living resources. Several legal instruments were issued: one to propose the required constitutional amendment; one to amend the Ley Agraria; a third to amend the Civil Code; and, some time later, Legislative Decree 25 of 17 January 1951, approving Executive Decree 96 of 28 January 1950, which unlike the other instruments did not require ratification in order to take effect and in which Honduran sovereignty was extended to the continental shelf and the "waters which cover it."

In short, regardless of the language in which they were framed,[24] all the claims referred to in this section aimed to extend the coastal state's sovereignty to the continental shelf or other submarine areas, as well as to the superjacent waters. With respect to the living resources found in these waters, these legal instruments have claimed the same exclusive exploration, conservation, and exploitation or utilization rights claimed with respect to the resources of the sea bed and subsoil of submarine areas.

THE 200-MILE MARITIME ZONE

A new type of Latin American claim that also appeared on the scene soon after President Truman's two proclamations was enunciated within a subregional context in the Santiago Declaration signed by Chile, Ecuador, and Peru on 18 August 1952. Before this, five countries had already claimed a 200-mile zone. As will be shown, this other type of claim later took on other features, some of which differ significantly from the original claims and from the maritime zone established under the Santiago Declaration, which was the first multilateral expression of a 200-mile zone.

The Chilean Claim of 1947 and the Four Other Claims That Preceded the Santiago Declaration

It was Chile that took the initiative in proclaiming a 200-mile limit by means of the presidential declaration of 23 June 1947.[25] Peru followed this lead and enunciated its claim in Supreme Decree 781 of 1 August 1947. The two claims pursued common objectives and were even framed in similar language. Specifically, they proclaim national sovereignty --or "national sovereignty and jurisdiction" in the Peruvian decree-- over submarine areas, regardless of their size or depth, as well as over the adjacent seas extending as far as necessary "to reserve, protect, maintain, and utilize natural resources and wealth." By virtue of this declaration of sovereignty, marine fishing and hunting protection zones in the respective countries' continental and island seas were established, but "protection and control" was immediately declared over the adjacent sea up to a distance of 200 nautical miles. The Chilean and Peruvian claims also paralleled each other in stating expressly that the declaration of sovereignty did not affect the freedom of navigation on the high seas recognized under international law.

The other three claims that preceded the Santiago Declaration were made by Central American countries. One of these was the claim by Costa Rica, which initially appeared in Decree-Law 116 of 27 July 1948, proclaiming "national sovereignty" over adjacent seas "to protect, conserve, and utilize the natural resources and wealth" and proclaiming "the protection and control of the State" over a 200-mile zone. This decree-law was amended by Decree-Law 803 of 2 November 1949. In the next text, the term "national sovereignty" was replaced with "rights and interests of Costa Rica," and the word "control" was deleted in reference to the 200-mile zone, with only "the protection of the State" with respect to this maritime zone being declared. Another Central American claim was that of El Salvador, the only one of the 200-mile claims to be entrenched in a constitution. This provision, contained in Article 7 of the Constitution of 1950 --and reproduced verbatim in Article 8 of the

Constitution of 1962-- states that "The territory of the republic within its present boundaries is irreducible; it includes the adjacent sea within a distance of 200 marine miles measured from the line of lowest tide, and it embraces the air space above, the subsoil, and the corresponding continental shelf." The third Central American claim, and the last of the five unilateral claims that preceded the Santiago Declaration, was that of Honduras. The wording used in the decrees of 1950 and 1951, cited above in regad to Honduras's claim to the continental shelf and its superjacent waters, was reiterated in declaring "State protection and control" with respect to the 200-mile zone.

It is not difficult to identify the aims of these early 200-mile claims. Like the Chilean and Peruvian declarations, the Costa Rican and Honduran decrees and the Salvadorean constitutional article stated expressly that the claim did not affect freedom of navigation. It is clear, then, that no attempt was made to extend the state's full territorial sovereignty, as would be the case if the outer limit of the territorial sea were extended. On the contrary, these coastal states claimed only certain rights in the zone in question, with specific purposes. All of these claims except for that of Costa Rica --which, as one may have appreciated, wound up by declaring simply a right of conservation-- explicitly or implicitly declared the right "to reserve, protect, maintain, and utilize" the zone's natural resources.

The Santiago Declaration of 1952: Its True Legal Nature

The Declaration on the Maritime Zone, or the Santiago Declaration as it is better known, was signed on 18 August 1952 at the Conference on the Exploitation and Conservation of the Maritime Resources of the South Pacific by Chile, Ecuador, and Peru, the three countries taking part in the conference. Because of the declaration's legal force, it had subsequently to be submitted to a process of ratification in the three signatory countries. Following are key passages from the declaration:[26]

> For the foregoing reasons the Governments of Chile, Ecuador, and Peru, being resolved to preserve for and make available to their respective peoples the natural resources of the areas of sea adjacent to their coasts, hereby declare as follows:
>
> (I) Owing to the geological and biological factors affecting the existence, conservation, and development of the marine fauna and flora of the

waters adjacent to the coasts of the declarant countries, the former extent of the territorial sea and contiguous zone is insufficient to permit of the conservation, development, and use of those resources, to which the coastal countries are entitled.

(II) The Governments of Chile, Ecuador, and Peru therefore proclaim as a principle of their international maritime policy that each of them possesses sole sovereignty and jurisdiction over the area of sea adjacent to the coast of its own country and extending not less than 200 nautical miles from the said coast.

(III) Their sole jurisdiction and sovereignty over the zone thus described includes sole sovereignty and jurisdiction over the sea floor and subsoil thereof.

(IV) The zone of 200 nautical miles shall extend in every direction from any island or group of islands forming part of the territory of a declarant country. The maritime zone of an island or group of islands belonging to one declarant country and situated less than 200 nautical miles from the general maritime zone of another declarant country shall be bounded by the parallel of latitude drawn from the point at which the land frontier between the two countries reaches the sea.

(V) This declaration shall not be construed as disregarding the necessary restrictions on the exercise of sovereignty and jurisdiction imposed by international law to permit the innocent and inoffensive passage of vessels of all nations through the zone aforesaid.

(VI) The Governments of Chile, Ecuador, and Peru state that they intend to sign agreements or conventions to put into effect the principles set forth in this Declaration and to establish general regulations for the control and protection of hunting and fishing in their respective maritime zones and the control and coordination of the use and working of all other natural products or resources of common interest present in the said waters.

Clearly, the maritime zone established by the Santiago Declaration also involves an extension of special competences, or, to use an expression that was very much in vogue for a time at the Third United

Nations Conference on the Law of the Sea, an extension of "special jurisdictions." Indeed, although in the declaration the three governments proclaim exclusive sovereignty and jurisdiction to be a principle of their international maritime policy, the declaration is clearly concerned with nothing more than "the conservation, development, and use of those resources, to which the coastal countries are entitled." In another part of the declaration, the "exclusive sovereignty and jurisdiction" claimed are said to apply to the sea bed and subsoil appertaining to the maritime zone. Thus, even though the declaration's primary purpose is to enunciate a claim of fishing and hunting rights, it also claims submarine areas, although it does so by rather different means from those usually employed at the time to claim such areas.[27]

With regard to the nature of the maritime zone, one should consider the interpretations given from time to time by authorized representatives of the three countries, particularly within United Nations bodies and at United Nations conferences, which fully confirm the essence of the zone to be indeed a set of special competences and jurisdictions. Thus, when the Santiago Declaration speaks of "the necessary restrictions on the exercise of sovereignty and jurisdiction imposed by international law to permit the innocent and inoffensive passage of vessels through the zone aforesaid," what it is really talking about is freedom of navigation.

Since the right of innocent passage is an integral element of the legal regime of the territorial sea, it need not have been expressly mentioned.[28] This leads one to conclude, particularly when the specific and exclusive objectives of the claim are borne in mind, that what the declaration is actually referring to and recognizing, like the five claims that preceded it, is freedom of navigation, certainly in that part of the maritime zone that does not form part of the territorial sea of any of the three countries.[29]

As one may have gathered, it is in the maritime zone conceived in 1947 and ordained at the multilateral level in 1952 by the Santiago Declaration that the essential elements of the EEZ were brought together for the first time.[30] These elements are (1) the object of the claim: the claim covers all resources-- that is, it takes in the living resources in the waters of the zone as well as the renewable and non-renewable resources of the sea bed and the subsoil beneath the zone; (2) the nature of the rights claimed: the rights are exclusive rights of exploration, conservation, and exploitation or utilization; and (3) the area covered by the claim: the area takes in 200 miles of the sea adjacent to the coastal state. In short, the Santiago Declaration created a "maritime zone" in which, as in the present-day EEZ, sovereign rights --in other words, exclusive rights-- were claimed in a certain area of the sea with respect to all resources found within that area, and, since the nature of the rights claimed was strictly economic, without prejudice to the recognition of freedom of navigation and the other freedoms enjoyed under the traditional regime of the high seas.

NOTES

1. For the claims on mineral resources, Sir Cecil Hurst: "Whose is the Bed of the Sea?" The British earbook of International Law. 1923-1924. Vol.4. pp. 34 et seq.
2. A principal source in the matter is still the article cited in Note 1.
3. R. Young: "Sedentary Fisheries and the Convention on the Continental Shelf." The American Journal of International Law, 1961, Vol. 55, p. 361.
4. On this arbitration, Leonard L. Larry: International Regulation of Fisheries. 1944. pp. 55-82.
5. Ibid., p. 89.
6. Ibid., pp. 48-55.
7. Minutes of the Second Committee of the Conference. In League of Nations, Acts of the Conference for the Codification of International Law. Vol. 3. Minutes of the Second Committee, Territorial Waters. Off. No. C 351(b). M 145(b). 1930. V. pp. 20 et seq.
8. Ibid., pp. 19, 125, 120, 193, respectively.
9. Ibid., p. 134.
10. Ibid., pp. 142, 189.
11. Ibid., p. 25.
12. The full text of the resolution is reproduced in ibid., p. 212.
13. Mention should also be made of two earlier claims. In 1927 Canada enacted legislation prohibiting certain fishing activities in its territorial sea, which at the time had a three mile width, or restricting those activities in a twelve-mile area during other periods of the year. In 1934, Ecuador regulated certain activities in the high seas contiguous to its territorial sea.
14. Full text in United Nations Legislative Series:Laws and Regulations on the Regime of the High eas (1951) Vol. 1. pp. 112-113.
15. Full text of the declaration was published in El Universal, Mexico City, October 30, 1945.
16. For the texts of these regulations and legislation, see United Nations Legislative Series, op. cit. pp. 12-13, and Supplement. 1959. p. 11.
17. Hurst, op. cit.
18. Ibid., p. 40. See also D. M. Johnson: The

International Law of Fisheries. 1965. p. 229.
19. José Luis de Azcarraga: La Plataforma Submarina y el Derecho Internacional. Madrid: 1952. pp. 27-31.
20. See United Nations Legislative Series, op.cit., pp. 112-113.
21. Ibid. Vol. 1. Part I. For the Israeli Claim, Doc.A/CN.4/99/Add.1. p. 22.
22. See, generally, F. V. García-Amador: América Latina y el Derecho del Mar. Santiago: Instituto de Estudios Internacionales de la Universidad de Chile. 1976. pp. 48-98.
23. On the legislative history, see Bernardo Sepúlveda: "Derecho del Mar. Apuntes sobre el sistema legal mexicano." Foro Internacional. 1972. Vol. 13. p. 244.
24. The term "epicontinental sea" appears in the Declaration of Antigua, Guatemala, signed on 24 August 1955 by the Ministers of Foreign Affairs of Central America. See also the Uruguayan Resolution of 26 December 1963 and Decree 235/969 of 16 May 1969.
25. El Mercurio, Santiago, Chile, 29 June 1947, p. 27.
26. See García Amador, op.cit.
27. In this regard it has been correctly stated that the 200-mile Latin American proclamations "claimed rights over the seabed and subsoil as well as over the superjacent waters in a manner unrelated to the geological definition of the continental shelf, recoursing instead to the criterion of distance, irrespectively of whether it coincided or not with the shelf." Francisco Orrego Vicuña:Los Fondos Marinos y Oceánicos. Santiago, Editorial Andrés Bello, 1976. p. 76.
28. F. V. García-Amador: The Utilization and Conservation of the Resources of the Sea. Sijthoff, 1963. pp. 77-79.
29. On further diplomatic interpretation that rejects the territorial sea approach, see the Agreement among Chile, Ecuador and Peru of 12 April 1955, related to a reply to the observations by the United States and the United Kingdom to the Santiago Declaration. Text in: Ministerio de Relaciones Exteriores del Peru: Instrumentos Nacionales e Internacionales sobre Derecho del Mar. Lima, 1971. pp. 225-228.
30. It might be pertinent to insist in that the real origins of the EEZ are to be found in the 200-mile maritime zone of the Latin American countries of the South Pacific. Recent studies seem to suggest that it would originate in the proposals of other countries and regions in the early stages of the Third United Nations Law of the Sea Conference. See, for example, N. S. Rembé: Africa and the International Law of the Sea, 1980. pp. 117-118. Also T. O. Elias: New Horizons in International Law. 1979. pp. 25-26.

Pilar Armanet

3. The Economic Interest Underlying the First Declaration on a Maritime Zone

BASIC PRINCIPLES

The preamble to the Official Declaration of 23 June 1947 sets forth the principles that led to President Gabriel González Videla's decision to proclaim national sovereignty over the continental shelf and waters adjacent to the coast of Chile. These principles represent recognition of the right of coastal states to protect, preserve, regulate, and supervise the exploitation of all known natural resources, as well as those discovered in future, that are deemed essential to the welfare and progress of their peoples.[1]

These same principles were later reaffirmed in the declaration by the president of Peru, Bustamante y Rivero, and Foreign Minister Enrique García Sayan, published on 1 August 1947. Again, in the Santiago Declaration of 18 August 1952 the governments of Chile, Ecuador, and Peru expressly declared their sovereignty over waters within 200 nautical miles in order to protect and preserve their marine resources, stating that they were "resolved to preserve for and make available to their respective peoples the natural resources of the areas of sea adjacent to their coasts."[2]

These historical events marked the beginning of a long process by which the institution known as the Exclusive Economic Zone has been elaborated--an institution with roots in Latin America, but one that has come to be recognized by the international community.

This process, which has had such a profound effect on international law in general and on the new law of the sea in particular, began at the initiative of private Chilean entrepreneurs who were pressing, at both the national and international level, for the creation of a legal instrument to protect the natural resources of coastal states.

ORIGINS OF THE INITIATIVE

During World War II, the Industrial Company of Valparaíso (INDUS), along with many other firms, repeatedly ran short of the raw materials necessary for its processing operation, particularly for the manufacturing of oil. This led the technical department of INDUS to concentrate on the search for alternative methods of processing whale, and these efforts eventually culminated in the discovery of a dehydrogenization formula that placed the company in a position to exploit this fisheries resource independently. Shortly thereafter, this formula was patented by the technical manager of INDUS, Alans Appuhn Becker.

The importance of this discovery did not go unnoticed in scientific and industrial circles, and it led the Lever Brothers Corporation, an international concern, to seek an association with INDUS for the purpose of acquiring and making use of this process.

Despite these developments, INDUS remained a small company, with only one plant for whale processing. Consequently, it became increasingly difficult for the company to compete with the factory ships of industrial nations that were then fishing in the South Pacific.

The wartime suspension of fisheries activities in the Antarctic zone by European firms was a stroke of luck for INDUS, since it temporarily eliminated foreign competition. However, with the end of the war, and in the knowledge that factory ships from Europe would soon be returning to the South Pacific endangering the incipient Chilean fisheries industry, the general manager of INDUS, Helmut Heinzen, asked the company's legal counsel, Fernando Guarello, to seek arguments—either within Chilean legislation or in the form of international precedents—that might enable the Chilean government to regulate the utilization of marine resources in waters adjacent to the coasts of Chile.[3]

It is interesting to note that at the same time Guarello was conducting legal research on this matter, Heinzen was also attempting to coordinate the interests of private Chilean firms with those of Peruvian and Ecuadorian firms that, although not specifically concerned with whaling, nevertheless found themselves—for a variety of reasons—facing the same task of convincing their governments of the need to restrict access to limited fisheries resources in order to permit rational management of these, taking into account available technologies and capacities. Ecuadorian firms were primarily interested in restricting access to the tuna fishery, thus preventing stiff competition from U.S. fishermen. For its part, Peru was hoping to increase fish meal production based on the anchovy fishery, since it had invested heavily in equipment imported from California for this industry.

THE SEARCH FOR PRECEDENTS

When Fernando Guarello was unable to find anything in national legislation that would permit the Chilean government to protect its fisheries sector from foreign competition, he undertook a search for international precedents that might support a claim of sovereignty over the seas, thus enabling coastal states to achieve the objective of regulating, preserving, and supervising utilization of marine resources.

In this search he requested the cooperation of international law expert Jerman Fisher, who uncovered an article in the January 1940 issue of the magazine Semana Internacional, written by Juan Bardina. In his article, Professor Bardina discussed the Panama Declaration of 1939 in which Great Britain and the United States agreed to establish a zone of security and neutrality in the Americas, in order to avoid the resupplying of Axis ships in South American ports. The article contained a map showing this zone of neutrality, and off the Chilean coast the boundary coincided approximately with the 200-mile limit. As described in the Panama Declaration, the width of this zone of neutrality actually varied between 300 and 500 miles; for Chile, it was closer to 300 miles. However, the map in Bardina's article showed a zone of much smaller dimensions than that described in the Panama Declaration.

When Guarello and Fisher presented this information to the company, INDUS executives were reluctant to support the idea of a 200-mile limit since their own whaling operations required only a 50-mile-wide zone of protection and preservation. However, legal counsel succeeded in convincing them that a claim of sovereignty over adjacent waters beyond the recognized territorial limit of 3 nautical miles would only be recognized if some international precedent could be found to lend it legitimacy.[4]

These views were later presented to President Gabriel González Videla and were adopted by him in the Official Declaration of 1947. Also, the contacts made with Peruvian and Ecuadorian firms opened the way for diplomatic and political negotiations that later culminated in the signing of the Santiago Declaration of 1952.

ADVANCEMENT OF MARITIME INTERESTS

It is interesting to note that both President Gabriel González Videla's declaration and the Santiago Declaration established the right of coastal states to protect, preserve, and supervise the utilization of all of the resources of the adjacent sea and continental shelf, thus creating a legal regime for the 200-mile limit that is much broader in scope than that of a fisheries zone for the protection of living resources.

This fact is of particular importance if one considers that the initiative of the INDUS company resulted from an observed shortage of natural resources--especially the whale--and the need to find a juridical formula for safeguarding this species in order to ensure the growth of the fledgling Chilean fisheries industry.

Consequently, it may be said that in defending the interests of a private firm, a long-term national and regional interest began to emerge, namely the need to protect and conserve the resources of the sea and to ensure that these are effectively employed for the development and benefit of the peoples of coastal states.

The creation of an Exclusive Economic Zone therefore reflects a most advantageous integration of the private interests of business with the national interest--the latter represented by public institutions--in the design of a maritime policy that is of great importance for the country and region, and the development of which provided the basis for the new law of the sea.

NOTES

1. Official Declaration of President Gabriel González Videla on Maritime Jurisdiction, 2 June 1947; in Francisco Orrego Vicuña: Chile y el Derecho del Mar; Editorial Andrés Bello, Santiago, 1972, p. 33.
2. "Declaración sobre Zona Marítima" Santiago 18 August 1952; in F. V. García-Amador: "Latin America and the Law of the Sea." Law of the Sea Institute, Occasional Paper 14, July 1972, pp. 43-44.
3. Ann Hollick: "The origins of 200-miles offshore zones." American Journal of International Law. Vol. 71, No. 3. July 1977, pp. 494-500.
4. Tobías Barros: "Las Doscientas Millas Marinas." El Mercurio, Santiago, 19 July 1974.

Reynaldo Galindo Pohl

4. The Exclusive Economic Zone in the Light of Negotiations of the Third United Nations Conference on the Law of the Sea

THE HISTORICAL APPROACH

Various means may be employed to analyze a juridicopolitical entity. The choice of any one method does not imply that the others are to be condemned. Each method has its place, depending on the nature of the entity and the aims of the investigation. For any given situation, one method may be more appropriate, in the sense that it is more productive, and other methods may be rejected as unsatisfactory or inadequate.

When one endeavors to grasp the significance of a juridicopolitical entity--which means penetrating its nature and anticipating how it will develop in time and space, in other words, its historical unfolding--the historical approach seems most apt. This is especially applicable to entities that are still evolving or that retain the fire of the political forces that gave them birth and have fueled their development and that are still far from reaching the phenomenon of sedimentation that reduces living processes to cold, tidy, lifeless rules that to some extent exist outside of time.

When the evolutionary process of a juridicopolitical entity has come to an end, or when it has become sedimented in habits and customs, formalism may be useful and even necessary at times. But dry and rigid formulas, understood as the symbolic language of the connections of logic, seem to lose their humanity alongside the living process to which they are applied. To treat them as incorporeal and intemporal species at a very high level of abstraction and generalization is to fall into the abyss of logics that provoked Ihering's reaction. Since one is not endeavoring simply to satisfy the interests of reason or discursive preciosities but rather to reconcile interests and aims within a framework of cooperation, peace, and security (all the while striving for fairness), continuing contact with the surrounding circumstances places common sense, which is historical, concrete, and rooted in fact, on the side of the harmonious progress of international relations and the enrichment of the international community.

Formalism, with its diligent examination of words, its comparison of texts, and its intemporal exegesis, is ill suited to determining the significance and consequences of juridicopolitical entities whose development is still continuing. The historical approach is better suited to this, for by examining the relevant factors, particularly political ones, it can tie events together as the elements of an evolutionary process and, without being wholly dominated by them, can make use of certain formalistic approaches and conclusions.

Stressing differences, considering intentions and agreements outside the immediate context of circumstances, meticulously searching for words, particularly new ones, and making the subtle distinctions between various hues all fit in with distinguishing among claims of parentage and originality. There is in this process a certain throwback to myth and legend, a certain pleasure in spontaneous generation, which seems to satisfy some of the deep anxieties expressed in the birth of Aphrodite full-blown from the mere foam of the sea. The historical approach, on the other hand, focuses on similarities and sequences of events and is concerned more with the heart of the matter than with names, with intentions and context rather than with the text.

Another pitfall is to judge the events of the past according to criteria that are valid for the present. It is common to read--and understandably to be surprised at--papers judging unilateral claims of the 1940s and 1950s as though they were claims made today. Any number of qualifications and objections can be made to such judgments. The fact is that what is now known by the term "Exclusive Economic Zone" (EEZ) was some thirty years ago a creation whose survival was doubtful but whose parentage no one disputed. What is today a victory was then an adventure of consequences for which the minimum penalty was ridicule. Although defeat is an orphan, victory is claimed by many parents, so claims of parentage of the Exclusive Economic Zone abound. Failure, as usual, would have brought on charges of blame, accusations of miscalculation, and political evasions.

The plain fact is that, when seen in historical perspective, the EEZ had its origins in the South Pacific in 1947, finding support and acquiring economic emphasis in the Central Pacific from 1950 onwards. It did not spring forth like the legendary Aphrodite born fully formed, but evolved through a long and slow gestation period, surviving crises and setbacks that threatened to consign it to the dust of the archives.

The pioneering countries, to be sure, tied their own hands with laws and declarations, particularly because their unilateral acts aroused a watchful, and to a point militant, public opinion. These unilateral acts reduced the flexibility that is so necessary in international negotiations and thus restricted the maneuvering space available in the process of transforming unilateral claims into generally accepted rules. But these actions imposed a consistency of policy on successive governments and provided a shield against the pressures of the great powers, which at the time were still able to conduct themselves daringly while provoking little or no international reaction. Without that loss of flexibility, the little group of pioneers could well have disbanded in the 1950s and 1960s. One need only consider what happened to some claims at that time, piously forgotten in highly significant inaction. To gain a full picture of the process whereby the Exclusive Economic Zone was born and has developed, one must examine and evaluate instances both of support and of opposition and, even more, instances of temporary or persistent inaction.

The pioneers formed the EEZ negotiating group in the ad hoc sea bed committee and its successor. But in the 1950s and 1960s, and particularly at the time of the First United Nations Conference on the Law of the Sea in 1958, they were the outcasts of international law. The first unilateral actions aroused irate protests from the naval powers, and some incidents, such as that of the Onassis whaling fleet, captured headlines throughout the world. It is worth recalling the atmosphere of persuasion and pressure within which the 1960 Conference on the Law of the Sea was carried on. To be sure, it was not the same to support the Exclusive Economic Zone at the Caracas session of the Third United Nations Conference on the Law of the Sea held in 1974.

THE PROCESS OF SHAPING THE EXCLUSIVE ECONOMIC ZONE

This process had its beginnings in the unilateral acts of certain Latin American countries bordering on the Pacific Ocean. Concern over conservation both of the marine environment and of living species played its part. But the main driving force was the desire to develop the resources of coastal waters, under a more or less imprecise notion of compensation vis-à-vis the then-recent claims to extensive continental shelves. From coastal headlands, fishing fleets could be seen coming and going at will thanks to the freedom of fishing, a freedom that meant the developed countries had access to fisheries in every ocean without exception. The earliest claims to waters and their resources had a certain compensatory quality because a country with a small continental shelf was denied riches of the sort claimed under the Truman proclamation. This notion of compensation, of which traces could be found in the preparatory work of the International Law Commission for the 1958 Conference on the Law of the Sea thanks to José María Yepes, the Colombian jurist, was lost as the economic zone won general acceptance, particularly since the Third Conference on the Law of the Sea was inclined, among other things, to accommodate opposing interests by accepting them in maximum terms. Thus, in large measure it has been a maximalistic forum.

The process of the EEZ's evolving and being given shape can be divided into three stages: Stage 1, stretching from the first Central and South American claims to the establishment by the United Nations General Assembly of the ad hoc Committee to Study the Peaceful Uses of the Sea Bed and the Ocean Floor beyond the Limits of National Jurisdiction (1947 to 1967); Stage 2, covering the years of the ad hoc committee and its successor, the Committee on the Peaceful Uses of the Sea Bed and the Ocean Floor beyond the Limits of National Jurisdiction (1968 to 1973); and Stage 3, the period covered by the Third United Nations Conference on the Law of the Sea (from December 1973 to December 1982), the longest conference in the history of the United Nations and probably in the entire history of international negotiations as well.

The two sea bed committees had no mandate to consider the law of the sea in general, for they were limited to examining the new principle of the sea bed area beyond the limits of national jurisdictions as a common heritage of mankind. These national jurisdictions had been the subject of the 1958 Convention on the Continental Shelf, but their extent and limits were not firm. The fact is that any expansion of the international zone that is subject to the principle of the common heritage of mankind is wholly at odds with the interests of national jurisdictions on the continental shelf. By implication, then, the committees had to reduce jurisdiction from coastal states. Latin America's position was to refuse to recognize the Committees' competence to consider the question of limits and to maintain that examination of the attributes of the sea bed area was a matter quite apart from the consideration of its limits, as the latter required the express mandate of the General Assembly. The Latin American position was sufficient to make limits a sort of taboo subject. Consideration of limits at that time would have been inopportune for the unilateral claims made by Latin American countries.

The first stage was particularly difficult, a

period of political and diplomatic isolation, of pure adventure characterized by constant outside pressure and some noteworthy incidents. The so-called tuna war erupted at that time. Its aim was so nebulous that even some countries in the region regarded it as excessive and unreal. The first subregional agreement dates from that time, that of the Commission on the South Pacific (1952). In 1950, El Salvador included an economic zone in its constitution in an exclusively economic sense and with freedom of navigation. The group of pioneers mounted a generally weak and largely uncoordinated effort at the 1958 Conference on the Law of the Sea. There were so few of them that they were on the defensive. Latin America's voices were isolated, submerged, and drowned out in an atmosphere in which the overwhelming strength of the European masters of international law was seen in one of its last displays. These gentlemen, well schooled in the art of savoir faire, discreetly chuckled at claims that they whispered were out of all proportion; but at no time, not even in the corridors, did they attribute such claims to ignorance or stupidity. These were rare ideas from an underdeveloped corner of the world, what some considered stunted offshoot of European culture that, as Papini said at the time, had no cultural legacy to hand down. At the 1960 conference, the situation was handled much more in political than in academic circles, and the famous "arm twisting" was carried on with full vigor. One vote made the difference concerning the proposal to define the width of the territorial sea and hence the start of the high seas and thus determined whether or not Latin America's claims were to be buried. A single vote usually carries very little weight, but when opinion is nearly evenly divided it can be worth everything, like that vote in San Francisco that gave veto power to the permanent members of the United Nations Security Council.

The years of the two sea bed committees were decisive for the development and recognition of the Exclusive Economic Zone. The importance of those years is shown by the fact that a swarm of countries moved to become adherents of the zone at the first session of the Third Conference on the Law of the Sea to deal with matters of substance, held in Caracas. This indicates that the matter had been examined and had gained growing support within the committees.

Some of the committees' decisions shaped the character of the Third Conference on the Law of the Sea. One such decision was that concerning the rule of consensus, which originally provided a shield for that minority of pioneers. The solid and concerted opposition to the notion of a conference restricted to three subjects (the twelve-mile territorial sea, certain fishing rights beyond the territorial sea, and navigation through international straits), as propounded by the great naval powers, and the alternative proposal of a conference to examine all aspects and questions of the sea, with the consequent possibility of global negotiations, made a decisive mark on the immediate future. In the course of global negotiations, there was a potential for the economic zone to find approbation, albeit, to be sure, at a price, either real or invented. The real price was the participation of other states, under certain conditions, in the exploitation of living resources; the collateral price (or rather, the fall-back position known in advance) was the adoption of some of the freedoms of the high seas; and the invented price was navigation through international straits.

If one considers the composition of the two sea bed committees in their early years, one notices that all the Latin American members were already adherents of the 200-mile zone and had economic interests as a common denominator, although there were differences in regard to the rules of navigation. The activists coordinated their efforts swiftly and effectively. Some Latin American countries displayed a complete lack of interest in the committees and chose to stay on the sidelines. Latin America's representatives at the time constituted the "200-Mile Club."

That concerted effort within the United Nations opened the way for the first manifestations of a common policy in the Montevideo and Lima declarations of 1970. The Montevideo Declaration was followed by critiques and explanations of why the dissenting votes were cast and what the declaration and its consequences would mean. But while the differences have been emphasized, the broad areas of agreement have been overlooked. In any case, those dissenting votes deprived the Montevideo Declaration of its political force. The Lima Declaration was an opportunity for the landlocked countries in the region to express their disagreement, not with what it contained but with what it did not contain. This disagreement has persisted at the Third Conference.

The Santo Domingo Declaration of 1972 came at the right time to strengthen, refine, and press claims to a 200-mile zone. This declaration did not receive a negative vote from any of the participants, although there were some abstentions. The Santo Domingo Declaration, except for its imprecision as to the spatial character of the zone called the patrimonial sea, placed its adherents in a position similar to that of the countries that claimed a 200-mile zone of adjacent sea under various names for economic purposes while recognizing freedom of navigation in that zone. When it was made plain that adherents of the patrimonial sea intended to define it as having a certain spatial character, the two positions in essence became one. This is the thesis of the Exclusive Economic Zone as a zone sui generis that was debated at the Third Conference on the Law of the Sea.

Other regions and countries also played a part in shaping the zone. Norway and Canada, soon followed by Australia and New Zealand, noted that such a zone was favorable to their interests. But the turning point was the push by the African countries. As early as 1971, the Afro-Asian Legal Consultative Committee took a position favouring the new zone. This process led from Colombo to Yaoundé and Lagos (from 1971 to 1972) and culminated in the declaration of the Organization of African Unity (Addis Ababa, 1973). Africa's support tipped the scales in favor of the Exclusive Economic Zone. As a footnote, for names are of little importance in the matter, it was the Africans that brought into official use the term "economic zone," which had been used in meetings and informal discussions as well as in the diplomatic correspondence of the time.

During the 1972 meetings of the sea bed committee, Kenya indicated its formal support for the new zone. That Kenyan speech cast a glow like that of the promised land, beckoning wanderers in the desert. But in 1971 someone had had a vision of the future: in that year, Ambassador Augusto Espinosa of Colombia had declared that the 200-mile economic zone would emerge victorious from this process.

During those years, certain African countries strove for something more than an economic zone, for a sort of territorial sea modified to provide for rules of navigation that tended more towards innocent passage than towards freedom of navigation. As often happens, these new converts were more radical than the original leaders of the cause they had adopted. The worrisome specter of a 200-mile territorial sea, with the problems between major naval powers and small countries that it would create, helped motivate the search for a compromise. For it is a bad thing for the major powers when they have disputes with small countries. Nothing leaves the same impression as a recognised abuse of power. As early as the Middle Ages, lawyers knew that a middling settlement out of court was worth more than a courtroom victory.

An entire chapter of interregional relations has been given little or no attention, perhaps because the diplomatic correspondence of the time is not yet available to scholars. It concerns the campaign waged by the pioneers of the 200-mile zone to gain the adherence of developing countries. At the crucial meeting of the Afro-Asian Legal Consultative Committee in Colombo in 1971, Argentina, Chile, Ecuador, and Peru attended as observers. Other members of the 200-Mile Club did not attend, quietly citing a lack of funds as the reason--the usual refrain of foreign ministries when they have other priorities. But attendance at that meeting was not casual or of little significance; its importance and consequences were fully intended, planned, and understood.

The Montevideo, Lima, and Santo Domingo declarations, elements in an ongoing process, could have been formally and officially linked by means of a Latin American conference on the law of the sea. Such a conference could have been held on two occasions. After the Santo Domingo conference, Mexico was willing to sponsor and host a conference, as was Argentina after the sessions of the Third Conference on the Law of the Sea held in Caracas. In both cases, a certain pessimism prevailed as to the outcome, with a resulting negative impact on the development of the Exclusive Economic Zone. Nonetheless, a linking of positions was theoretically possible. The proof of this is to be found in the Latin American consensus on Part V of the 1982 convention, entitled "Exclusive Economic Zone."

The third stage in the process takes in the period covered by the Third Conference on the Law of the Sea, which came to an end in December 1982 with the signature of the final act and the convention. In Caracas, in 1974, the EEZ emerged as a respected and respectable institution. Professor Gilbert Gidel said that the victim of the aborted Codification Conference of 1930 had been the three-mile territorial sea. Of the Caracas meeting of the Third Conference on the Law of the Sea it could be said that a new star achieved worldwide renown: the 200-mile Exclusive Economic Zone. The number 200 has entered the ranks of mystic numbers whose secrets numerologists try to divine. And it was the Chileans who, in 1947, with the inspiration of the Humboldt current, discovered it and made it part of international relations and international law.

INTERESTS RECONCILED IN THE ECONOMIC ZONE

The Third Conference on the Law of the Sea has examined two exciting topics, the Exclusive Economic Zone and the international sea bed area. The complex negotiations can be explained and analyzed in terms of these two questions. Of the 24 items on the agenda, broken down into 244 subitems and sub-subitems, 15 were assigned to the Second Committee; but none was as decisive as the EEZ.

The zone, as framed in the Convention on the Law of the Sea, covers 36 percent of the oceans and embraces 94 percent of the fisheries now being exploited.[1] It involves, therefore, a substantial redistribution of the sea's living resources.

Given the conflicting interests, and especially the existence of development and underdevelopment side by side, as well as disparities in political and military power, the political compromises that the text embodies and translates into legal language have not been without ambiguities. In some cases, attempts to clarify terms have resulted in <u>obscurum</u> <u>per</u> <u>obscurius</u>: explaining the obscure in terms yet more obscure. The array of problems--the military uses of the zone and of the high seas, the economic rights of third parties in the zone, delimitation of the zone, and residual rights--indicates that an extensive period of negotiation in search of compromise was indeed necessary. Ambiguity is a necessary ingredient in intricate negotiations where an effort is being made to reconcile contrary and often mutually exclusive interests, in that any victory or advantage for one side involves a defeat or disadvantage for the other. Through ambiguity, the actual reaching of solutions is put off to a later time while present harmony is maintained through agreements in which in each party hopes to protect its own interests. The interpretation of the text is in the eye of the beholder. Clarity and logic could simply pose an insurmountable barrier to agreement. And in the end it is preferable to have an agreement tinged here and there with a certain ambiguity than not to have an agreement at all, particularly if specific steps are to be taken for the settlement of disputes. In some cases, then, ambiguity is a desirable and sought-after feature, a sort of modus vivendi that shields politicians and diplomats and creates the problems that make for lawyers and judges a paradise of complexities of interpretation. They seem wont to toast ambiguity, with all due apologies and respect to logic and to wise Aristotelian syllogisms.

Through the Exclusive Economic Zone one can follow the threads of international relations. The problems of world military strategy, the play of the superpowers, and the military uses of the sea have all served as filters to smooth the edges of the EEZ and refine it into an acceptable institution. The fact is that inoffensive but very abstract language lends itself to drawing a veil over the thorniest issues, as it provides a means for dealing with them by implication only, thus leaving them open to a variety of interpretations.

For small and medium-sized countries, the Exclusive Economic Zone is, as its name signifies, a part of the sea adjacent to the territorial sea in which the coastal state has exclusive right to the exploitation of natural resources. To be sure, this essentially economic interest may in some cases be at odds with other uses of these waters, and this fact explains the apprehension with which naval powers received early claims, since certain questions concerning navigation were raised. Arguments relating to navigation did not only concern commercial shipping but also navigation by warships. It was only when the new zone was accommodated to the interests of the various groups of states and survived successive bouts of scrutiny, and was thus developed, refined, and modified, that it became fit for general widespread acceptance. With regard to provisions for commercial shipping, namely the sacred freedom of navigation, there has been full agreement. Since the introduction of the principle of the use of the zone for exclusively peaceful purposes as laid down with respect to the high seas (Article 88) and incorporated in the regime of the EEZ (Article 58, paragraph 2), certain doubts have arisen with regard to its scope, doubts that were manifested in the discussions of the Third Conference but that no one has suggested be clarified.

Since its inception, the zone has been characterized by purposes existing side by side that taken to their extremes, are mutually exclusive: economics and security. The present characterization of the zone is the result of a balance's being found, although areas of overlap still exist between economics, with which all nations' commercial shipping is concerned, and security, which relates to the military uses of the seas by coastal and other states. Carried on in an atmosphere of suspicion and loaded with dual intentions, the accommodation process went forward taking as a point of reference the extreme position of a modified territorial sea--that is to say, of a zone under a regime assimilated to innocent passage. Faced with this position and its possible consequences, a slow but steady effort was mounted by naval powers and developed countries in an effort to limit the scope of such claims as far as possible. Successive attempts at accommodation took the form of recognition of preferential fishing rights for coastal states, of a resource zone, of a special interest zone, of exclusive fisheries jurisdiction, of a resource conservation zone. Full and open opposition was thus not forthcoming; instead, there was opposition in the form of alternatives, which shows the skill of the naval powers' and developed countries' representatives in handling the affair. In the end, with compromises being accepted on economics and security, the dispute came to center on the question of whether the economic zone was a zone sui generis or part of the high seas.

The Single Negotiating Text, which was the product of the third session held in Geneva in 1975, granted economic concessions to the coastal states having jurisdiction over the zone, upheld the rule of the flag state and related codified rules with respect to navigation contained in the 1958 Convention on the High Seas, and recognized the security interests of naval powers, but without going beyond the claims presented by the naval powers in this respect. Each delegation wanted its own points to be included in the text in order to gain tactical advantage, which led to a struggle for influence, campaigns of persuasion, comings and goings by consultative groups, interminable meetings, the repeated stating of positions, and so forth. But there was no coercion of any kind. Noblesse oblige, as must be recognized in respect to those countries that could have exerted pressure. There were no machinations by foreign ministries. It was an independent effort in which all parties concerned endeavored to win by persuasion alone.

The most critical point was that of the zone's having a status of its own, separate from the status of the high seas. Here, accommodation was achieved by opting for the distinction set forth in the 1958 Convention on the High Seas and adapting this distinction to the EEZ. There was no need to go back to the beginning and reinvent the wheel; it was simply a case of finding viable alternatives and choosing those that seemed best suited as acceptable compromises balancing disparate interests. Vast amounts of reference material were available, for besides the many proposals received at the Caracas session, many papers had been presented by informal consultative groups. The final texts in respect to the Exclusive Economic Zone were provided for consideration by the Evensen Group and the Group of 77. Elements were taken from both as a basis for the design of the zone; the design, as so often happens in the case of draft texts, was modified during subsequent sessions. During that summer in Geneva, there was no time to ponder because those involved were working against the clock, although preparatory work on the single text had begun some days before the general committee made its decision, since it had been felt that the assignment of such a task to the committee chairmen would be inevitable if a proper working basis were to be established. That text reflects the progress made up to that time. Of course, the situation changed in subsequent sessions, and the changes were therefore reflected in later versions of the text.

There was one particularly difficult and complex problem, certainly for those who had taken part in the aborted restricted conference: that of navigation through international straits. This question arose in the difficult process of accommodating economic and security interests; although it had no direct connection with the Exclusive Economic Zone, it became a linked issue during the negotiating process because if the states that were propounding a zone had supported the demands of states bordering on international straits, many such straits would have become subject to the regime of the territorial sea because they were less than twenty-four miles wide. Many supporters of the Exclusive Economic Zone, especially in the developing world, had expressed their support for these demands. In the event, many developed countries said that without a satisfactory regime for navigation through international straits they could never recognize an economic zone. Was this a tactical move or a true position? Given the circumstances, it was meet to accept the position as genuine and act accordingly. The states that wanted the zone established had to make their choice. They also faced another wrangle, this one over archipelagic states, to whose aspirations they gave full and unwavering support. Some nations' interest had to be restrained or moderated. Here, the aspirations of states adjacent to international straits had to be, if not dispensed with, at least attenuated enough that objective, nondiscriminatory navigation rules might be established.

Days went by and consultations amongst the delegations concerned yielded no results. The same news was repeated every day: the parties were maintaining their positions. What could be done to break the impasse? How could a text be produced that stood a chance of acceptance? Could it be assumed that the support given by coastal states favoring an economic zone to the aspirations of states adjacent to international straits was of a tactical nature? How could the blockage be overcome with a text containing objective and reasonable rules? Were there any more rabbits to be pulled out of the hat? Could a Solomonic compromise between the extreme positions be reached? Could something be put forward to help break the log jam? Where could the measured judgment, the technical competence, the experience, and the diplomatic finesse be found? Among whom? It finally was found in the British. One must give Sir Roger Jackling his due, for it was under his discreet and effective guidance that the section on international straits was produced, an accomplishment that had eluded the consultation process and that, if missing or inadequate provided for, could have caused the entire exercise to founder.

The last chapter to take shape was the one concerning archipelagic states. But here the parties involved managed to settle the question even though time had nearly run out. Nobody was especially concerned with the high seas, and so this question remained on the sidelines in the intricate negotiations. The suggestion that its resources be considered the common heritage of humanity under a regime of joint exploitation was quickly dropped when it seemed that this would torpedo the Third Conference. This explains the loose regime of the high seas, in contrast to that of the Exclusive Economic Zone. Prince Vann of Thailand, the chairman of the 1958 Conference on the Sea, referred to the high seas as the "common heritage of mankind." And Hsu, the Chinese member on the International Law Commission, suggested for the continental shelf a regime that has now been adopted for the international sea bed area. And still there are those who would dispute the wisdom of the saying in Ecclesiastes that "there is no new thing under the sun"!

SPECIFIC QUESTIONS RELATING TO THE ECONOMIC ZONE

Delimitation

The term "zone" signifies space. Physically, the Exclusive Economic Zone takes in the area lying between 12 and 200 miles offshore from standard or low-water coastal baselines. The width of the zone cannot exceed 200 nautical miles. The first 12 miles of the zone--in other words, the area lying between 12 and 24 miles from the baselines--constitutes the contiguous zone in which the coastal state has competences in regard to customs, taxation, immigration and emigration, and health (Article 33 of the convention). It may be concluded that the coastal state does not have these competences in the rest of the EEZ.

Demarcation of the outer and side boundaries of the zone, and of the continental shelf, is a particularly sensitive problem that is aggravated by political complexities and the situation of one state's having sovereign islands on the continental shelf of another state. Both the principle of equidistance and the principle of special circumstances linked to equity have been cited as the proper means for resolving the matter. Those who favor application of the principle of special circumstances linked to equity argue that equidistance is protected under this principle, inasmuch as equidistance often results in the establishment of equitable boundary lines. But equity is an imprecise notion while equidistance is a precise one, and equity is something to be achieved in certain specific cases while equidistance is a general principle. Here is an instance, then, of the eternal problem of applying a general principle to a specific case.

The principle of equidistance has lost ground vis-à-vis that of equity. In 1969, in the case of the North Sea Shelf, the International Court of Justice found that equidistance was a method within the corresponding article of the 1958 Convention on the Continental Shelf, although that article seemed to suggest equidistance as a principle rather than as an absolute rule. The case of the Anglo-French continental shelf in the English Channel (1977-1978) applies both equidistance and equity and is particularly important because it resolves the problem of islands adjacent to the coasts of another state-- here, Jersey and Guernsey off the coast of France.

At the Third Conference on the Law of the Sea, successive versions of the negotiating texts diminished the importance of equidistance. In the first version, the order of precedence was (1) agreement of the parties concerned, (2) equidistance, and (3) equity according to special circumstances. Authorization to draw an interim boundary line on the basis of the principle of equidistance was intended to exert pressure that would encourage the channeling of any disagreement to diplomatic, political, or judicial mechanisms for the settlement of disputes and would thus prevent the problems inherent in the regime from dragging on because of the lack of adequate provision in the United Nations Charter.

In another version, the principle of equidistance was to be used "when appropriate" and after all special circumstances had been taken into account. To find the difference in meaning between the two versions requires a surgeon's precision. But the intransigence of the parties (with some backing the principle of equidistance, albeit making allowances for special circumstances, while others uncompromisingly advocated the principle of equity) seemed destined to halt indefinitely the process of reaching a consensus on the convention. A solution was reached by dropping reference to the two principles and stating simply that boundary lines would be drawn by agreement between the parties concerned in accordance with international law. In other words, instead of resolving the matter the Third Conference turned it over to the parties concerned to make an agreement. A thorny question will be determining to what extent procedures for the settlement of disputes may apply in regard to this issue.

When the Exclusive Economic Zone extends into open areas of the sea on which no other state borders, the coastal state may establish the outer limits unilaterally, but the boundary lines thus drawn must conform to international rules in order to be valid with respect to third parties, in accordance with the doctrine established by the International Court of Justice in the Anglo-Norwegian fisheries case (1951).

Coexistence of Competences

Coastal states and other states have competences that coexist in the Exclusive Economic Zone; those of coastal states relate primarily to the exploitation of resources, while those of other states relate to navigation, transport, and communications. The competences of coastal states include both matters pertaining to the exploitation of resources and matters that cannot easily be separated from resource exploitation, such as scientific investigation and pollution control. Competences with respect to resources are well defined and clearly delimited, but competences relating to scientific research and pollution are concerned with the whole of the zone, and are thus <u>competences with respect to the zone itself rather than just competences with respect to certain activities within the zone</u>.

Other states enjoy within the zone some of the freedoms of the high seas (Article 55). The fact that certain provisions from the regime of the high seas have been included in the regime of the EEZ has been cited as evidence that the zone continues to constitute part of the high seas. The fact is that these rules are associated with other very special rules and thus help give shape to a new juridicopolitical entity that has a unified and coherent character that cannot be properly defined in terms of its constituent elements. If this is found acceptable, it would not be possible to assimilate the EEZ either to the high seas or to the territorial sea if the determining criterion were the existence of certain rules common to other areas of the sea. The chapter on the EEZ and its corresponding regulations together constitutes a complete unit whose structural harmony and workability would be destroyed if the zone were assimilated to any other preexisting entity. The existence of intermediate forms is not ruled out in nature, and even less is it in international relations, where newly generated entities often take on such a character.

The sum of a coastal state's competences with respect to the natural resources in the economic zone may be called simply <u>economic sovereignty</u>. To be sure, even though the word "economic" is used to modify "sovereignty" in this case, it is not suggested that this term denotes the perpetual and absolute power that made the Bobino's <u>Tratado sobre la República</u> (Treatise on the Republic) so celebrated. If sovereignty is defined as a full and complete set of competences--that is, the sum of specific competences of every conceivable kind with respect to a given area of subject matter, in this case resources, plus the attribution of residual rights--then this definition achieves by other means the same effects as the attribution of sovereignty with respect to a specific object--which is to say, the effects of economic sovereignty with respect to the Exclusive Economic Zone. Although the question of residual rights hovers in the shadows in the convention, because the relevant clause (Article 59) is indicative rather than prescriptive and instead of establishing a rule turns to individual cases and invokes equity, it may be assumed that residual rights in economic matters will be attributed to the coastal state. Full competence of an economic nature--which is meant by the term "economic sovereignty"--flows from the sum of specifically attributed competences, with the presumptive addition of residual rights. To be sure, the addition of residual rights has yet to be proven as the convention is implemented and thus for the time being is subject to a certain degree of uncertainty.

For the coastal state, sovereignty over the zone expressed in plain, absolute, and unqualified terms is expressly excluded by the corresponding provision relating to the high seas (Article 58 and articles 88 to 115). Hence, the rule stating that "no state may validly purport to subject any part of the high seas (in this case, any part of the Exclusive Economic Zone) to its sovereignty" is included (Article 89).

When in the preparatory work for the 1958 Conference on the Law of the Sea the International Law Commission studied the nature of a state's rights with respect to its continental shelf, the term "sovereign rights" emerged to denote not only the incontrovertible force of those rights but also their limited nature in regard to the object to which they apply. Full sovereignty, unqualified, would have implied mastery over the zone and thus would have prohibited other activities, including those of a military nature. To preserve and protect such activities, the term "sovereign rights" showed itself to be more appropriate than "sovereignty." Similarly, in the term "economic sovereignty," sovereignty is limited to the object to which it is applied (in this case, the sphere of economics) and hence does not prejudice any activities that the parties may wish to leave in the shadows, thus excluding them from a debate that could have an uncertain outcome.

Assimilation of the Exclusive Economic Zone to the territorial sea would also be excluded because sovereignty--in other words, a full and complete set of competences of every kind, not only economic competences--exists in this area of the sea. These full competences permit the prevention, control, and prohibition of every kind of activity, innocent passage alone excepted. Insofar as the EEZ is concerned, albeit with certain limitations--servitudes of a sort in favor of other states--the coastal state enjoys considerable power. Moreover, acknowledgment that a coastal state has discretionary competence in setting the permissible catch and its own capacity to work the fishery, and recognition that the conciliation committee cannot replace the state in the use of this discretionary power, means that a coastal state has the powers that count in regard to economic exploitation.

That the case is not entirely free of ambiguity is shown by the fear often expressed in English-speaking countries concerning "creeping jurisdiction," jurisdiction that expands gradually and eventually comes to prevail as competing jurisdictions are edged out. Actual implementation will shed light on points that now remain obscure. The EEZ could become entrenched as a zone sui generis, become merged into the high seas, or become closer to the territorial sea as predicted by Andrés Aramburu Menchaca: "The Exclusive Economic Zone is destined to become a territorial sea with freedom of navigation, whilst retaining its character."[2]

The Sovereign Rights of Coastal States

The competences of a coastal state in the Exclusive Economic Zone are listed in the convention with various names, depending on their force vis-à-vis other states' powers. The terms "sovereign rights," "jurisdiction," and "other rights" are used in these instances (Article 56 of the convention). Such competences are invariably qualified by the object to which they apply and its purpose.

Determination of the scope of sovereign rights is one of the many important questions raised by such competences. Much elucidative information in this regard is to be found in the documents of the International Law Commission[3] and in the records of the 1958 Conference on the Law of the Sea. The Third Conference on the Law of the Sea heard occasional references to the meaning of this term, in which the idea of identifying these rights with exclusivity predominated. No new in-depth debate has taken place on this matter, and one must therefore look back to the antecedents in the 1950s.

The International Law Commission set forth the meanings of this term in the commentary with which it prefaced its proposed draft articles that later, with additions and amendments, evolved into the four conventions on the law of the sea concluded in Geneva. According to the commission, sovereign rights comprise: (1) necessary rights for natural-resource exploration and exploitation; (2) powers to prevent and punish infractions of the law; (3) the exclusivity of such rights and powers, in the sense that if a given coastal state does not exercise them no other state may exercise them without its consent; and (4) the independence of such rights with respect to real or nominal occupation. As a corollary, they include the power to make laws and, implicitly, to exercise discretional powers.

It does not appear that this theory can simply be transplanted to cover sovereign rights in the Exclusive Economic Zone. For instance, a coastal state could not simply pursue a policy of inaction with respect to the utilization of the EEZ's living resources even if it retained its sovereign rights. Inaction may have a place with respect to the shelf, but it has no place with respect to the Exclusive Economic Zone. A coastal state has rights and obligations in the EEZ, and so far as resources are concerned it must exploit them and do so in the best possible way. In a world hungry for protein, rational exploitation becomes an obligation. To a degree, this philosophy parallels the one that recognizes private property in the context of its social function.

The Attribution of Exclusivity to the Economic Zone

The convention invariably qualifies "economic zone" with the word "exclusive." This qualification may seem superfluous or appear to reflect aims that do not materialize in the text. Indeed, even in economic matters there are certain moderating factors that are scarcely compatible with exclusivity, such as fishing rules with respect to highly migratory species or anadromous species, the true scope of which will probably be mind-boggling when the time comes for implementation.

Nevertheless, this qualification is much more than a relic reminiscent of the arduous discussions and negotiations between territorialists, patrimonialists, zonists, and preferentialists; it is much more than a political whim. In a carefully negotiated text it must of necessity have a meaning that answers an explicit or unstated, but identifiable, purpose. The qualification will have an effect on the interpretation of the provisions agreed upon. It indicates the primacy of the coastal state's interests and rights in the economic sphere and is a factor to be taken into account in allocating residual rights. It is, then, a qualification that brings with it certain consequences as regards interpretation. Hence the idea that, in the absence of a prescriptive stipulation with regard to residual rights, and taking into account an expressed principle of direction or preference (Article 59), the qualifying term "exclusive" can influence interpretations and support the thesis that the sum of a coastal state's economic competences, together with its residual rights in economic matters, constitute full competence in the economic sphere, which may be termed "economic sovereignty." To be sure, states' practice, as well as the settlements that are reached to disputes and especially the actions of international jurisprudence, will provide firm grounds much more apt than mere speculation to indicate the true scope of the part on the Exclusive Economic Zone in the convention.

Scope of the "Pactum de Contrahendo"

"Pactum de Contrahendo" occupies a prominent place in the convention on the sea. Many provisions contained in this treaty simply put off agreement between the parties to a later time, with the parties concerned being bound to negotiate such an agreement. Normally such an obligation could bring either positive or negative results. It is understood that this obligation is fulfilled by negotiation in good faith and that it does not require that any settlement actually be reached. In other words, it is an obligation that is fulfilled in the seeking of an agreement, leaving the actual reaching of an agreement an open question. This obligation would not necessarily be accompanied by results.

In the new law of development, the "Pactum de Contrahendo" has taken on considerable importance. The present situation of the international community and the new impetus given to cooperation and interdependence are causing objective rules in economic and social matters to be brought forth. It is not compatible with the good faith that must direct international agreements that solemn promises of cooperation should be treated simply as intentions that have a role to play or can be used to skirt some political difficulty. A great many provisions of the Convention on the Law of the Sea would only undermine the new system if they were used to avoid definitive results and were fulfilled by the mere act of negotiating. In the "Pactum de Contrahendo" respecting this convention there is something more than a mere undertaking to negotiate; in some cases there is an absolute obligation to achieve results, and the obligation is not fulfilled unless results are achieved. What those results are and when they will be achieved cannot be foreseen, but even if it takes years the obligation will continue and will only be fulfilled when results are achieved. The assumption usually made regarding the "Pactum de Contrahendo" could be turned on its head in that instead of the mere seeking of an agreement constituting an element of fulfillment, it could be understood that in the circumstances of contemporary international life the agreement aims at producing results and entails a solemn commitment to achieve them except where it is evident that the intention of the parties has been to be content with the act of negotiation regardless of the outcome. The Convention on the Law of the Sea, instead of establishing peace in the oceans, would simply help promote interminable wrangling if these clauses were given their usual scope.

The part on the EEZ contains provisions relating to highly migratory species (Article 64). The third conference received proposals to internationalize the fishing of highly migratory species, which for Latin Americans on the Pacific coast concerns mainly tuna. Other proposals aiming to grant preferential rights to the states in whose exclusive economic zones the species in question happened to be found. The approach adopted focuses on the obligation of the countries concerned to cooperate in conserving this resource and ensuring that it is put to the best possible use.

Because of the obligation to make a concerted effort in conservation and optimum utilization, a coastal state may find its catch limited. The provision does not say that other states have automatic fishing rights in the EEZ; such rights, if they exist, must be the result of an agreement concluded with the coastal state, subject to the applicable regulations (Article 62). The fulfillment of this obligation may imply a limitation on catches in the zone. Such limitations would, moreover, be reasonable because, if a species originated and fed in other zones, it would constitute an abuse of rights if a state attempted to take the largest catch possible on the high seas or in its economic zone, leaving the leftovers for other states reached by the species later in their annual migration. It would remain permissible to fish for highly migratory species on the high seas but not for andromous species that could only be caught in waters on the landward side of an EEZ's outer limits (Article 66, paragraph 3).

The doctrinary elaboration of the scope of the "Pactum de Contrahendo" in the international community of today, with the elucidation and identification of the various consequences according to the corresponding system of the convention and the framework of aims and commitments, seen as a whole rather than individually, could constitute an advance in legal analysis imposed by new forms of international cooperation as an objective rule of international relations. By diversifying the agreement into various kinds, taking into account the function of each in the corresponding body of the convention, it would be possible to help strengthen the law of development and lay firmer foundations for cooperation between nations.

The Economic Zone and the High Seas

The nature of the Exclusive Economic Zone gave rise to serious confrontations at the Third Conference on the Law of the Sea. The situation was eventually calmed with certain changes of approach. This means not that the problem has been resolved but rather that each party thinks the problem was settled in its favor or prefers ambiguity to a net loss, as if to say that if no one can win then no one should lose or that the question should be left in the air to be decided by states' practice and by the courts' decisions. If questions are decided by practice the big powers have an advantage, but if by legal decisions then big and small, strong and weak are equal before the law and the impartiality of the courts.

The question centers on whether the Exclusive Economic Zone forms part of the high seas. The Single Negotiating Text of 1975, which survived for a time, said that the high seas comprise all waters not included in any state's EEZ, territorial sea, or inland waters, or in the archipelagic waters of any archipelagic state. The high seas were thus clearly separate from the Exclusive Economic Zone.

Subsequent meetings, which often took place in a tense atmosphere, produced a new wording: "The provisions of this Part apply to all parts of the sea that are not included in the exclusive economic zone, in the territorial sea, or in the internal waters of a State, or in the archipelagic waters of an archipelagic State" (Article 86 of the convention). The first version was based on the relevant clause of the 1958 Convention on the High Seas, adapted to take into account the creation of the Exclusive Economic Zone as a new juridicopolitical entity. The later version concerns rules applicable to a certain area of the sea. Despite the shift in emphasis, the nature of the EEZ as a zone sui generis remains, although the compromise wording, in spite of its enabling agreement to be reached, will spark increased controversy when the Convention on the Law of the Sea becomes binding.

It is worthwhile examining briefly the arguments of those who support the thesis that the Exclusive Economic Zone remains part of the high seas.[4] The arguments in favor of the EEZ's remaining part of the high seas were put forward during the course of the Third Conference on the Law of the Sea. When sixty coastal states proclaimed the sui generis character of the EEZ as a consequence of sovereign rights with respect to natural resource exploration and exploitation, the immediate reaction was the banding together of countries that were landlocked or in a disadvantaged geographical position and states having large merchant fleets, including the United States, the

Soviet Union, Japan, Greece, and of course Liberia. For the EEZ to remain part of the high seas seemed to be linked "to the preservation of the freedoms of the high seas in the economic zone."

The arguments of those who support the doctrine that the economic zone continues to form part of the high seas may be summed up as follows:

1. International law recognizes special jurisdictions on the high seas, but without such jurisdictions altering the nature of the area to which they apply. For example, there exist jurisdictions over the contiguous zone, which the 1958 Convention on the High Seas considered to be part of the high seas. Sovereign rights and jurisdictions in the Exclusive Economic Zone are perfectly compatible with the doctrine that the zone forms part of the high seas.

2. The essential characteristics of the high seas are to be found in the Exclusive Economic Zone: for example, the same inherent freedoms of the high seas apply to the zone except for the freedom of fishing, and no state has sovereignty with respect to the zone. The zone thus constitutes a part of the high seas from which freedom of fishing and related activities have been eliminated.

3. It is recognized that navigation has priority. In the event of incompatibility in legitimate uses, navigation takes precedence over economic exploitation. Indeed, "Artificial islands, installations and structures and the safety zones around them may not be established where interference may be caused to the use of recognized sea lanes essential to international navigation." (Article 60, paragraph 7).

4. The right of hot pursuit may be initiated only from inland waters, the territorial sea, or the contiguous zone, and it ceases when the ship being pursued enters the territorial sea either of the country to which it belongs or of a third state (Article 111, paragraphs 1 and 3). In these respects, it is clearly evident that the Exclusive Economic Zone is assimilated to the high seas. (This argument, which carries a certain weight, nonetheless loses some of its force when examined more closely, since this is a matter of functional competences and the safeguarding of the specific rights of a coastal state that extend up to the contiguous zone.)

5. Finally, a philosophical and logical argument holds that only two entities can exist, the high seas over which no sovereignty exists and the territorial sea over which it does exist, with the existence of an intermediate entity thus precluded. This application of the principle that if two mutually exclusive entities exist then no third entity can exist is founded on the mutual exclusivity of sovereignty and absence of sovereignty. But in fact, much more complex

situations exist in international affairs. As far as sovereignty is concerned, intermediate situations do exist between totality and nullity according to the definition of specific competences with certain areas of application and purposes. Thus, a strict dualism of this sort is at odds with international practice.

Maximum Sustainable Yield and Optimum Utilization

The maximum sustainable yield and optimum utilization of marine species have been described as opposing aims. Biggest is not always best. The Exclusive Economic Zone has to be managed in such a way that fish populations are maintained at or restored to levels that can achieve the maximum sustainable yield in keeping with the relevant economic and environmental factors (Article 61, paragraph 3). In addition, coastal states must promote the optimum utilization of the zone's living resources (Article 62, paragraph 1).

While optimum utilization may coincide with the maximum sustainable yield, it may also mean a smaller yield. Indeed, the maximum yield in purely quantitative terms does not always lead to larger revenues or more jobs. Other factors have a bearing on optimum utilization, such as sport and recreational fishing, tourism, marine parks, and the need to maintain breeding stocks of fish and other marine animal life. In striving for optimum utilization, the economics of fisheries must be considered within the economy as a whole, and particularly as regards the allocation of material and human resources to each productive activity. Convergence of the maximum food yield and the greatest economic utilization of resources must be achieved by means of complex mechanisms for administering the fishery, referred to in the text as the management of resources.

Thus, the experts define optimum utilization as a deliberate mix of biological, economic, social, and political objectives intended to result in the greatest social benefit as a consequence of the development of fishing resources. The use of the Spanish word ordenación as an equivalent for the English word "management" needs to be defined, for this equivalence is not to be found among its common meanings. The new technical meaning of ordenación would be "the art of carrying on an activity or enterprise in a judicious and efficient manner with respect to predetermined goals." Coastal states acquire rights, but also obligations, in the EEZ. Among their obligations, that of resource management should be stressed, for the fulfillment of that obligation implies a scientific understanding of the marine environment and the habits of exploitable species, and the formulation of policies aimed at the optimum utilization of resources.

Military uses

The military uses of the Exclusive Economic Zone, which were brought up for discussion from time to time at the Third Conference on the Law of the Sea, have been the subject neither of detailed examination nor of proposals of clarification. The matter has been left to fall back on precedents, which are to be found both in practice, in connection with the uses of the sea, and in the 1958 conventions on the law of the sea and their preliminary documents.

On this question there are several points to be elucidated, including: the possible effects of sovereign rights with respect to resources, the consequences of the principle of utilization for solely peaceful purposes, and the results of the application of the freedoms of the high seas.

As far as sovereign rights are concerned, the precedents of their being recognized with respect to the continental shelf in 1958 indicate that they are compatible with the military uses of the zone. In the International Law Commission, use of the term "sovereignty" to describe a state's rights over the continental shelf was rejected essentially because of possible interference with military uses by other countries. The term "sovereign rights" was chosen, among other reasons, in order to leave military uses untouched. The 1958 Conference on the Law of the Sea rejected several proposals aimed at prohibiting the use of the continental shelf by foreign powers for military purposes. Even an Indian proposal to prohibit the military use of the continental shelf entirely, whether by foreign powers or by the coastal state, was defeated.

The principle that the Exclusive Economic Zone must be used for solely peaceful purposes has been included in the convention by incorporating the rule expressly mentioned in this respect with regard to the high seas (Article 58, paragraph 2, and Article 88). Enunciation of this principle was motivated by the proclamation of the principle that the international sea bed area constitutes a common heritage of mankind. This principle has thus come to apply to other areas of the sea as well. Its scope has given rise to contradictory and irreconcilable statements, but not to efforts to reach a consensus. According to one position, this principle is to be interpreted as requiring complete demilitarization and the banning of all military activities.[5] Another position states that the principle of peaceful uses does not prohibit military activities, since military activities for peaceful ends may exist, and that the banning of military uses would have to be expressly agreed on, since the United Nations Charter provides a general framework for this. In the myths that surround this question, it has been asserted that the navigation of warships is expressly authorized in the Exclusive Economic Zone, an activity that is interpreted as a military use. This is true in that navigation by warships is authorized as a result of the inclusion of the rules of the high seas, but it would seem excessive to construe this one activity as grounds for the military use of the zone, because there is a good deal of difference between navigation and naval maneuvers, a naval presence the installation of sensing apparatus, arms testing, and so on.

The other point has to do with the freedoms of the high seas. Since military uses are accepted in the regime of freedoms of the high seas, it is concluded that the transfer of these regulations to the Exclusive Economic Zone brings the same consequences. This question was debated and settled at the 1958 Conference on the Law of the Sea. At that conference, the United Kingdom and Ireland introduced a proposal that received majority support and was incorporated in the Convention on the High Seas. The clause in question reads as follows: "These freedoms, and others which are recognized by the general principles of international law, shall be exercised by all states with reasonable regard to the interests of other states...." An adaptation of this clause was included in the draft of the current convention (Article 56, paragraph 2, and Article 58, paragraph 3).

The freedoms of the high seas have been incorporated (Article 58, paragraph 1) by means of a provision that makes reference to the freedoms of navigation, overflight, and laying of submarine cables and pipelines, in accordance with the freedoms laid down in the corresponding article of the chapter on the high seas (Article 87 of the convention) and is extended to "other internationally lawful uses of the sea related to these freedoms." What freedoms? Navigation, overflight, and the laying of submarine cables. The text omits the phrase "and others (freedoms) recognized by the general principles of international law," but the listing is not exclusive. Language and precedents lend themselves to sibylline exercises.

Reservations and the Compatibility Clause

The convention establishes that no reservations shall be admitted except those expressly authorized (Article 309). Among the reservations authorized, those relating to binding procedures or binding adjudication with respect to disputes figure prominently (Article 298).

In this context, the question arises as to the

nature, meaning, and scope of the clause that appears under the title "Declarations and Statements" (Article 310 of the convention), which reads as follows: "Article 309 shall not preclude a State Party, at the time of signing, ratifying or acceding to this Convention, from making declarations or statements, however phrased or named, with a view, _inter alia_, to the harmonization of national laws and regulations with the provisions of this Convention, provided that such declarations or statements do not purport to exclude or to modify the legal effect of the provisions of this Convention in their application to that State Party."

A technical difference is here admitted between reservations and interpretive declarations, but each case must be considered on its own merits since what matters is not the name used but the actual content of any declaration or statement put forward. Considering who are the proponents of this clause--the countries known as "territorialists," which advocate that the EEZ be a modified territorial sea--it may be asserted that the main purpose of the clause has to do with the EEZ. If its purpose were simply to allow interpretive declarations, inclusion of the clause would perhaps be pointless. But the clauses contained in agreements must have some meaning, and this clause does indeed serve some purpose, namely, as stated in the clause itself, to make the convention compatible with national laws and regulations. This authorized purpose could only be served if the declarations and statements made tended, in effect, to be reservations. But then the condition comes into play that such declarations or statements may not have it as their purpose to nullify or modify the legal effect of the provisions contained in the convention. Here, ambiguity provides sufficient latitude that even though these declarations of compatibility may not be called reservations they will in fact function as such and are authorized to do so. How could two texts be made compatible without certain accommodations being initiated by one party albeit subject to subsequent acceptance by the other parties, as is always the case with reservations? If two bodies of law could mesh without difficulty, there would be no need for declarations of compatibility. If such declarations are needed, it is because the bodies of law in question do not fit together neatly and because in order to work well some intervening factor is necessary, something specific on the part of a given state. If this something were worthless or pointless, the clause would undermine itself so far as its fulfilling a useful function is concerned (another gold mine for the lawyers). Practice and the decisions of the courts will have the last word, but in the meantime some states will probably use this clause to defend their national positions.

The Exclusive Economic Zone and International Custom

The Exclusive Economic Zone has received so much support and has become so much a part of international practice that in the unlikely event that the Third Conference on the Law of the Sea had come to naught, the zone would have become a part of international law by general practice or custom. The question can be looked at both within the context of traditional doctrine and in the present-day functioning of multilateral forums, particularly those of the United Nations. The establishment of international custom through the United Nations continues to be hotly disputed. Nevertheless, there is good reason to believe that custom can be affirmed and sometimes even created in this way. Since conferences are negotiative in nature and the positions adopted are tentative, tactical, and subject to conditions, their impact is more debatable than usual. But there can be no doubt that in the United Nations and at international conferences the legal conscience of the community of states is expressed, identified, and established.

The International Court of Justice set forth in detail the elements of international custom in handing down certain decisions, such as the asylum case of 1951 and the North Sea shelf case of 1969. In the relevant 1974 decisions, between the United Kingdom and Iceland and between the Federal Republic of Germany and Iceland, the court did not recognize the Exclusive Economic Zone as a matter of custom. It should be noted, however, that on 25 July 1974, the date on which both decisions were announced, the second session of the Third Conference on the Law of the Sea was being held in Caracas, and so the court had had neither the time nor the opportunity to examine the many declarations in support of the EEZ.

Consideration of the case by the traditional means of coincident and continuous practice, together with expressed court opinion, leaves no doubt in the matter. In fact, a great many states, large and small, developed and developing, in every part of world are involved in this practice. And it should be noted that this goes on without protests or reservations--that is, with the tacit acceptance of other states.

The main argument put forward to challenge this conclusion consists of pointing out that great differences exist between the practices of individual states in this regard. Certainly this is true: such differences do exist, in regard not only to the names used but also to the scope of the competences claimed and exercised. But a broad common base also exists. The fact that differences exist does not preclude the rule of custom, but rather is a normal additional factor. It is precisely because of such differences and points of uncertainty that some codification is being suggested. But custom can exist even if the specific details and standardized concepts that can only be obtained by means of codification are lacking. To be sure, the Exclusive Economic Zone, now rooted in international custom, will be given its final shape by careful comparison of states' practices and the finding of a common denominator. But it does not seem likely that the definitive codification of the EEZ will differ greatly from the text hammered out by the Third Conference on the Law of the Sea, because it is this text that has served as a model for a number of individual states' practices and laws.

THE ECONOMIC ZONE IN THE NEW INTERNATIONAL ECONOMIC ORDER

The advent of the new international economic order in international relations came about while the Third Conference on the Law of the Sea was underway. Efforts to link the conference to the new order yielded uncertain results. Or rather, the new order had little or no real influence on the conference, owing to impropitious timing. Application of the principles implicit in the new order would have required whole chapters of the convention to be rewritten. Such a reevaluation would have required a considerable change in states' aspirations.

The Exclusive Economic Zone entails a redistribution of resources that favors not only developed countries but also those countries that are said to be developing and for the moment are underdeveloped. The circumstance that, in global terms, developed countries may acquire a large share of the resources available does not detract from the fact that developing countries are acquiring those resources that lie within the reach of their technology and working tools. So far as the continental margin is concerned, on the other hand, the gains made by the developed countries are massive, in respect not only of area but also of natural resources. The potential surface of the international sea bed area subject to the principle of the common heritage of humanity is thus reduced to whatever is left over from states' claims, since these claims preceded the common heritage principle by many years. In particular, the movable frontier of the continental shelf established in the 1958 Convention on the Continental Shelf has contributed to this result.

It is noteworthy that one of the claims of the new order was accepted and put into practice at the Third Conference on the Law of the Sea: true and effective participation by developing countries in the decision-making process with respect to matters of general interest. All countries took part, their motives were fully understood, and they defended their own interests properly. On this point, the Third Conference on the Law of the Sea has become a model of global negotiations, and its results took on greater and greater importance as states that at some conferences have sat on the sidelines took a more active and more useful part.

Two cardinal principles of the new order, however, are noticeable by their absence from the convention: compensation as a means to correct objective imbalances, and application of the principle of nonreciprocity in the elaboration of specific agreements and rules.

The Convention on the Law of the Sea will be a particularly illustrative reflection of the status of the society of states in its period of transition to a community of states.

NOTES

1. Lewis M. Alexander: "New approaches to the Control of Ocean Resources." In: R. G. Wirsing (ed.): *International Relations and the Future of the Oceans*. Columbia, S.C.: University of South Carolina Press, 1974. p. 88.
2. Andrés Aramburu Menchaca: "El Derecho del Mar del Porvenir." *Revista de Política Internacional*. No. 154. 1977. p. 70.
3. International Law Commission: *Plenary meetings*. Vol. 1, 1953. pp. 83-86.
4. J. Symonides: "Maritime Economic Zone." *Studies in International Relations*. No. 9, 1977. pp. 56-65.
5. P. Rao: "The Legal Regime of the Sea Bed and the Ocean Floor." In: *Indian Journal of International Law*. No. 9, 1969. p. 17.

_____ Vicente Marotta Rangel

5. The Role of Informal Negotiations in the Search for a Consensus on the Law of the Sea

THE EXPANDING SCOPE OF THE LAW OF THE SEA

Nine years after its opening procedural session in New York (3 to 15 December 1973), the Third United Nations Conference on the Law of the Sea came to an end.[1] In view of the difficult negotiations that took place during this period, several observations may be made regarding the role of informal negotiations in the conference. Despite beginning its immense task without any background documents on which to objectively base itself, the conference ended up with a most complete convention.

R. Eudis has written that this conference represents the most ambitious, extensive, and complicated international negotiation in history.[2] These negotiations have been, to say the least, "the most unique, the most original, and the least susceptible to the ordinary rules of international negotiations."[3] Because of the number of subjects included in its agenda, the scope of this conference exceeded that of any previous negotiations. Included within its competence were topics not dealt with in previous negotiations and arising primarily from technological advances, overfishing, pollution, and the risk of conflict between superpowers bent on exploiting the resources of the sea bed. Such materials have contributed to a revival of interest in areas not previously discussed, and in others that, although well known, have had to be subjected to new political, economic, strategic, and legal evaluations. This reevaluation is justified by the fact that a great many of the members of the international community--the new states--have only recently had the opportunity to contribute to the formulation and advancement of the rules governing the law of the sea.

The content that is now included within the scope of the law of the sea has grown substantially. To the extent that the multifaceted nature of our oceans is recognized--including their role as an instrument of communication between peoples, as a theatre of operations for military strategists, as a cornucopia of biological resources, as a source of mineral riches--to this extent does our view expand from a unifunctional perception to a multidimensional perspective.

From the multiplicity of uses of the oceans, one may deduce that the economic factor has been instrumental in the creation and development of the law of the sea. Over 80 percent of the world's freight is still shipped aboard oceangoing vessels, despite competition from air transport. World fisheries produce about $14 billion in annual income, roughly one-quarter of the amounts produced by the maritime shipping industry or by the oil rigs working over the continental shelf. Based on these figures, it is easy to see why the economic factor is of primary importance in maritime legal relations. Viewing these relations in historical perspective, it is well to remember, as we are reminded by Francoise Thibaut, that traditional sea law was created by the nations of Western Europe, which discovered and explored the other continents (and which were later joined by the United States, Japan, and the Soviet Union), and that it therefore corresponds "to the colonial trade era, in which only a few industrialized countries benefitted."[4] Arising as a reaction against this unequal distribution of wealth, the new law of the sea became less an ideological confrontation between East and West (which was still the case in the 1958 and 1960 conferences) and more an economic confrontation between North and South, as became evident in the course of the Third Conference in regard to some matters. Thus, the rules of the new law of the sea are coming to be seen as the driving force for a new international economic order and as a mechanism for weaving the many loose strands together into a single interdisciplinary fabric.

THE CREATION PROCESS

The new law of the sea not only is a set of rules but also is the result of a special process by which these rules were created.[5] This process, which is linked to a complex and prolonged systematics carried on by the members of the international community (transcending the membership of the United Nations itself), has taken on a pedagogical function, namely, that of clarifying these rules even as the content of the future treaty is being shaped, provision by provision, whether by consensus or majority vote.

Following are the principal elements of the process of negotiation carried out at the Conference on the Law of the Sea:

1. The "global package" mechanism, under which individual articles were given provisional status until each state had the opportunity to determine whether all articles of the treaty were equally acceptable, and the text as a whole was put to a final vote in which each delegation voted either for or against.
2. The methodology in which each of the chairmen of the conference committees was given responsibility for drafting the articles concerning matters falling within the competence of his own commission.
3. The consensus rule.
4. The process of informal negotiations.

THE CONSENSUS RULE

A relevant point in negotiating the new treaty on the law of the sea was the use of the consensus rule. This rule concerns the decision-making process and was elaborated in the General Assembly and other agencies of the United Nations and within other international bodies. It is a process in which decisions do not depend upon voting but are adopted after due consideration provided no delegation voices formal opposition. At the 1973 Helsinki Conference on Security and Cooperation in Europe, this process was defined negatively as "the absence of any clear objection expressed by a representative and raised as an obstacle to adoption of the decision in question."[6] As stated by Mario Amadeo, consensus "is a collective procedure aimed at obtaining a positive result by seemingly negative means. In this case, silence is taken as acquiescent since 'silence gives consent.'"[7]

The validity of the consensus process depends upon the extent to which the chairman of the organization investigates whether there are objections to a given proposal. If there are no objection then the chairman may immediately announce--without taking a vote--that the proposal has been approved. However, things are seldom this simple: "This result, which may be achieved in little more than a minute, is generally preceded by weeks or even months of strenuous negotiations and pourparlers."[8]

Article 18 of the United Nations Charter specifies that in the General Assembly, decisions on important questions are to be taken by a two-thirds majority vote of members present and voting, while other questions require a simple majority only. The other United Nations bodies (except the Security Council), as well as those of the specialized agencies of the United Nations, also take decisions by simple or qualified majority, as the case may be. Matters dealt with in the Security Council are classified as either procedural or nonprocedural questions. The veto mechanism applies to the latter type.

There is no rule in the charter concerning consensus. Rather, this process developed gradually in practice, with the encouragement of developed states that --being in a minority within the General Assembly--were opposed to the rule of "one nation, one vote" and with the (somewhat reluctant) acceptance of the other states who found that it possessed a certain degree of flexibility enabling it to overcome political differences and marshal general support for solutions whose effectiveness is dependent upon the approval of the superpowers.

As indicated by the secretary general of the United Nations Conference on Trade and Development (UNCTAD), Raul Prebisch, during the first session of that conference in 1974, "There is clearly nothing of practical value to be gained in adopting recommendations by a simple majority vote of developing countries, but without the support of developed countries, where the application of these recommendations depends upon their acceptance by the latter group."[9]

The consensus process has also been used to overcome rivalries that have arisen between the superpowers, such as the confrontation between the United States and the Soviet Union over financing of United Nations military operations in the Belgian Congo (Zaire). The question that arose was whether or not the sanctions specified in Article 19 of the charter should be applied, and the answer to this question would have had very serious consequences for the future of the United Nations. For this reason, Secretary General U Thant eventually ruled that questions that could not be solved without opposition would not be entertained.[10]

As is often the case, the consensus process began as a means used by international organizations to approve motions regarding procedural questions. Later, its use was gradually extended to the approval of substantive motions. Such was its evolution within two committees of the General Assembly (those dealing with the outer space and with the question of friendly relations) whose practices served as antecedents in the development of the consensus process. Perhaps the earliest use of consensus was by the Outer Space Committee. On 19 March 1962, in the second meeting of this committee, its chairman made a statement to the effect that through informal consultations he had learned that all members shared the objective to conduct the committee's business in the manner most likely to achieve agreement without the need for a formal vote. The chairman then concluded that if there were no objections, he would announce that the committee was in agreement regarding this procedure, and it was so decided.[11]

Whether in the practice of the United Nations Secretariat or in that of the above mentioned committees, it has been noted that the process of consensus developed against a background in which the East-West dichotomy was the central issue. However, it was in relation to the North-South polarization, which was fundamental to the formation, principles, and objectives of the UNCTAD, that the consensus process achieved its greatest consistency and strength.[12] General Assembly Resolution 1995 (XIX) of 30th December 1964, by which the UNCTAD was created as a permanent agency of the United Nations, established a process of mandatory conciliation before any vote could be taken. This process was designed to provide an adequate basis for the adoption of recommendations regarding proposals of a specific nature that would substantially affect the economic or financial interests of particular countries. The search for a consensus in this stage of mandatory conciliation was in the interests of the industrialized countries and was accepted by other countries as the lesser of two evils, the other of which would have meant adoption of the veto system or a means of weighted voting.[13]

APPLICATION OF THE CONSENSUS PROCESS IN THE LAW OF THE SEA

With respect to negotiations on the law of the sea,[14] it has been noted that the consensus rule as a decision-making method was introduced in the ad hoc committee created in 1967 by means of United Nations General Assembly Resolution 2340 (XXII). The consensus process continued to be applied in the sea bed committee created under General Assembly Resolution 2467 (XXIII) on 21 December 1968. The Third United Nations Conference on the Law of the Sea, which met in New York for the first time in December 1973, decided to postpone its decision regarding the rules of procedure until its second session. Accordingly, the rules were approved by consensus in Caracas following arduous negotiations. But the fundamental rule of the third conference concerning consensus did not figure in these rules themselves; it was detailed separately.[15] This is explained in part by the fact that the model for the conference rules (i.e., the rules of the General Assembly) does not contain the consensus rule, this being the first time in the history of international conferences and organizations that that rule had been incorporated in a document of positive law.[16]

There were three fundamental reasons why consensus was employed within the context of the negotiations concerning the treaty on the Law of the Sea.

The first was the delegations' fear of finding themselves in the minority on matters they considered vital. This occurred particularly with the United States delegation, as it had occurred in the past with the countries of Latin America. Galindo Pohl offers the following comment regarding the use of consensus: "There was a fundamental political reason for it. The Latin American position with respect to traditional sea law was clearly a minority view: consensus served as a safeguard."[17]

The second reason was based on the conviction that the creation of a new order within sea law would only be possible with the support of the greatest number of states.

The third reason was the assumption that the many questions being introduced regarding the law of the sea, and the conflicting interests related to these questions, would lead to formulation of a global package of solutions, and that such a package would be less compatible with the traditional consensus mechanism in which sectoral views dominate and more compatible with a consensus method in which overall solutions might find greater acceptance. As was stated in the Gentleman's Agreement contained within the conference rules, the problems of the sea are tightly interrelated and must be considered as a whole.

These three reasons explain the introduction of the consensus rule as the principal (although not final or definitive) decision-making procedure of the conference. To these three may be added the positive experiences of the General Assembly ad hoc committee and the sea bed committee. As also pointed out by Galindo Pohl, both committees operated under the consensus rule, and through it they achieved the Declaration of Principles Regarding the International Sea Bed Area and the List of Topics and Questions for the Third Conference on the Law of the Sea.

The question of the concept of consensus is different from that of its legal effects, which depend upon the context and the respective subject. Thus, the questions negotiated in the Conference on the Law of the Sea have had as their objective the search for bases of agreement concerning the various points on the agenda and the various proposals regarding same. After ten conference sessions, the negotiation phase ended with the adoption of the convention. With respect to consensus, then, it is necessary to distinguish between the process itself and the result of this process. In the latter case, consensus is seen as a rule or set of rules. The question has been raised as to whether, in this case, consensus might not be a new type of source for law or a new category of legal acts.[18] The answer to this question is in the negative. On the other hand, it is also necessary--as proposed by Barry Buzan[19]--to distinguish between <u>passive</u> consensus, employed simply to avoid a vote, and <u>active</u> consensus, which acts as a stimulus and an innovation in the search for positive results in negotiations.

The consensus process was the method generally used, with active consensus being employed particularly after the fifth session of the conference. It is true that the decision to hold a vote has been adopted, for example in the case of President Amerasinghe, when it was necessary to decide whether he could continue to hold the chair when he had ceased to be a member of the Sri Lanka delegation, and again in the case of the choice between Portugal and the Federal Republic of Germany as the site of the Law of the Sea Tribunal. These cases have several explanations: at least the second case was in effect an election that was dealt with under articles 46-49 of the rules; neither case was a substantive issue; and finally, every other method had been exhausted in the effort to reach general agreement.

In a vote, procedural questions are decided by a simple majority of the representatives present and voting, while substantive matters must have the approval of two-thirds of the representatives present and voting, providing those voting in favor include a majority of states participating in that session of the conference.

It is interesting to note that the final stage of the process of consolidation and incoporation of the consensus took place during the later sessions, when agreement was obtained on one of the crucial questions facing the conference: the question regarding the decision-making process in the Council of the Sea Bed Authority. It was decided then that substantive questions would be decided, in accordance with the case under consideration, in three different manners: (1) by a two-thirds majority, (2) by a three-fourths majority, or (3) by consensus. Among the questions to be decided by consensus were amendments to Part XI of the convention. In addition, the term "consensus" was defined as the "absence of any formal objection" (Article 161, paragraph 8(e) of the convention).

CONFLICTING INTERESTS

Bearing in mind the nature and practice of consensus, it is possible to comprehend one of the main reasons for the slow pace of negotiations at the conference. Such negotiations can be easy and rapid when the voting method is used. But where that method is dispensed with or rejected as contrary to the consensus process, there is no other way to assess the mood in committees, plenary sessions, and negotiating groups, except through the presentations of each delegation on the various items of the agenda and on the various proposals concerning each of these items.

Another principal reason for the slow pace was the diversity of factors to be considered in the law of the sea. Within the economic sphere, for example, there was the distribution of jurisdiction over the biological and mineral resources of the waters and sea bed, the commercial shipping regime, and the impact of development. Military interests included freedom of navigation and undetectability of nuclear-armed submarines; scientists are concerned with the regime governing research in oceanography; ecologists are interested in the assignment of responsibility for conservation of the marine environment; geographers have such concerns as the opposition between coastal states and the landlocked states; while politicians concentrate on conflict between opposing sovereignties, projection of the concept of the common heritage of mankind and confrontation between blocs formed along lines of regional and ideological interests. These broadly diversified but very relevant factors necessarily engendered a balance of forces that was unmatched by those of any other negotiating forum.

It is on the basis of these interests that the traditional regional groupings arose, essentially within the United Nations: (1) Asian, (2) African, (3) Latin American, (4) East European, and (5) West European and other states. The chairmanships of the first, second, and third committees, as well as the drafting committee, were assigned to these regional groups. The African states are the most numerous (forty-nine members), followed by the Asians (forty-four members), Latin Americans (thirty members), and West European and other states (twenty-six members).

Other groups were also formed, however, mostly on the basis of specific problems facing the conference, and the degree to which these were perceived as vital to a given state's well-being or as affecting its strategic, political, economic, or scientific interests or communication. Often such issues resulted in new and sometimes surprising polarizations as states formed parts of more than one group, depending on the different voting criteria of each and the topic being dealt with. The largest such grouping is the Group of 77, which included close to 120 members--over two-thirds of the conference membership.

Only fifty-four states were members of the group of landlocked states (twenty-eight members) and states with special geographical characteristics (twenty-six members), which meant that the group of coastal states had a significant majority. The overwhelming majority of coastal states favored the concept of the Exclusive

Economic Zone rather than that of extending the territorial sea. If necessary, the group of landlocked states and states with special geographical characteristics would also align themselves with this majority, in opposition to the so-called territorialists. Only twenty-three states were in the latter category, and of these six were in Latin America: Brazil, Ecuador, El Salvador, Panama, Peru, and Uruguay. The others were: Benin, Cape Verde, Congo, Democratic Yemen, Equatorial Guinea, Gabon, Guinea-Bissau, Libya, Madagascar, Mauritania, Mozambique, Sao Tomé and Principe, Senegal, Sierra Leone, Somalia, and Togo. Angola was included in the territorialist group as an observer.

Another interest group worth noting, because of its influence in the conference, was the group of archipelagic states: Cape Verde, Fiji, Indonesia, Japan, Madagascar, Mauritius, the Philippines, Sao Tomé and Principe, the Seychelles, Tonga, and Trinidad and Tobago.

Two groups of states polarized around the question of how to determine the boundaries of maritime zones, one advocating the principle of equidistance (twenty-three members) and the other favoring use of the "equity" criterion (twenty-nine members), making this one of the most crucial issues facing the conference.

These groups concerned with the delimitation of maritime zones, particularly in respect to the continental shelf and the Exclusive Economic Zone, were the last to be formed at the seventh session of the conference (1978) for the purpose of examining the crucial issues that at that time remained unresolved. Other issues in this category included exploration and exploitation of the sea bed and the policy regarding its resources; financial arrangements in regard to this exploration and exploitaion; the choice of agencies responsible for this exploration and exploitation, including their respective duties and jurisdictions; access by landlocked and geographically disadvantaged states to the living resources of the Exclusive Economic Zone; settlement of disputes relating to the exercise of the rights of sovereignty of coastal states over the Exclusive Economic Zone; and definition of the outer limits of the continental shelf.

IMPORTANCE OF INFORMAL NEGOTIATIONS

Among the semiofficial and unofficial groups within the conference there were two others that merit our attention, one formed at the beginning of conference negotiations and the other organized in the 1981 Geneva meeting. The first was the so-called Evensen Group, chaired by the head of the Norwegian delegation and formed for the purpose of solving the problems encountered in the Second Committee. This group began its work in the first session of the conference and gradually increased its numbers from an initial group of eighteen to some forty participants--all of whom were chosen on strictly personal grounds. Operating without mandate and without express ties to any other group or delegatiton, the Evensen Group attempted to apply a "purely legalistic methodology," "without prejudice to any position," in order to reduce the various texts to increasingly precise and complete proposals capable of obtaining the consensus of the conference. This method was to a certain extent innovative. The chairman took upon himself the responsibility of preparing a text that included proposed amendments that had been submitted for discussion by the group and that circulated without any indication of either date or authorship. Afterwards, the text was revised by the chairman and resubmitted to the members of the group as often as necessary to arrive at a proposal that could be accepted by consensus.

In April 1975 the Evensen Group, having completed the sixth revision of its texts, agreed to have Ambassador Evensen forward these to the chairman of the Second Committee, in his capacity as chairman of a semiofficial group and as a personal undertaking. The group's contribution toward formulation of the final text of that committee was extremely positive, primarily with regard to the articles on the Exclusive Economic Zone, its definition and utilization, and its biological resources.[20]

It is very interesting to evaluate the work of the various negotiating groups of the conference, taking into account their nature as formal or informal bodies. Of even more relevance than this division between formal and informal groups is the distinction between formal and informal negotiations per se, for it is common knowledge that the formal groups of the conference engaged in both types of negotiations and that informal negotiations have had a profound influence on the development and growth of the codification process. The advantages of informal meetings are well-known: (1) they serve as a stimulus for negotiations; (2) they allow delegates to candidly examine actual points of disagreement and to put forward compromise formulas; (3) they permit greater flexibility on the part of negotiators; (4) they facilitate the formation of ad hoc groups for the purpose of reconciling opposing positions; and (5) they save money since it is possible to dispense with (or at least reduce the size of) the staff required for formal meetings, including secretaries, translators, and interpreters.

Informal negotiations may have an added advantage or significance in that they can serve as a means for avoiding situations that could arise within the official or semiofficial procedures, but they do not prevent new negotiations that might eventually lead to a revision of these very situations. This is precisely what happened in the 1981 Geneva session when the United States delegation disagreed with the other delegations with respect to formalizing the draft convention and attempted to reopen negotiations primarily in reference to Part XI on the regime governing exploration and exploitation of the sea bed. A compromise was sought between the alternatives of accepting this proposal, and thus sounding the death knell of everything that had been so laboriously negotiated over the course of several years, and rejecting it, which would likewise have put an end to all hopes of reaching an agreement. The solution was to create a new forum independent from the conference in which the U.S. initiative could be discussed informally. This forum was instituted under the joint chairmanship of Ambassador Koh, conference president, and Ambassador Engo, chairman of the First Committee.

We should also make mention of the parliamentary device known as the "contact group," which is intended as an informal stimulus to negotiations and which had much use in the course of the conference. The contact group consists of representatives appointed by regional groups and is generally open to other members of these groups as well.

All these various methods and factors that we have considered here have contributed to the development of the negotiating process of the conference and positively led to the approval of the new treaty on the law of the sea.

NOTES

1. Regarding negotiations at the Third Conference on the Law of the Sea see, among others:

John R. Stevenson and Bernard H. Oxman: "The Preparation for the Law of the Sea Conference," American Journal of International Law, 1974, pp. 1 et seq.

..........: "The Third United Nations Conference of the Law of the Sea: The 1974 Caracas Session,"American Journal of International Law, 1975, pp. 1 et seq.

..........: "The Third United Nations Conference of the Law of the Sea: The 1975 Geneva Session," American Journal of International Law, 1975, pp. 763-797.

Bernard H. Oxman: "The Third United Nations Conference on the Law of the Sea: The 1976 New York Session, *American Journal of International Law*, 1977, pp. 247-269.
..........: "The Third United Nations Conference on the Law of the Sea: The 1977 New York Session," *American Journal of International Law*, 1978, pp. 57-82.
..........: "The Seventh Session" (1978) *American Journal of International Law*, 1979, pp. 73-89.
..........: "The Eighth Session" (1980) *American Journal of International Law*, 1981, pp. 211 et seq.
Francoise Thibaut: "Le Continent Américain et la Crise du Droit de la Mer," RGDIP, 1976, p. 785.
F. V. García-Amador: The Latin American Contribution to the Development of the Law of the Sea, *American Journal of International Law*, 1974, pp. 33 et seq.
David L. Ganz: "The United Nations and the Law of the Sea," ICLO, 1977, pp. 1 et seq.
Edward Miles: "The Structure and Effects of the Decision Process in the Sea Bed Committee and the Third United Nations Conference on the Law of the Sea," *International Organization*, 1977, No. 31.

2. Robert D. D. Eudis: "Procedures and Techniques of Multinational Negotiation: The LOS III Model," *Virginia Journal of International Law*, 1977, vol. 17, no. 2, p. 217.

3. Guy De Lacharrière: "Le Nouveau Droit de la Mer," *Politique Etrangère*, March 1980, p. 88.

4. "L'Amerique Latine et L'Evolution du Droit International de la Mer," RGDIP, 1971, p. 745.

5. Barry Buzan has written in this regard, "The Third Nations Conference on the Law of the Sea (UNCLOS III) is important not only because of the scope and substance of the issues with which it is concerned, but also because it represents a major interest international experiment in decision-making by consensus." Barry Buzan: "Negotiating by consensus: Developments in Technique at the United Nations Conference on the Law of the Sea," *American Journal of International Law*, 1981, p. 324.

6. Amadiou-Mahtar M'Bow: "Le Consensus dans les Organisations Internationales." *Le Consensus et la Paix*, Paris, UNESCO, 1980, p. 12. If the objection is not in the nature of an obstacle to adoption of the decision, as in the case of reservations and interpretations, then it is understood that consensus has been obtained. See Rachid Daker: "Quelques Aspects Politiques et Juridiques du 'Consensus' dans le Monde Arabe et dans l'Islam," *Le Consensus et la Paix*, op. cit., p. 165.

7. Mario Amadeo: "Le Consensus dans les Relations Internationales," *Le Consensus et la Paix*, op. cit., pp. 128 and 131.

8. Mario Amadeo: "El Consenso en las Relaciones Internacionales" *Anuario Hispano-Luso Americano de Derecho Internacional*, 1979, no. 6, p. 19.
9. M'Bow, op. cit., p. 19.
10. Ibid., op. cit., p. 18.
11. Michael Hardy: "Decision Making at the Law of the Sea Conference," *Revue Belge de Droit International*, 1975, p. 447.
12. On consensus in general, see, in addition to notes 1, 6, 7, and 8 above, W. Jenks: "Unanimity, the Veto, Weighted Voting, Special and Simple Majorities and Consensus as Modes of Decision in International Organizations," *Cambridge Essays in International Law, Essays in Honour of Lord McNair*, London, 1965, pp. 48-63.

Guy de Lacharrière: "Consensus et Nations Unies," *Annuaire Francaise*, 1968, pp. 9-14.

Anthony D'Amato: "On Consensus," *Canadian Yearbook of International Law*, 1970, pp. 104-222.

F. Y. Chai: *Consultation and Consensus in the Security Council*, New York, Unitar, 1971.

S. Bastid: "Observations sur la practique du consensus," *Multitudo legum, jus unum*, Festschrift fuer Wilhelm Wengler, Berlin, 1973, vol. 1, pp. 11-25.

L. Sohn: "United Nations Decision-Making: Confrontation or Consensus?" *Harvard International Law*, 1974, pp. 438-445.

H. Cassan: "Le Consensus dans la practique des Nations Unies," *Annuaire Francais de Droit International*, 1974, pp. 456-485.

A. Cassese: "Consensus and some of its pitfalls," *Rivista di Diritto Internationale*, 1975, pp. 456-485.

W. Wengler: "Rechtsvertrag, Konsensus und Absichtserklaerung in Voelkerrecht" (Agreement, Consensus and Intent in International Law), *JuristenZeitung*, 1976, pp. 193-197.

L. Sohn: "Voting Procedures in United Nations Conferences for the Codification of International Law," *American Journal of International Law*, 1975, pp. 310-353.

13. Hardy, op. cit., p. 446.
14. On the use of consensus at the Conference on the Law of the Sea, see, in addition to notes 2, 5, and 11 above, the following: D. Vignes: "Will the Third Conference on the Law of the Sea Work According to the Consensus Rule?", *American Journal of International Law*, 1975, pp. 119-129.

Tullio Treves: "Devices to Facilitate Consensus: The Experience of the Law of the Sea Conference," *The Italian Yearbook of International Law*, pp. 40-60.

Giuseppe Barile: "Uguaglianza e Disuguaglianza degli Stati alla Conferenza sul Diritto del Mare" (Equality and Disparity of States at the Conference on the Law of the Sea), *Rivista di Diritto Internationale*,

1979.

15. Reynaldo Galindo Pohl: "Contribución de América Latina en la Conferencia de Caracas" (The Latin American Contribution at the Caracas Conference), *Derecho del Mar: Una Visión Latinoamericana*, Jorge A. Vargas and Edmundo Vargas C. (editors), Mexico, Editorial Jus, 1976, page 55. According to various authors, consensus is incorporated in the conference rules themselves since item 1 of Article 37 refers to the obligation to take every effort to arrive at a *general agreement* before taking a vote on substantive issues. See Daniel Vignes, op. cit., pp. 119-129, and Tullio Treves, op.cit., p. 41.

16. The Rules of Procedure of the Third United Nations Conference on the Law of the Sea were approved by the conference on 27 June 1974 with the appendix containing the chairman's declaration regarding the requirement to submit substantive issues to consensus before voting on them. Some weeks later (19 August 1974), the Bucharest Conference on Population adopted in an annex of its internal rules a statement that it was "highly desirable" that decisions be taken by consensus before reaching the voting stage. See Cassan, op. cit., pp. 469-470.

17. Galindo Pohl, op. cit.
18. Bastid, op. cit., p. 25.
19. Buzan, op. cit., p. 329.
20. Daniel Vignes: "Deux prolégomenes du nouveau Droit de la Mer: le Texte unique de négociation du 7 mai 1975 et le Groupe nommé Evensen," *Revue Iranienne des Relations Internationales*, 1975-1976, pp. 18-25. Also Eudis, op. cit., pp. 247-249.

_____ *Julio César Lupinacci*

6. The Legal Status of the Exclusive Economic Zone in the 1982 Convention on the Law of the Sea

THE ORIGINS OF THE EXCLUSIVE ECONOMIC ZONE

The earliest antecedents of the Exclusive Economic Zone are to be found in the declarations of sovereignty and jurisdiction over waters within a 200-mile limit, made by certain Latin American states. The first of these were the unilateral proclamations contained in the official declaration by the president of Chile of 23 June 1947 and Executive Decree 781 of the government of Peru of 1 August 1947. These similarly worded documents established a maritime zone extending 200 miles offshore for the purpose of reserving, protecting, conserving, and exploiting existing resources within that area, without affecting the freedom of navigation in the zone.

Five years later (18 August 1952), the Santiago Declaration on a maritime zone was signed by the three South American countries that border the South Pacific: Chile, Ecuador, and Peru. This was the first international instrument to proclaim a 200-mile limit, and it states that the three signatories, "being resolved to preserve for and make available to their respective peoples the natural resources of the areas of sea adjacent to their coasts," declare that in view of the geological and biological factors affecting the existence, conservation, and development of the flora and fauna in those waters "the former extent of the territorial sea and contiguous zones is insufficient to permit of the conservation, development, and use of those resources, to which the coastal countries are entitled." As a consequence the three nations "proclaim as a principle of their international maritime policy that each of them possesses sole sovereignty and jurisdiction over the area of sea adjacent to the coast of its own country and extending not less than 200 nautical miles from the said coast."

The declaration adds that this shall not be construed as disregarding the necessary limitations on the exercise of sovereignty and jurisdiction established under international law in favor of innocent passage. In this respect, the Santiago Declaration differs from the Chilean and Peruvian instruments that preceded it and that refer to freedom of navigation.

In commenting on the differences of interpretation on the juridical nature of this area, Alfonso Arias Schreiber states that the important factor here is that it was from this point onward that the idea of extending the jurisdiction of the coastal state to include waters within a 200-mile limit, in order to ensure that marine resources were preserved and used to satisfy the needs and promote the well-being of the people, began to take hold.[1]

To implement the policy proclaimed in the Santiago Declaration of 1952 the three signatories began to enact regulations relating to the fisheries of the South Pacific and provided for the establishment of a Permanent Commission for the Conservation and Exploitation of the Marine Resources of the South Pacific in order to coordinate the activities of member countries in achieving various objectives, including research and the adoption of measures aimed at the conservation, protection, and utilization of marine fauna and other resources. A system of sanctions to be imposed against those who violate fishing regulations approved by the conference was also enacted, and other regulations referred to monitoring and supervising maritime zones, granting permits for exploitation of the resources, and other matters. In addition, a Protocol of Accession to the Santiago Declaration was signed in Quito on 6 October 1955, by which states of the Americas were free to accede to the fundamental principles of the declaration.

There are also a number of antecedents in the resolutions, opinions, and reports issued by several bodies within the Inter-American Systems and in drafts prepared by Latin American countries.[2] One of the most important of these is Resolution XIII of the Third Meeting of the Inter-American Council of Jurists (held in 1956), which is entitled "Principles of Mexico Concerning the Law of the Sea." This document set forth and recognizes several principles as expressing the legal perceptions of the Americas and as applicable by the American states, including the principle that each state has the right to set reasonable limits to its territorial sea on the basis of geographical, geological, and biological factors, the economic means of its people, and its own security and defence requirements. This resolution was the subject of various declarations and reservations, as was the Resolution of Ciudad Trujillo, adopted by the Specialized Inter-American Conference on Conservation of Natural Resources: Underwater Shelf and Marine Waters (15-28 March 1956), which was particularly important as a forerunner of the 1958 Geneva Convention on the Continental Shelf.

In the first and second United Nations conferences on the law of the sea held in Geneva in 1958 and 1960, the criteria set forth by Chile, Peru, and Ecuador in favor of extending jurisdiction over a 200-mile area gained little support and left these three South American countries in an isolated position. However, following these conferences--particularly during the 1960s--several Latin American countries issued unilateral declarations that, although differing in detail, extended their jurisdiction over maritime areas within the 200-mile area. These countries were[3] thus endorsing the movement begun by Chile, Ecuador, and Peru and subsequently followed by El Salvador, whose constitution of 1950 extended sovereignty over waters within 200 miles. By means of Executive Decree 1L of 5 April 1965, Nicaragua established a "National Fisheries Zone" extending 200 nautical miles from its Atlantic and Pacific coasts "for improved conservation and rational exploitation" of its fisheries and other resources.

Argentina followed with its Law 17094 of 29 December 1966 concerning "Argentinian sovereignty over waters adjoining the national territory," in which jurisdiction was extended over maritime zones adjacent to its coasts for a distance of 200 miles measured as a general rule from the low-water line.[4] Article 3 of the law specifies that its provisions do not affect freedom of navigation or overflight.

Although Law 17094 does not use the words "territorial sea," this phrase does appear in a law promulgated on 22 April 1968 to amend Article 2340 of the Civil Code. The latter law, however, makes no reference to a 200-mile limit, but rather to "that distance which is set forth in special legislation, independently of the jurisdictional power over the contiguous zone." This "special legislation" would appear to be the above-mentioned Law 17094 and Law 17500 (the Fisheries Act) of 25 October 1967, which refers to the "territorial sea of Argentina," apparently in reference to the adjoining waters up to the 200-mile distance. While the use of terminology is not entirely consistent--some provisions contain yet another expression "jurisdictional waters"--it is nevertheless clear that Argentinian sovereignty or jurisdiction is being proclaimed over a maritime zone extending 200 nautical miles from Argentina's coast.

By its Law 31 of 2 February 1967, Panama extended its sovereignty "beyond its continental and insular territory and its island waters to a zone of territorial sea 200 nautical miles wide, to the sea bed and subsoil of that zone and to the air space above it." Panama had already been promulgating laws and decrees relating to fisheries and its territorial sea or jurisdictional waters for several years preceding its 1967 legislation. Presumably, these provisions are applicable to its subsequent extension of the 200-mile limit.

In Decree 604/969 of 3 December 1969 and in its Fisheries Act of 29 December 1969--Law No. 13833-- Uruguay extended its territorial sea to 200 nautical miles, as measured from the baselines.[5] The Uruguayan legislation is particularly interesting in that it embodies the so-called plurality of regimes within the territorial sea, under which two well-defined zones are distinguished within the 200-mile territorial sea: (1) a 12-mile zone measured from the baselines, within which there is innocent passage and fishing and hunting of marine life are exclusively reserved for vessels of Uruguayan registry, without prejudice to any international agreements signed by Uruguay on the basis of reciprocity; and (2) the remaining 188-mile zone in which the freedoms of navigation and overflight are recognized and living resources may be exploited by foreign vessels under permits issued by the Office of the President in accordance with Uruguayan legislation and regulations, or under international agreements to which Uruguay is a signatory.

Therefore, two separate regimes are applied within Uruguay's territorial sea: that of the territorial sea per se, within the 12-mile limit; and that of sovereignty, limited by the recognition of freedom of navigation and overflight, within the area between the 12-mile and 200-mile limits, which--because there was no official term in international law--continued to be referred to as the territorial sea, taking into account the broad competences that Uruguayan legislation assigns to the state and the residual application of the principle of sovereignty within that area.

Of all the various formulations used to extend sovereignty and jurisdiction over coastal waters to the 200-mile distance before the Third United Nations Conference on the Law of the Sea, Uruguay's legislation comes closest to that adopted in the convention with regard to the territorial sea and the Exclusive Economic Zone, although certain differences of substance exist between the latter and the concept of plurality of regimes within the territorial sea.[6]

Brazil expanded its territorial sea to the 200-mile limit under Decree-Law 1098 of 25 March 1970, which also specifies that Brazilian sovereignty extends to the airspace above such area and to its sea bed and subsoil. Within Brazil's 200-mile territorial sea, the right of innocent passage of all vessels is recognized, regardless of nationality, and fisheries activities are made subject to Brazilian regulations governing rational utilization and conservation of the living resources of the sea, as well as research activities and exploration. Decree 68459 of 1 April 1971 established two 100-mile fisheries zones, one of which includes coastal waters within 100 miles of Brazil's coastline, the other consisting of the remaining maritime zone out to the 200-mile limit. The first zone is reserved for Brazilian vessels only, whereas foreign vessels are allowed to fish in the latter area under duly authorized permits.

When the United Nations General Assembly adopted Resolution 2750 (XXV), in December 1970 under which a conference on the law of the sea was convened for 1973 and the mandate of the Committee on the Peaceful Uses of the Sea bed and the Ocean Floor beyond the Limits of National Jurisdiction was extended to include preparation of a draft treaty to be considered by the Conference, an important group of nine Latin American countries had declared sovereignty and jurisdiction over all waters within 200 nautical miles of their coasts.

The legal scope of these declarations varies depending upon whether the entity established is (1) a regime in which the classical concept of the territorial sea has been applied to the entire area within the 200-mile limit, so that the coastal state claims complete sovereignty with the only limitation being that of innocent passage (Ecuador, Panama, and Brazil); (2) a zone of sovereignty (whether or not it is called a territorial sea) in which freedoms of navigation and overflight are recognized, in some cases establishing two separate and precisely defined zones, one of innocent passage and the other of freedom of navigation and overflight (as in the case of Uruguay with its plurality of regimes within the territorial sea), and in other cases simply placing the matter under international law or stating that such freedoms will not be affected without specifying particular areas (Chile, Peru, El Salvador, and Argentina); or (3) a "national fisheries zone" established to ensure proper utilization and conservation of the living resources of the sea (Nicaragua).

Despite these differences, all of these proclamataions are remarkably similar, and all share a common denominator: namely, their purpose of establishing the legal framework within which coastal states may preserve and exploit the natural resources of the waters adjacent to their coasts.

The basic elements of this position shared by the Latin American countries become evident in two documents signed in 1970: the Montevideo Declaration on the Law of the Sea and the Declaration of Latin American States on the Law of the Sea (Lima

Declaration).

BASIC ELEMENTS OF THE LATIN AMERICAN POSITION: THE MONTEVIDEO AND LIMA DECLARATIONS

Toward the end of 1969, the United States and the Soviet Union approached all maritime nations regarding the possibility of convening a new conference on the law of the sea in order to deal with the following topics: 1. limiting the width of the territorial sea to a maximum of twelve miles; 2. freedom of passage through international straits; and 3. certain regulations intended to protect the "special fisheries interests" of coastal states in the waters of the high seas beyond the twelve-mile limit to be established as the maximum width of the territorial sea.

At the same time, the twenty-fourth Session of the United Nations General Assembly, acting on a proposal originally put forward by Malta, adopted Resolution 2574A of 15 December 1969, recommending that the secretary general conduct a much broader survey regarding the convening of the new United Nations Conference on the Law of the Sea for the purpose of revising the regimes of the high seas, the continental shelf, the territorial sea and the contiguous zone, and the conservation of the living resources of the high seas, with particular emphasis on arriving at a clear, precise, and internationally accepted definition of the area known as the sea bed and the ocean floor beyond the limits of national jurisdiction, in the light of the international regime to be established for such area.

In accordance with this resolution, the secretary general sent an inquiry to member governments on 29 January 1970, requesting a reply by 30 June 1970. As a reaction to these events, the government of Uruguay, itself having recently joined the 200-Mile Club, invited the other Latin American countries that had declared their sovereignty over waters within the 200-mile limit to a meeting in Montevideo for the purpose of exchanging views and coordinating their positions.

As a result, representatives of Argentina, Brazil, Chile, Ecuador, El Salvador, Nicaragua, Panama, Peru, and Uruguay met in Montevideo from 4 to 8 May 1970, where they approved the Montevideo Declaration on the Law of the Sea.[7]

This declaration proclaimed two fundamental rights:

> 1. the right of coastal states to utilize the resources of the waters adjoining their coasts, as well as those of the sea bed and subsoil underlying such waters, in order to promote

maximum economic development and raise the standard of living of their peoples; and
2. the right of coastal states to establish the limits of their sovereignty and jurisdiction over maritime areas on the basis of their geographical and geological characteristics, the factors affecting the existence of marine resources, and the need for rational utilization of said resources.

From these are derived a number of other rights relating to exploration, conservation, and utilization of the natural resources in adjacent waters and the continental shelf and to the adoption of regulations to enforce these rights within waters under their sovereignty or jurisdiction "without prejudice to the freedom of navigation and overflight by the vessels and aircraft of all nations."
At the Montevideo meeting, the government of Peru proposed a conference of all Latin American states to be held in Lima. Accordingly, the representatives of twenty Latin American states came together in the Peruvian capital for the Latin American meeting on aspects on the law of the sea, which was held from 4 to 8 August 1970.[8] At this meeting, the Declaration of Latin American States on the Law of the Sea[9] was approved by a majority of fourteen states, including the nine signatories of the Montevideo Declaration plus Colombia, the Dominican Republic, Guatemala, Honduras, and Mexico.
In addition to reiterating the concept of the Montevideo Declaration, this new declaration introduced, among other things, the notion of "reasonable criteria"[10] under which coastal states are to exercise the right to delimit their maritime sovereignty or jurisdiction according to the geographical, geological and biological characteristics of adjacent waters. Likewise, two principles that also figure prominently as antecedents of the Latin American conception of the Exclusive Economic Zone are set forth in explicit form, namely the rights of a coastal state (1) to prevent pollution and other dangerous and noxious effects that might result from the use, exploration, or exploitation of the waters adjacent to its coasts and (2) to authorize, monitor, and participate in all scientific research activities conducted in waters subject to its sovereignty or jurisdiction, and to receive the data and results of such research.
The paragraph in the Montevideo Declaration that refers to "the freedoms of navigation and overflight by the vessels and aircraft of all nations" is repeated in the Lima Declaration with identical wording. At the time the respective declarations were signed, this

passage was interpreted differently by various delegations. By some, it was viewed in the traditional sense in which the term is used in international law; others interpreted it to mean the right of innocent passage and overflight in accordance with the regime normally applicable to the territorial sea and superjacent airspace.

The basic features of the Latin American position are set forth in these two declarations and are none other than those elements that have inspired the creation of the Exclusive Economic Zone. Thus the emergence of the latter is the result of an evolutionary process of international practice and represents the attempt to reconcile and coordinate, within new programs and institutions of the law of the sea, the desire to ensure juridical protection of the traditional interests of individual states and the international community in maritime waters, with the new requirements and approaches brought about by profound political and social changes, growing economic needs, and the phenomenal progress in science and technology that has characterized the second half of the twentieth century.

Socioeconomic and ecological factors played a decisive role in the efforts made by Latin American countries to formulate new approaches to the law of the sea. These nations were soon joined in their efforts by other developing countries, particularly those of Africa, which were similarly motivated to elaborate the concept of the Exclusive Economic Zone and to develop, on the basis of this concept, a new institution within the law of the sea.

The wording of the preambles to the Montevideo and Lima declarations show this clearly. Both declarations begin by recognizing the existence of "a geographic, economic and social link between the sea, the land, and its inhabitants, Man, which confers on the coastal peoples legitimate priority in the utilization of the natural resources provided by their marine environment." The Lima Declaration continues by stating that "as a result of that preeminent relationship, it has been recognized that coastal states have the right to establish the limits of their sovereignty or jurisdiction over the sea on the basis of reasonable criteria, taking into account their geographical, geological, and biological situation and their socioeconomic needs and responsibilities." The Montevideo Declaration contains a similarly worded passage.

Another factor affecting the exercise of this right is the concern for the ecology. In its pramble, the Montevideo Declaration states that scientific and technological progress in the utilization of the natural resources of the sea has created the danger of depleting biological resources through overfishing or by disturbing the ecological balance. This fact serves as the basis for the right of coastal states to take the necessary measures to protect their resources over wider areas than those traditionally claimed. The preamble to the Lima Declaration also states that certain methods of utilizing maritime resources have resulted in a serious risk of polluting the waters and disturbing the ecological balance. Faced with this risk, coastal states must adopt measures designed to protect the health and interests of their peoples.

Closely tied to this concern is the progress being made in scientific research in the maritime environment. Coastal states are seen as having the right to authorize, supervise, and participate in such research, as well as the duty to promote it, all of which implies the exercise of exclusive jurisdiction.

The process by which the Exclusive Economic Zone was created began with the extension of sovereignty, or at least the rights of sovereignty, of coastal states over maritime areas that were more extensive than those traditionally claimed. At the same time we must bear in mind that there existed no formal rule in international law determining the width of the territorial sea. Whether or not the areas claimed were called the territorial sea, it is clear in the traditional terminology that they no longer belonged to the high seas.

Balanced against the economic interests, the preservation of the marine environment, and related factors requiring extension of the sovereignty or jurisdiction of coastal states, are the interests of international communications enshrined in the freedoms of navigation and overflight. This explains the references to these freedoms in the Montevideo and Lima declarations, as well as the reservations contained in the legislation of various Latin American countries. However, since the principle of sovereignty within the new maritime zones was generally applied in order to defend economic interests, which were given priority, the recognition of these freedoms appears not to have its traditional meanings.

Therefore, in this first stage of the process there is a certain lack of precision concerning the scope of these freedoms, which is seen in the various formulations contained in Latin American legislation regarding the 200-mile zone and in the different interpretations given to the phrase "freedom of navigation and overflight" by the signatories of the declarations.

Illanes Fernández[11] observes that, faced with the growing economic requirements of their people and the urgent need to provide the means for development, certain states--in order to extend their competence--

have made use of the concept of the territorial sea as the only institution that international law had to offer capable of providing the legal framework within which to protect the economic interests of coastal states. In the words of this author, "The only difficulty was that achieving the desired economic goals would unnecessarily damage the interests of other countries since major extensions of the territorial sea would endanger freedom of communication. This is a very important difficulty since, as we have seen, the superpowers have a 'vital interest' in seeing that maritime routes remain open for their navigation. It is also of strategic importance since submarines are required to navigate on the surface of the territorial sea, which limits the margin of safety with which the submarines of superpowers may fulfill their essential function as nuclear deterrents ('second strike capability')."

What we have here, in fact, is a renewal of the dilema of the principles of sovereignty and freedom, which goes back to the origin of the law of the sea and which--in its classical formulation--resolved the long-standing dispute between the mare liberum of Grotius and the mare clausum of Selden by establishing two well-defined zones: the territorial sea and the high seas. This traditional and widespread system has been replaced by the profound changes taking place in the international sphere, changes that have given rise to new circumstances that the law of the sea has been forced to deal with by creating new rules and institutions. The Exclusive Economic Zone is one of these institutions. Moreover, within the current restructuring process that the law of the sea is undergoing, it constitutes the clearest example of the new formulation of the sovereignty-freedom equation, as will be shown below.

THE CONCEPT OF THE PATRIMONIAL SEA: THE SANTO DOMINGO DECLARATION

One of the immediate antecedents of the Exclusive Economic Zone is found in the concept of the patrimonial sea, which first appeared in the Santo Domingo Declaration adopted by the Meeting of the Specialized Conference of Caribbean Countries on Problems of the Sea, held on 9 June 1972.

The concept of the patrimonial sea originated in a project submitted in 1971 to the Inter-American Juridical Committee by the Chilean jurist Edmundo Vargas Carreño.[12] Although Vargas was the first to use the term "patrimonial sea," Luis Valencia Rodríguez[13] has pointed out that many people had a hand in formulating and defining the concept in the course of various inter-American meetings and during sessions of the sea bed commission, which began to meet in 1971. As the statement by Illanes Fernández, quoted above, indicates, proclamations extending the territorial sea to the 200-mile limit raised certain difficulties. The author added that these proclamations were met by resistance not only from major maritime powers seeking greater freedom of movement for their fleets but also from other countries, not in the superpowers category, that nevertheless saw potential problems arising from the fact that their ships and planes used routes crossing the newly expanded territorial seas of their neighbors. Such countries put forward this reason for supporting the patrimonial sea as a new concept that would permit adequate protection of economic interests and yet maintain respect for jus communicationis. Certain Latin American countries viewed the patrimonial sea as a technically superior means for safeguarding liberties of navigation and overflight, when compared with the plurality of regimes within the territorial sea.

In his report, Edmundo Vargas Carreño states that, "In general practice, it appears that the territorial sea has ceased to be the only legal instrument available to states for protecting the resources of waters adjacent to their coasts, since the same end may be achieved through the creation of other maritime zones." On the basis of the Lima Declaration, he defines the patrimonial sea as "that maritime zone in which the coastal state has exclusive rights to the exploration, conservation, and exploitation of the natural resources of waters adjoining its coasts, the sea bed and subsoil thereof, and the continental shelf and its subsoil to a limit determined by said state in accordance with reasonable criteria and based on its geographical, geological, and biological characteristics, and the need for rational utilization of its resources."[14]

According to this same report, the patrimonial sea would include the territorial sea and a further zone located beyond the territorial sea to a distance that would be determined unilaterally--but not arbitrarily--by the coastal state, and whose maximum limit, in line with the current practice and legislation of a large number of developing countries, would be 200 nautical miles.[15]

The author states, "The patrimonial sea transcends the concepts of territorial sea and high seas in classical international law of the sea, participating to a degree in the characteristics of both concepts." Later, he concludes that "by means of this new concept of the patrimonial sea, it is perfectly possible to reconcile the legitimate rights of the international community with the equally legitimate--if not more legitimate--socioeconomic aspirations of coastal states."[16]

As mentioned above, the first official use of the concept of the patrimonial sea was made in the Santo Domingo Declaration,[17] an international instrument of subregional scope, adopted by the Specialized Conference of Caribbean Countries on Problems of the Sea with the participation of fifteen Caribbean and Central American states and Mexico.[18] The declaration was signed by Colombia, Costa Rica, the Dominican Republic, Guatemala, Haiti, Honduras, Mexico, Nicaragua, Trinidad and Tobago, and Venezuela. The principles proclaimed in this declaration refer to the following: the territorial sea, the patrimonial sea, the continental shelf, the international sea bed, the high seas, marine pollution, and regional cooperation.

With respect to the territorial sea, the declaration adopts the definition of the 1958 Geneva Convention on the Law of the Sea but adds that until an international agreement regarding its width is reached (preferably one of worldwide scope), every state has the right to set this limit at twelve nautical miles as measured from the applicable baseline.

The principles referring to the patrimonial sea are particularly pertinent to the subject of this chapter. Following are the two principles that define the patrimonial sea:

1. The coastal state shall exercise rights of sovereignty over the natural resources, both renewable and nonrenewable, of the waters, sea bed, and subsoil adjacent to the territorial sea, to be known as the patrimonial sea.
2. The freedoms of navigation and overflight, and the laying of submarine cables and pipelines, shall be respected within this zone, with no other restrictions than those that may result from the exercise of the coastal states' rights within the patrimonial sea.

The declaration also includes the principle that within the patrimonial sea, the coastal state has the duty to promote and the right to regulate scientific research and to adopt the necessary measures to prevent pollution of the marine environment and maintain sovereignty over its resources. It states that the width of the patrimonial sea should be the subject of an international agreement--preferably one signed by all countries--and that the territorial sea and the patrimonial sea together, depending on geographical circumstances, ought not to extend beyond the 200-mile limit.

The Mexican jurist Jorge Castañeda, whose country has been among the strongest supporters of this concept, had the following to say regarding the scope of the Santo Domingo Declaration and the nature of the patrimonial sea: "An analysis of these provisions reveals that the patrimonial sea is actually a zone of jurisdiction--particularly economic jurisdiction--rather than a zone of sovereignty. Unlike in its 12-mile territorial sea where it exercises true sovereignty, the coastal state does not in fact exercise sovereignty over its patrimonial sea. Instead, it enjoys "rights of sovereignty" only over the resources found within this zone, and not over the patrimonial sea itself. The objective in establishing this zone is purely economic and not political or strategic. Consequently, there is no need to grant the status of a sovereign territory to this economic zone. There is thus an enormous difference between the two zones."

The same author also writes: "In view of the reason for establishing the patrimonial sea, the regime of the high seas will continue to be applicable to this new zone--to the extent, naturally, that it is compatible with the rights which the coastal states exercises over it."[19] Valencia Rodríguez[20] indicated that, despite efforts to prevent it, the Santo Domingo Declaration created a split within Latin America between "territorialists" and "patrimonialists."

Mention should also be made of the Resolution on the Law of the Sea, which was adopted by the Inter-American Juridical Committee on 9 February 1973 by a majority of nine of its members. The resolution appears to support the plurality of regimes within the territorial sea, since it states that the sovereignty or jurisdiction of the coastal state extends to the waters adjacent to its coasts to a maximum distance of 200 nautical miles, as well as to the superjacent airspace and the sea bed and subsoil beneath these waters. Within this area, two zones are distinguished: one within 12 miles of the coast, and another between the 12-mile and 200-mile limits. Within the latter zone, the vessels and aircraft of all states enjoy rights of navigation and overflight, subject to the pertinent regulations of the coastal state, in accordance with international law.

Of the nine members who voted for the resolution, eight submitted briefs in favor of their decisions. From these briefs it is clear that they held different--sometimes diametrically opposed--interpretations of key paragraphs of the resolution. Thus, one member maintains that no state may unilaterally extend its territorial sea beyond the 12-mile limit, while another notes his objection to setting this limit and supports the claim of sovereignty over the entire 200-mile area.

Although lacking in precision, the resolution in

fact attempts to reconcile the position of the radical territorialists with that of the patrimonialists. In the words of Edmundo Vargas Carreño: "The balancing of these two opposing concepts resulted in a document which is in some ways contradictory and lacking in juridical rigor."[21] Efforts at reconciliation within the inter-American sphere were continued during the lengthy negotiations of the Third United Nations Conference on the Law of the Sea, with the gap between the two positions gradually diminishing.

AFRICAN AND ASIAN STATES AND THE CONCEPT OF AN EXCLUSIVE ECONOMIC ZONE: THE ADDIS ABABA DECLARATION

As a result of the measures of coordination adopted at the Montevideo meeting on the law of the sea, contacts were established between the countries of Latin America and those of Asia and Africa. These latter handled law of the sea questions principally through the Afro-Asian Legal Consultative Committee.

At the twelfth meeting of this committee, held at Colombo (Sri Lanka) in January 1971, several states' members firmly advocated the concept of a "zone of exclusive economic jurisdiction" in the high seas contiguous to the territorial waters, although this zone was not clearly defined and its maximum width was not as yet determined, nor were the precise nature and scope of the rights of the coastal state in the zone, which, in any case, related to the exploitation of resources. Nevertheless, as far as the extent of the zone was concerned, it was stipulated that a state could establish its territorial sea up to a distance of twelve miles but that there was an organic linkage between the acceptance of a territorial sea of that width and the establishment of a zone subject to the exclusive economic jurisdiction of the coastal state.[22]

Subsequently, and especially in a working paper presented by Kenya, a clearer definition of the concept of the zone was gradually shaped on the basis of determining the rights and obligations of the coastal state and of the international community, with the aim of reaching a settlement that would harmonize the economic interests of the developing states in maritime spaces that in accordance with latin American practice, would extend up to a 200-mile limit and the innterests of international communication.

From 20 to 30 June 1972, that is, a few days after the Santo Domingo meeting, a Regional Seminar of African States on the Law of the Sea met in Yaoundé (Cameroun) and took up the idea put forward by the delegation of Kenya in the Afro-Asian Legal Consultative Committee, adopting, by unanimous agreement of the sixteen participation states, what are known as the conclusions, the content of whose main recommendation is very similar to that of the Montevideo and Lima declarations. Thus, Recommendation 1 lays down, inter alia, two basic principles:

> 1. The African states have the right to determine the limits of their jurisdiction over the sea contiguous to their coasts in the light of reasonable criteria, taking particular account of geographical, geological, biological, and national security factors.
> 2. The African states have likewise the right to establish, beyond their territorial waters, an <u>economic zone</u> over which they shall have exclusive jurisdiction for the purposes of controlling, regulating, and rationally exploiting the living resources of the sea and of reserving them primarily for the benefit of their peoples and their respective economies and also for the purpose of prevention and control of pollution

The recommendation states that the establishment of this zone should not affect the freedom of navigation, of overflight, and of laying submarine cables and pipelines. It further declared that the exploitation of living resources within the economic zone should be open to all landlocked or near landlocked African states, on condition that enterprises pertaining to these states be effectively under the control of African capital and personnel.

The recommendation did not define the exact width of this zone because of the disagreement on this point existing between the coastal states and the landlocked states, but it proposed that the extent of the territorial sea should not exceed twelve miles. Winston Conrad Extavour notes, however, that inasmuch as Recommendation 2 declares that the zone includes the continental shelf, in practice it would extend, in some cases, up to hundreds of miles from the coast.[23]

At the twenty-first ordinary session of the Council of Ministers of the Organization of African Unity (OAU), held at Addis Ababa, the Declaration of the Organization of African Unity on Questions of the Law of the Sea, also known as the Addis Ababa Declaration, was adopted, and, according to Extavour, constituted the best authorized and most representative manifestation of the African states' position with respect to the progressive development of the law of the sea.

The declaration comprises several sections: (1) territorial sea and straits; (2) regime of islands; (3) concept of the Exclusive Economic Zone, including the exclusive fishing zone; (4) regional agreements; (5) fishing activities in the high seas; (6) training of personnel and transfer of technology; (7) scientific research; (8) preservation of the marine environment; and (9) international regime and international mechanism for the sea bed and ocean floor and their subsoil outside the limits of national jurisdiction. The preamble of the declaration states the socioeconomic grounds for these new approaches to the law of the sea, and a reminder is given that many African countries did not participate in the Geneva conferences in 1958 and 1960.

With respect to the Exclusive Economic Zone, it recognizes the right of every coastal state to establish such a zone beyond its territorial waters, the limits of which should not exceed 200 nautical miles measured from the baseline of its territorial sea, in which it would exercise permanent sovereignty over all the living and mineral resources, and in managing which it should not unduly hamper other legitimate uses of the sea, i.e., freedom of navigation, of overflight, and of laying cables and pipelines. The declaration also states that the African states consider that scientific research and the control of pollution of the marine environment in the Exclusive Economic Zone should be subject to the jurisdiction of the coastal states.[24]

As can be seen, a clear definition of the concept of the Exclusive Economic Zone emerges in the declaration. In this respect, it is substantially similar to the proposal put forward a year before by Kenya at the meeting of the Afro-Asian Legal Consultative Committee.[25] Unlike the latter, however, it does not determine a maximum limit for the width of the territorial waters, leaving this to be negotiated at the forthcoming United Nations Conference on the Law of the Sea; but, in contrast, it does stipulate a maximum limit for the Exclusive Economic Zone, whereas the Kenya proposal did not. Lastly, it should be noted that both documents recognize the right of landlocked states and others in a disadvantageous geographical situation to participate in the exploitation of the living resources of neighboring exclusive economic zones.

The international meetings, documents, and instruments to which reference has been made, especially those dating from the early 1970s and onward, represent the final stage in the emergence of the concept of the Exclusive Economic Zone, which culminated in the negotiations of the Third United Nations Conference on the Law of the Sea. Besides these joint efforts, an increasing number of coastal states have taken unilateral measures to extend their jurisdiction, especially for economic purposes, over maritime spaces contiguous to their territorial waters, up to a distance of 200 miles measured from the applicable baselines.

THE CONCEPT OF THE EXCLUSIVE ECONOMIC ZONE IN THE NEGOTIATIONS OF THE THIRD UNITED NATIONS CONFERENCE

The Committee on the Peaceful Uses of the Sea Bed and the Ocean Floor beyond the Limits of National Jurisdiction, called upon under Resolution 2750C (XXV) of the General Assembly of the United Nations to prepare the Conference on the Law of the Sea that was convened under that same resolution, placed on its draft agenda for the conference the topic of an "Exclusive Economic Zone outside the Territorial Sea," including as subtopics the nature and characteristics of the zone, the rights and jurisdiction of coastal states in respect to resources, control of pollution and scientific research, duties of states, freedom of navigation and overflight, and so forth. During the preparatory work of the committee, several states and group of states brought before Subcommittee 2 draft proposals on an Exclusive Economic Zone that, despite some differences of nuance, were essentially concordant, except in the case of one referring to regional or subregional economic zones.

The first <u>draft articles</u> on the zone were submitted by Kenya. In this draft the Exclusive Economic Zone was defined as a zone contiguous to the territorial sea within which the coastal state would exercise sovereign rights over the natural resources existing in the surface waters, the water column, and its sea bed and subsoil and could establish special norms for the following purposes: (1) exclusive exploration and exploitation of nonrenewable marine resources; (2) exclusive or preferential exploitation of renewable resources; (3) protection and conservation of renewable resources; (4) control, prevention, and elimination of pollution of the marine environment; and (5) scientific research. It was added that the establishment of this zone would in no way detract from the exercise of the freedoms of navigation, overflight, and laying of submarine cables and pipelines. Furthermore, the coastal state would authorize neighboring countries that were landlocked or near landlocked or had a small continental shelf to exploit living resources within its Exclusive Economic Zone. The limits of the zone were not to exceed 200 nautical miles measured from the baselines used to delimit the territorial sea.

Among the Latin American countries, Colombia, Mexico, and Venezuela presented draft treaty articles that included references to the patrimonial sea, in terms exactly resembling those of the Santo Domingo Declaration.[26] The term "patrimonial sea," however, was a source of conceptual difficulties in other languages, particularly in English, and this problem, combined with the fact that the expression "Exclusive Economic Zone" was accepted by the African and Asian countries (which were a larger percentage of the participating states), decided the Latin American countries who had backed the former term in the meetings of the committee on the sea bed to use only the term "Exclusive Economic Zone" while reaffirming their support of the recognition of continental shelves extending beyond 200 miles, as far as the outer edge of the continental margin.

All this background material was brought before the Third United Nations Conference on the Law of the Sea, at whose second session, held in Caracas from June to August 1974, new drafts were presented and the relevant opinions of the vast majority of the delegations were heard. There it clearly transpired that most of the coastal developing states supported the institution of an Exclusive Economic Zone of up to 200 miles. These states included not only the patrimonialists and zonists but also most of the so-called territorialist countries, which advocated territorial seas 200 miles in extent and declared themselves willing not to haggle over a question of nomenclature and to accept the term "Exclusive Economic Zone," provided that this was defined as a zone of national jurisdiction in which the coastal states would exercise sovereign rights in the economic field and exclusive jurisdiction in respect of associated activities (installations, preservation of the marine environment, scientific research), with attribution of the corresponding residual rights, due recognition being accorded to freedom of international communication.

The great maritime powers, in their turn, also declared their readiness to accept the establishment of a zone of the high seas, to be called an economic zone (they did not yet use the qualifying adjective "exclusive"), of up to 200 miles, wherein the coastal state enjoys projection of certain powers or exercises specific rights, much more modest than those contemplated by the creators of the concept of the Exclusive Economic Zone.

The developing coastal countries, particularly those of Latin America, had won the first battle with the recognition of the 200-mile limit; but the second battle was beginning, which was to be waged over the "content" of those 200 miles, that is, over what would be the nature and scope of the rights and powers of the coastal state in that zone, or, in the last analysis, what would be the legal status of the zone. Moreover, the landlocked states and others with special geographical characteristics, which defined themselves as being in a disadvantageous geographical situation or geographically disadvantaged,[27] also adopted a restrictive attitude and made their support for the new institution conditional upon recognition of their right to participate in the exploitation of natural resources in neighboring countries' zones.

In short, although the formulation of the concept of an Exclusive Economic Zone stemmed--as has been shown--from a whole gamut of positions with manifold nuances, in the first phase of the deliberations of the United Nations Third Conference on the Law of the Sea three basic trends of opinion could be distinguished. The <u>territorialist</u> trend, starting from the postulate of 200-mile territorial seas, gradually accepted restrictions to the jurisdiction of the coastal states, beyond the first 12 miles, until it reached the point of recognizing, in the remaining 188-mile belt, the freedoms of sovereignty for the sake of international cooperation (preservation of the marine environment, scientific research, access of third states to surplus living resources). This point of view, as it was originally formulated, has virtually disappeared, giving way to positions in favor of a "strong" economic zone. Another trend was at first called <u>preferentialist</u>, because it recognized only preferential rights of the coastal states beyond the territorial sea in respect of the exploitation of living resources; its point of departure was therefore the recognition of certain special rights or a projection of specialized powers of the coastal states in areas of the high seas contiguous to the territorial waters. This approach has evolved since it was first formulated, to the extent of accepting an Exclusive Economic Zone of up to 200 miles and listing the rights and duties of the coastal state (including sovereign rights over resources and jurisdiction in respect of associated activities) and of the other states. It is weakened, however, by the conception that the zone forms part of the high seas. The final trend was <u>zonist</u> within which the patrimonialist attitude was subsumed (shades of difference might be found between the two, but fundamentally they have upheld the same position) and which presupposed the creation of a new juridical institution to regulate a maritime space possessing characteristics of its own and therefore not forming part either of the territorial waters or of the high seas. This trend was evolved and matured, absorbing elements from the other two.

The history of the conference's deliberations records the conflict among these trends, whose adherents gradually fell into groups representing two basic positions: those who wanted a more or less strong economic zone, in which cause zonists and territorialists essentially joined forces, although there are differences--even fundamental ones--between them; and those who wanted a "weak" economic zone. The bone of contention between the two groups of opinion, as will be seen, was the legal status of the Exclusive Economic Zone.

This conflict was reflected in the formulation of the compromise texts that gradually emerged as the result of very arduous negotiations during the years subsequent to the Caracas meeting. The 1975 text, like the revised text of 1976, incorporated an initial compromise between the positions referred to above, called by Arias Schreiber[28] internationalist and territorialist, and was negotiated especially in the Evensen Group.

During the fifth session (August-September 1976) efforts were made to arrive at more acceptable texts, particularly in an ad hoc negotiating group to consider the legal status of the Exclusive Economic Zone, within which a small consultative group was set up. In this the delegation of Uruguay proposed an article intended to take the place of Article 44 of the revised text that strengthened the rights of the coastal state in the zone.[29] As Ambassador Andrés Aguilar, chairman of the Second Committee, stated in his report on the work of that committee on 16 September 1976 (Doc.A/Conf.62/L.17), the discussion within the consultative group in fact centered on reformulating articles 44 and 46 to avoid assimilating the Exclusive Economic Zone in any way into the territorial sea or the high seas. For that purpose, formulas were presented that were favorably received as a basis for the final settlement of that difference of views.

Lastly, at the sixth session (May-July 1977), the consultative group, taking as a basis articles 44 and 46 of the revised text, considered the Uruguayan draft, a British draft representing the inclination to weaken the Exclusive Economic Zone, and a draft of article 46 presented by the United Arab Emirates that sought, by way of compromise, to clarify the scope of the freedoms of navigation, overflight, and laying of submarine cables in order to leave no room for doubt as to their being the same as those enjoyed on the high seas. Although the negotiations came to a standstill, during the last days of that session a group of delegations met privately to make a concerted effort to settle the difficulties, and they produced a reformulation of articles 44 and 46 and of Article 75, on the definition of the High Seas.

These new texts were discussed at the plenary meeting of the Second Committee. The chairman of the committee felt that they constituted a better basis for continuing negotiations, for which reason he decided to incorporate them into the Informal Composite

Negotiating Text, emanating from the sixth session (Doc.A/Conf.62/WP.10).

THE CONCEPT OF AN EXCLUSIVE ECONOMIC ZONE IN THE CONVENTION, THE PRACTICE OF STATES, AND THE FORMATION OF A CUSTOMARY RULE

Articles 55, 56, and 58 of the convention constitute the backbone of the concept of an Exclusive Economic Zone, being essentially complemented by Article 86, which defines the application of the legal regime of the high seas, and by Article 59, which, in a somewhat confused and technically defective fashion, attempts to settle the question of residual rights.[30] Article 57, for its part, establishes the width of the zone, which shall not extend beyond 200 nautical miles from the baselines used in measuring the breadth of the territorial sea.

In brief, according to these articles, the Exclusive Economic Zone is an area beyond and adjacent to the territorial sea, constituted by a part of the sea not included in the high seas and subject to a specific legal regime governing (1) sovereign rights for economic purposes; (2) jurisdiction, under the relevant provisions of the convention, with regard to given activities (establishment and use of artificial islands, installations, and structures; scientific research; and protection and preservation of the marine environment); (3) other rights and duties contemplated in the convention as appertaining to the coastal state; and (4) the freedoms of navigation, overflight, and laying of submarine cables and pipelines, together with other internationally lawful uses of the sea related to these freedoms, which all states enjoy under the relevant provisions of the convention.

The rights and jurisdiction of the coastal state described above carry with them given obligations in connection with the conservation and utilization of living resources, the promotion of scientific research, the protection and preservation of the marine environment, and so forth, which need not to be referred to here. Other states, in the exercise of their rights and fulfillment of their duties in the Exclusive Economic Zone, are to comply with the laws and regulations adopted by the coastal state in accordance with the provisions of the convention and with other rules of international law in so far as they are not incompatible with the legal regime established for the zone.

It is of interest, therefore, to note that the negotiations of the conference were the means of gradually defining all the characteristics of the Exclusive Economic Zone, with full opportunity for the participation of all states and effective contributions by many of them--both developed and developing--whose positions were representative of all trends of opinion; and that as a result a set of articles has been drawn up that has met with general acceptance in all fundamental respects, although there were some adjustments and amendments advocated by several delegations that did not affect the essence of the political agreement reached on this institution. At all events, through the negotiations in the world forum of the conference, total agreement has been evidenced by the states regarding the recognition of an economic zone of up to 200 miles in which the coastal state holds sovereign rights for economic and jurisdictional purposes with respect to specific activities and all states enjoy the freedoms of navigation, overflight, and laying of submarine cables, with other related lawful uses of the sea.

At the same time, as already pointed out, a vast majority of the coastal states of the world, accounting for a high percentage of the total length of continental and insular coastlines, have introduced unilateral measures extending their jurisdiction within the 200-mile limit in a greater or lesser degree, in most cases with the basic characteristics of the Exclusive Economic Zone, and even in many instances with the use of that same designation. These measures are pursuant, in general, to the lines proposed in the informal negotiating texts of the conference. It is important to note that the states that have adopted such unilateral measures include major maritime and fishing powers that had originally been opposed to the extension of jurisdiction up to the 200-mile limit and had shown themselves only willing to recognize preferential fishing rights in a zone of the high seas contiguous to the territorial sea. Some of these powers likewise submitted proposals at the conference on the establishment of an Exclusive Economic Zone.[31]

As Eduardo Jiménez de Aréchaga has observed,[32] during the past decade the International Court of Justice has adopted an innovative and potentially fruitful approach by concerning itself with customary international law, and it has accepted, in certain circumstances, the normative value of a practice that has been consolidated in a short time, thus acknowledging that custom must be measured in accordance with the tempo of contemporary life. In reality, when traditional doctrine insisted on a practice continued from time immemorial, it wished to ensure the generality and uniformity of a specific behavior pattern of states as a material element in custom. Today, however, this generality and uniformity can be checked up on much more rapidly because of the characteristics of contemporary international relations, the emergence of universal problems that provoke a more or less simultaneous reaction from many states, the immediate knowledge of attitudes or practices obtained through the modern communication media and often from general international conferences, and the convergence of opinions produced in such conferences, all of which are determining factors in the acceleration of the process of forming a custom. All of these factors also enable international law to keep pace with the brisk and dynamic developments of present-day international life and to adapt rapidly to the changes enforced by the new interests and requirements of peoples and of the international community.

Furthermore, the former president of the International Court of Justice recalls that in the two verdicts the court pronounced in 1974 on the Icelandic fishery questions, customary norms were recognized and applied that had been formed through the practice of states, the nucleus being a <u>lege ferenda</u> proposal submitted at the 1960 Conference on the Law of the Sea but not adopted for want of one vote. And he adds that the court attached considerable weight to what it called the general consensus manifested at the Second United Nations Conference on the Law of the Sea, which in recent years had crystallized as customary law on the basis of the subsequent practice of states. The implications of these judicial pronouncements for the Third United Nations Conference on the Law of the Sea, in which more states participated, were unquestionably of far reaching significance.[33] The relevance of this last comment becomes especially clear if it is borne in mind that the conference, as already mentioned, was composed by all the states members of the international community, between 140 and 150 countries normally attending its sessions, and that after eight years of negotiations, with maximum possibilities of expounding their positions open to all delegations, a text was signed that as far as the basic issue is concerned, undoubtedly reflects a consensus.[34]

According to legal doctrine, not only certain provisions of a multilateral agreement but even a proposal put forward at a diplomatic conference that has gained ample support may become a model or guide for the subsequent conduct of the states, thereby producing an effect that has been defined as generating or constituting customary norms. If this doctrine holds, the nucleus of what has been negotiated at the conference with respect to the Exclusive Economic Zone, which reflects the consensus of the states and is confirmed by a generalized practice on their part that has aroused no opposition from any state, has indeed crystallized in a legal custom.[35] In the light of the discussions held at Caracas in 1974 and the subsequent preparation of the single negotiating text in 1975, José Luis Meseguer maintained at that time that the concept of the Exclusive Economic Zone and the delimitation of its width as 200 miles, including the territorial sea, appeared to be such irreversible and almost unanimously accepted facts that they could be regarded as institutions consecrated in customary international law.[36]

CURRENT TRENDS REGARDING THE LEGAL STATUS OF THE EXCLUSIVE ECONOMIC ZONE

The legal status of the Exclusive Economic Zone was the subject of one of the most thorny controversies waged in the conference and likewise transmitted, of course, to the doctrine. Obviously this is no mere academic discussion, since whatever position is adopted will be the basis of significant implications for the amplitude and scope of the rights and obligations of the states involved. Underlying this issue, then, is the problem of residual rights, which, in a classic model, becomes a matter of deciding between residual application of the principle of sovereignty of the coastal state and residual application of the principle of freedom of all states, when it comes to the interpretation of the rights and duties of the one or the others in doubtful or unforseen situations. This problem may acquire particular importance in the future, considering, for example, the immense perspectives, impossible to predict or even to imagine, opened up by the development of science and technology. The section of this chapter on negotiations in the Third United Nations Conference referred to the main trends of opinion about the concept of the Exclusive Economic Zone, particularly in the first phase of the conference negotiations. It stated that the trends finally congealed into two basic positions, advocacy of a strong economic zone and advocacy of a weak economic zone, and that this confrontation is reflected in the question of the legal status of the zone. In this connection, accordingly, two fundamental positions emerge:

    1. The Exclusive Economic Zone is a part of the high seas subject to a special regime, under which the respecctive coastal states enjoy certain exclusive rights listed in the convention.
    2. The Exclusive Economic Zone is a zone sui generis, that is, with legal characteristic of its own, constituting a new institution in the law of the sea, different in its legal status from the territorial sea, where the principle of sovereignty is totally paramount, and from the

high seas, where the principle of freedom is totally paramount.

It is mainly the great maritime powers--interested in enjoying to the fullest the freedoms of navigation and of overflight so that there may be no obstacles whatever to the movements of their warships and related activities--that claim that the Exclusive Economic Zone is part of the high seas. Their purpose in making the claims is to ensure the full exercise of the freedoms in question as well as of residual rights in the zone, rights that would then belong to the international community, i.e., to all states. Furthermore, the maritime powers see the thesis that the Exclusive Economic Zone is a part of the high seas as a kind of insurance against the possibility of the so-called creeping jurisdiction, i.e., the tendency gradually to extend the jurisdiction of the coastal states until sooner or later the EEZ becomes "territorialized," or, in other words, assimilated in practice to the territorial sea.

The coastal states, for their part, lay stress on their priority interests in the zone, which in the sphere of economic and other associated activities are of an exclusive character, and claim they are entitled to the residual rights related to the said activities. This position rules out the classification of the Exclusive Economic Zone as part of the high seas.

The Exclusive Economic Zone as Part of the High Seas

Those who maintain that the Exclusive Economic Zone is part of the high seas, subject to a special regime, invoke certain precedents established under the law of the sea, either on a customary or on a conventional basis, such as fishing zones (the Icelandic fisheries being a case in point),[37] pollution control zones (for example, off the coasts of Canada in the Arctic), or defense zones (Panama Declaration or Inter-American Treaty of Reciprocal Assistance),[38] and, above all, the contiguous zone provided for in the 1958 Geneva convention (Article 24).

In these antecedent instances recognition is accorded to the existence of zones of the high seas in which coastal states exercise certain specialized powers. If, however, the precedents are analyzed, especially the institution of the contiguous zone, marked differences from the Exclusive Economic Zone will be found.

Article 24 of the Geneva convention on the territorial sea and the contiguous zone states that the contiguous zone is "a zone of the high seas contiguous to its territorial sea" in which the coastal state may adopt specific measures of control. The right to adopt such measures is an exceptional power restricted in scope, confining these states exclusively to the prevention of specific infringements that might be committed in the territory or the territorial sea of the state and to punishment for such infringements that already had been committed. Hence references are sometimes made to a "projection" of specialized powers, based on the premise that a coastal state may apply certain policing measures outside the limits of its sphere of territorial sovereignty to prevent or repress the potential or actual production by other states of specific effects that are exclusively within the sphere of sovereignty of the coastal state. Although the application of such measures within limit areas of the high seas contiguous to the territorial sea is a constraint on the principle of the freedom of the high seas, the essence of that principle is not really affected, since it cannot confer immunity on the violators of national laws any more than it can protect piracy.

In short, the contiguous zone, according to the Geneva convention, cannot be said to imply an impairment of the principle of the freedom of the high seas. At most it creates a privilege for a state, the coastal state that is potentially or actually affected, allowing that state to take measures against abuses of the freedom of navigation, the general validity of which is maintained.

In the 1982 convention the contiguous zone is subsumed in the Exclusive Economic Zone. Hence Article 33 of this convention repeats the definition given in Article 24 of the Geneva convention, but with a fundamental modification: It eliminates the reference to the high seas. In other words, the contiguous zone is no longer said to be a zone of the high seas; in the new law of the sea the contiguous zone is within the Exclusive Economic Zone.

In the Exclusive Economic Zone, in contrast, several of the basic freedoms of the high seas disappear, in particular the freedom of fishing, other freedoms relating to the exploration and exploitation of resources, and the freedom of scientific research. These freedoms are not restricted or limitated; they are replaced by the sovereign rights and jurisdiction of a single state. Those who maintain that the Exclusive Economic Zone is a part of the high seas, however, adduce in their favor the argument that the coastal state has sovereign rights in the Exclusive Economic Zone but not sovereignty over it. They allege that the adoption in the convention of the system of numbering the rights of the coastal state shows that those rights derive solely from the conventional regime established, and, however far they may seem to stretch, they are, at most, sovereign rights that cannot be interpreted as conferrinng sovereignty on the coastal state.

Accordingly--and herein lies the core of the argument--once a maritime space is not subject to any territorial sovereignty, it belongs to the high seas under international law, even if the coastal states may exercise certain specially legitimized powers in it. The Exclusive Economic Zone should be no exception, as would seem to be confirmed by the regime of freedom applied in it with respect to navigation and communication.[39] This reasoning is based on the assumption in classic law that in maritime spaces either sovereignty or liberty prevails, with the respective residual application of each principle, a concept reflected, as has already been remarked, in the existence of only two basic institutions, territorial sea and high seas.

Nevertheless, the radical changes that have taken place in the international maritime world, under the influence of manifold political, economic, social, technological, and other factors, have led to the emergence of new interests or reformulation of those already existing, a development that calls for adequate legal tutelage through the creation of new concepts in the law of the sea or the restructuring of some traditional ones; and all of these changes, as we have observed, have a bearing on the formulation of the sovereignty-freedom equation of the classic law of the sea.

In particular, the institution of the continental shelf has altered the classic conceptions. In the first place, there is an overlapping of the continental shelf and the superjacent waters subject to different legal statutes. This overlapping has recurred in the case of the international zone of the sea bed. In the second place, there is a limitation of sovereignty. Thus, within the limits of a given space--the continental shelf--the coastal state concerned has sovereignty for certain purposes, i.e., the exploration and exploitation of natural resources. What is involved, therefore, is functional sovereignty.

Accordingly, to go on abiding by the classic moulds and pigeonholing maritime spaces exclusively under the statute of freedom or under the statute of sovereignty implies dismissing the entire evolution of the law of the sea in recent years, especially the Truman declaration in 1945. The convergence of different and equally legitimate interests, the assignment to states of new duties vis-à-vis the whole international community, the expansion of the area of general interests, the demands of the international principle of social justice, and the legal concept of sovereignty as a cluster of power are giving impetus to the evolution, which is taking shape in new institutions and paving the way for a new juridical order. Thus there comes about an interpretation of classic legal institutions in maritime space governed by a statute in which for certain purposes the principle of sovereignty is applied and for others that of freedom is applied. In other words, new ways are being found of formulating the sovereignty-freedom equation.

Those who uphold the position that the Exclusive Economic Zone is part of the high seas also assert that another proof of this is the application to the Exclusive Economic Zone of the provisions relating to freedom of navigation and communications on the high seas, particularly the rule of the flags of ships navigating in the said zone, as well as the right of pursuit by third states and the fact that a coastal state cannot require that foreign warships leave its Exclusive Economic Zone or cannot adopt appropriate measures against such vessels in the event of infringements of its laws and regulations established within the limits of its competence. These provisions and, in general, the partial remission given in Article 58 of the convention to many of the provisions concerning the high seas would warrant the contention that the Exclusive Economic Zone is apparently something like an exclusive fishing zone of the type established by somme states beyond their territorial seas in waters that basically continue to function as high seas, despite the limitation that there shall not be freedom of fishing therein. Freedom of fishing, moreover, has ceased to be total under the new regime and would seem no longer to constitute an essential characteristic of the statute of the high seas.[40]

Although by taking some of the above-mentioned provisions separately the strongest arguments in favor of the idea that the EEZ is part of the high seas can be found, a contextual interpretation detracts from their value. In point of fact, it is obvious that in the Exclusive Economic Zone a basic regime of freedom of communications is applied. In it, therefore, all states enjoy in principle the rights deriving from freedom of navigation. Over this activity the coastal state has no jurisdiction save in those cases for which express provision is made and that relate to its sovereign economic rights and to its jurisdiction in respect of scientific research, preservation of the marine environment, and establishment and use of artificial islands, installations, aad structures. Thus, for example, the repression of piracy is a corollary of the freedom of navigation, and if this practice exists in the Exclusive Economic Zone it goes without saying that any state can perform the policing function that the international community has delegated to states to ensure the lawful exercise of that freedom.

Furthermore, while it is true that there is no specific reference in the convention to the power of the coastal state to require a foreign warship or any other vessel of a third state used in noncommercial government service to leave the Exclusive Economic Zone in the event of noncompliance with its laws and regulations, as is the case with the territorial sea (Article 30 of the convention), and there is no particular reference to the liability of such vessels in respect to loss or damage incurred by the state as a result of such noncompliance (as there is in the case of the territorial sea--Article 31 of the same convention), it must nevertheless be borne in mind that paragraph 3 of Article 58 does stipulate that in exercising their rights and performing their duties in the Exclusive Economic Zone third states shall have due regard for the rights and duties of the coastal state and shall comply with the laws and regulations adopted by the coastal state in accordance with the provisions of the convention and other rules of international law insofar as they are not incompatible with that part of the convention.

Again, Article 297 of the convention stipulates that any dispute concerning the interpretation or application of the convention with regard to the exercise by a coastal state of its sovereign rights or its jurisdiction, if not settled in the manner provided for (by diplomatic and conciliatory procedures), shall be subject to a legal procedure provided that, inter alia, it is alleged that a state, in exercising the freedoms and rights of navigation, overflight, laying of submarine cables and pipelines, or any other internationally lawful uses of the sea (specified in Article 58), has acted in contravention of the provisions of the convention or of laws and regulations adopted by the coastal state in conformity with the convention or with other rules of international law not inncompatible therewith (paragraph 1,(b)).

By virtue of these articles, the coastal state has the right to make effective the liability of a state in the situations envisaged, which unquestionably may involve warships and other vessels of a third state used in noncommercial government service. Further, in its Exclusive Economic Zone the coastal state has the power, exclusive in character and excluding every other state, to take such measures as may be necessary to ensure compliance with the laws and regulations adopted by it in the exercise of its sovereign rights in the economic field, including boarding, inspection, arrest, and initiation of judicial proceedings (Article 73).

Under Article 200, the coastal state is also empowered, within its Exclusive Economic Zone and given certain conditions, to institute proceedings in accordance with its legislation, including detention of a vessel, when there are clear grounds for believing that a vessel navigating in the Exclusive Economic Zone or in the territorial sea of the state has in the Exclusive Economic Zone committed a violation of international rules and standards on the prevention, reduction, and control of pollution from vessels or a violation of the relevant laws and regulations adopted by the coastal state. Similarly, with regard to marine scientific research, the coastal state has the right to require suspensionn of any such research in specific situations (for which provision is made in Article 253 of the convention), on the basis of a researcher's noncompliance with certain provisions; and, should any of these situations not be rectified, the coastal state is entitled to require the researcher to cease the activity concerned. In such a case, the coastal state is not obliged to submit to judicial procedings; the matter can only be submitted, at the request of either party, to a conciliation procedure (Article 297, paragraph 2(a),(ii)).

Lastly, some points should be cleared up in connection with the partical remission in Article 58 of the convention to articles 88 to 115 of the part on the high seas. In the first place, Article 58 states that these provisions shall be applied only insofar as they are not incompatible with the part on the Exclusive Economic Zone. This criterion of compatibility is a clear indication that the legal status of the Exclusive Economic Zone is of a character peculiarly its own. Second, it must be noted that the articles referred to in Article 58 include provisions applicable to all maritime spaces, including the territorial sea.[41] Cases in point are articles 91 to 96 on nationality of vessels, their legal status, duties of the flag state, and so on, as well as Article 98 on the duty to render assistance.

No one can suppose, however, that because the part on the high seas includes provisions that also govern the territorial sea the latter is in any way assimilated into the former. Obviously, since there is a much larger area of coincidence between the high seas and the Exclusive Economic Zone, i.e., everything relating to the jus communicationis, there are several more articles whose application is basically common to these two maritime spaces. The freedoms guaranteed by the jus communicationis are in fact ontologically the same no matter where they are recognized, notwithstanding the fact where the Exclusive Economic Zone is concerned their exercise must be kept compatible with the statute for that zone, as required in Article 58.

Moreover, in the new law of the sea there are other maritime spaces that are not part of the high seas--even if they formely were so--in which the freedoms of navigation and overflight are recognized with certain restrictions. This is the case in the waters of straits used for international navigation that are under the sovereignty (not merely the sovereign rights) or the jurisdiction of their coastal states, but through which all states enjoy the right of transit, this being taken to mean the exercise of the freedom of navigation and overflight solely for the purpose of continuous and expeditious transit (Article 38 of the convention). According to Article 34 of the treaty, this regime of passage "shall not in other respects affect the legal status of the waters forming such straits or the exercise by the state bordering the straits of their sovereignty or jurisdiction over such waters and their airspace, bed and subsoil."[42]

The Exclusive Economic Zone as a Zone Sui Generis

In the view of the great majority of the delegates participating in the conference, the Exclusive Economic Zone is not a part either of the territorial sea or of the high seas; it is a zone sui generis, with a statute of its own that does not fit into the classic moulds. As has already been shown, the classic clean-out division between maritime spaces subject either to the statute of sovereignty or to the statute of freedom has been left behind by the evolution of the law of the sea. And as a result of this evolution, new institutions in the law of the sea are emerging in response to a rearrangement of interests reflected in different approaches to the application of the principles of sovereignty and freedom. This is what is happening in the case of the Exclusive Economic Zone, and this is why the delegates affirmed that the Exclusive Economic Zone is a zone sui generis, that is, different in legal status from the two traditional institutions, the territorial sea and the high seas.

An initial argument in favor of this position is to be found in the very definition given in Article 55 of the convention, according to which the Exclusive Economic Zone "is an area beyond and adjacent to the territorial sea, subject to the specific legal regime established in this Part." In keeping with this statement, Article 86, on the high seas, says that the provisions of the part of the convention on the high seas "apply to all Parts of the sea that are not included in the exclusive economic zone, in the territorial sea or in the internal waters of a State, or in the archipelagic waters of an archipelagic State." From a contextual interpretation of the two articles it can be clearly inferred that the Exclusive Economic zone and the high seas are subject to different legal statutes and that the Exclusive

Economic Zone is a part of the sea not included in the high seas.[43]

Article 75 of the Revised Single Negotiating Text (Doc.A/Conf.62/WP.8/Rev.1/Part II), the forerunner of the composite text and other texts that followed, stated that the term "high seas" meant (for the purposes of the convention) that part of the sea not pertaining to the Exclusive Economic Zone, the territorial sea, the inland waters of a state, or the archipelagic waters of an archipelagic state. It has been pointed out that this article was clearer than Article 86 of the convention in differentiating between the Exclusive Economic Zone and the high seas. In reality, although it is true that the wording of the former Article 75 left no room for doubt on the subject, the fact that Article 86 replaces the definition of maritime space by a more formal definition relating to the legal regime does not make it any less clear in distinguishing and separating one institution from the other.

If there were no separation, that is, if the Exclusive Economic Zone formed part of the high seas, the group of articles relating to that zone should appear as a section of Part VII (on the high seas). In fact, they constitute entirely different part, Part V. Furthermore, in many provisions in the rest if the treaty the Exclusive Economic Zone and the high seas are mentioned separately or as distinct parts of the sea (see, for example, articles 35, 36, 37, 38, 45, 47, 48, 53, 111, 121, 122, and those relating to the protection and preservation of the marine environment, scientific research, and the settlement of disputes, such as articles 210, 211, 216, 218, 220, 234, 246, 249, 253, 257, 259, and 297).

But, in my opinion, the fundamental argument on which to base the claim that the Exclusive Economic Zone is a zone sui generis emerges from an analysis of the rights and duties of states in that zone and their sphere of application. In the Exclusive Economic Zone, one state only, the coastal state to which the zone belongs, has sovereign rights for economic purposes and jurisdiction over specific activities. The latter is exclusive in character, since in respect to such activities the coastal State alone exercises its powers of establishing rules of management, of control, and of implementation of its laws and regulations, within the framework of the convention. On the other hand, all states enjoy, in the Exclusive Economic Zone, the freedoms of international communication and other related rights.

Can it be maintained, then, that the Exclusive Economic Zone is a part of the territorial sea, insofar as the coastal state has sovereign rights and jurisdiction for some purposes, despite the fact that for other purposes all states enjoy corresponding freedoms? Even if the definition of an Exclusive Economic Zone did not include a reference to its being situated beyond the territorial sea, the conclusion would still have to be reached, on the basis that other states have rights in the EEZ, that it is not part of the territorial sea although in many respects it is a zone of national jurisdiction.

As Jean Pierre Quéneudec writes the coastal state has sovereign rights but not sovereignty. Conversely, therefore, can it be contended that the Exclusive Economic Zone is part of the high seas because in it all states enjoy certain freedoms, despite the fact that in that same space a single state has sovereign rights and jurisdiction for several other purposes? Again, the reply must be in the negative. The legal status of the high seas is characterized by the total prevalence of the principle of freedom. It is a zone of "no sovereignty," neither territorial nor functional, that is, a zone open to common use by all states. One section of the doctrine speaks of a res communis, but in any event what is common and shared is not the sovereignty of a state but the use of the sea as an artery of communication and a source of resources. Strictly speaking, as Jiménez de Aréchaga remarks, the high seas can be described neither as res nullius, because they are not susceptible to appropriation, nor as res communis omnium, because they do not fall under the condominium of the international community. Rather, they resemble what in public municipal law are termed national goods for public use. They are, in fact, a good that is equally accessible and open to all states, even those that are landlocked, but that is not subject to the territorial sovereignty of states, either individually or as a whole.[44] Accordingly, the basic rule of the high seas is that every state can make free use of that maritime space within the limits of equality of freedom for other states. Consequently, the existence of sovereign rights pertaining to a single state and of jurisdiction exercised by it alone over specific activities is not compatible with the concept of the high seas.

As Extavour asserts,[45] to call the Exclusive Economic Zone part of the high seas would be, strictly speaking, to disregard the considerable modification of the concept of the high seas resulting from the establishment of the Exclusive Economic Zone, which involves the derogation of clearly defined rights and obligations connotative with the high seas.

The setting of certain limits to the rights and jurisdiction exercised by the coastal state in the Exclusive Economic Zone, limits that simply stem from correlative duties to the international community that relate to principles of equity and of international cooperation, does not affect the EEZ's exclusiveness to the state concerned but rather reaffirms that state's sovereign status by assigning it a responsibility that is likewise exclusive. Cases in point are the duties connected with the conservation of living resources and the promotion of their optimum utilization (basically, articles 61 and 62); with the access, in certain cases and circumstances, of landlocked countries or countries with special geographical characteristics in the same region or subregion to the exploitation of living resources, subject to specific limitations, conditions, and procedures (articles 69 and 70); with the promotion of marine scientific research (articles 239, 246, and others); or with the protection and preservation of the marine environment (pertinent articles in Part XII, especially 211).

The recognition of these sovereign rights and this jurisdiction as pertaining to a single state in the Exclusive Economic Zone does not constitute an abridgment of the freedoms of the high seas, as does the projection of specialized powers that characterizes the contiguous zone. It implies a radical application in depth of the principle of sovereignty in the field to which those freedoms relate and in the area of activities placed under the jurisdiction of the coastal state. Freedom of fishing does not exist; nor does freedom to exploit any other living or nonliving resources or to extract energy; nor does freedom to establish artificial islands; nor does freedom to set up certain types, at least, of installations and structures; nor does freedom of scientific research.

It is not that the principle of freedom is restricted, but that it is superseded, for the abovementioned purposes, by the principle of sovereignty, which is essentially in force--notwithstanding certain precise limitations to its exercise--and is applied residually. This residual application stems from the comprehensive wording of paragraph (a) of Article 56 of the convention and incorporates the compromise reflected in the negotiated formula constituted by articles 56 and 58.[46] The latter article, in turn, recognizes the freedoms of international communication for all states and their residual application. In this respect, notwithstanding logical limitations to its exercise, the ruling principle is essentially that of freedom. As Eduardo Ferrero Costa points out,[47] these limitations, apart from certain regulations applicable to all states, relate precisely to the peculiar interests and rights of the coastal state, in contrast to what happens in the case of the high seas, where the equal interests and rights of all states are taken into consideration.

Article 59, aside from its defective formulation, settles the question of residual rights in one sense:

It is not a matter of residual application of one of the principles only, whether that of sovereignty or that of freedom, but in cases where no rights are attributed to the coastal state or to third states, the gap must be filled on the basis of equity, "taking into account the respective importance of the interests involved to the parties as well as to the international community as a whole." Fleischer writes that with regard to residual rights no provision has been established in the texts in favor either of the coastal state or of the other states. There are sovereign rights for the coastal state in some respects and freedom for the rest of the states in others. Thus, in my view, the Exclusive Economic Zone is a hybrid. In it there is no general predominance either of the principle of sovereignty or of the principle of freedom, as is confirmed by Article 59. Both coexist within the same spatial bounds and, depending upon the purposes and activities concerned, one or the other prevails or is applied in that connection residually.

Benedetto Conforti points out that the institution of the Exclusive Economic Zone shatters once and for all the traditional discipline of relations between the coastal state and the other users of the ocean. He brings forward interesting arguments to substantiate his view that the old concepts of the law of the sea are changing and that we must now speak of functional rights. In the Exclusive Economic Zone the coastal state has functional rights, in the sense that it can exercise only those powers that are necessary for the purposes of total, exclusive, and rational exploitation of resources. In turn, the freedoms enjoyed by all states are likewise nothing other than functional rights, by virtue of which those activities can be carried out that are strictly necessary for the purposes of communications, maritime transport, and air traffic. Hence Conforti concludes that in relations between the coastal state and other states in the Exclusive Economic Zone, the prevailing principle is that all states, including the coastal state, must keep strictly within the limits of their rights, whereby a solution is reached in the form of an equitable middle way between those favoring residual application of the principle of sovereignty and those supporting residual application of the principle of freedom.[48]

According to Meseguer, the Exclusive Economic Zone, as a maritime space subject to specific territorial powers of the coastal state, implies the definitive disruption of the traditional equilibrium between the principle of sovereignty over the territorial sea and the principle of freedom of the high seas.[49]

The fundamental characteristic of this maritime space is, as we have said, the coexistence of the two basic principles of the law of the sea without general prevalence either of one or of the other, but with sovereignty prevailing to provide for legal protection of certain interests and freedom prevailing for the legal protection of others. This means, in addition, that there is a distribution of residual rights in favor of the coastal state with respect, essentially, to economic and associated interests and in favor of all states with respect to the interest of international communication. There remains the no-man's-land, which would seem to be constituted of other interests with no welldefined legal protection and governed by the provisions of Article 59, whose application in each specific case may give rise at the time to serious difficulties of interpretation. Nevertheless, future developments in the interpretation of the convention together with the practice of the States may gradually reduce this no-man's-land.

All the foregoing observations justify the description of the Exclusive Economic Zone as a zone sui generis, on which point the great majority of the states participating in the conference were in agreement, as transpires from the speeches of the delegations and an important sector of the doctrine. Worthy of special mention is the authorized opinion of the chairman of the Second Committee, the Venezuelan Ambassador Andrés Aguilar, under whose leadership the present convention text was drafted. Aguilar writes in his introductory note to Doc.A/Conf.62/WP.8/Rev.1/Part II[50] that beyond a doubt the Exclusive Economic Zone is neither the high seas nor the territorial sea; it is a zone sui generis (paragraph 17). And he reaffirms this view in his report dated 16 September 1976 (Doc.A/Conf.62/217), expressing the belief that the coments made in relation to this point in various paragraphs of the introductory note, particularly in paragraphs 17 and 18, indicate the appropriate path for a compromise solution in connection with that subject.

On one of the many occasions on which he expressed his opinion on this subject, the Mexican ambassador Jorge Castañeda, said he thought the best way of ensuring that the classic concepts did not constitute an obstacle to the creationn of a useful new institution was merely to recognize that it is neither one thing nor the other, but an institution sui generis containing some elements of the old notion of the high seas, insofar as it fully recognizes freedom of navigation, and certain elements of the concept of the territorial sea, such as the fact that the coastal state can reserve for itself the entire exploitation of the living and nonliving resources of the sea.[51] The speeches of the delegations of many states at the sessions of the conference categorically upheld the view that the Exclusive Economic Zone is a zone sui generis. Mention may also be made of numerous doctrinal opinions in support of this approach.[52]

In this context it may be recalled that the International Court of Justice, when hearing the case relating to jurisdiction over fisheries (United Kingdom versus Iceland and Federal Republic of Germany versus Iceland) described the nature of the exclusive fishing zone as a <u>tertium genus</u> between the territorial sea and the high seas.

BASIS OF APPLICATION OF THE SOVEREIGN RIGHTS OF THE COASTAL STATE

It falls within the scope of this chapter to make one more observation relating to the legal status of the Exclusive Economic Zone. The sovereign rights and jurisdiction in the zone that are attributed to the coastal state under the legal regime, are exercised on a territorial basis, that is, over a given space. In other words, these rights and jurisdiction are valid within the zone, as Article 56 establishes, for specific purposes or activities.

The text of Article 56 is the result of lengthy negotiations and reflects a compromise between the different trends of opinion that, as we have seen, were expressed in connection with the legal status of the Exclusive Economic Zone.

In the embryonic phases of the concept of the Exclusive Economic Zone there was a good deal of vagueness as to the ways in which the rights of the coastal state would be exercised. Some took it that sovereignty should be extended to the entire zone, while others maintained that sovereignty covered not the zone but the resources. The patrimonialists specifically adopted this position, which was incorporated in the Santo Domingo Declaration and was reproduced in a draft presented to the committee on the sea bed, in 1973, by Colombia, Mexico, and Venezuela (Doc.A/AC.138/SC. II/L. 21). According to that draft, the coastal state exercises sovereign rights over the natural resources found in the waters, the sea bed, and in the subsoil of the patrimonial sea. In their turn, the earliest African documents (the Addis Ababa (1973), and Mogadishu (1974) declarations of OAU and several drafts submitted by African countries) took up a similar attitude.

However, the difficulties of delimiting the sphere of sovereignty or jurisdiction very soon became apparent, during the initial proceedings of the conference in some drafts submitted by countries tending toward patrimonialism, through formulas that Valencia Rodríguez[53] rightly describes as subtle or hairsplitting, such as the statement that the coastal states would exercise the rights referred to within or in every part of the zone (draft presented in 1974 by Canada, Chile, Iceland, India, Indonesia, Mauritius, Mexico, New Zealand and Norway, Doc.A/Conf.62/L.4). Concurrently a clear definition of the difference between sovereignty and sovereign rights was being worked out.

The texts that ultimately resulted from the compromise among territorialists, zonists or patrimonialists, and preferentialists clearly laid down that the coastal state had "sovereign rights" and not sovereignty, a distinction that set at rest the minds of those who wanted no sort of assimilation of the zone into the territorial sea; but at the same time the formulas referring to sovereignty over resources were discarded, and the territorial base--the maritime space termed the Exclusive Economic Zone--was established for the application of the sovereign rights of the coastal state, and obviously, its jurisdiction over specific activities such as installations, scientific research, and preservation of the marine environment.

Article 56 of the convention is very clear on this point: In the Exclusive Economic Zone, the coastal state has "sovereign rights for the purpose of..." "and with regard to other activities for..." In the other relevant articles in part V the wording of the text is consistent with this concept. Thus it is no longer accurate to speak of sovereignty over resources, which may lead to these being classified in order to exclude particular species, like those that are highly migratory, from the applications of sovereign rights when they are within the Exclusive Economic Zone, on the basis of the criterion that this resource moves away from the zone in question. Such a conclusion would invalidate the meaning of the texts and would introduce an unjustifiable abridgment of the rights of the coastal state in the Exclusive Economic Zone.

CONCLUSIONS

To describe the Exclusive Economic Zone as a zone sui generis is not, of course, to define its legal status. It is to say that the EEZ is not a part either of the territorial sea or of the high seas and that it has a status of its own, different from those of either of those other two maritime spaces.

That status is characterized--and herein lies the essence of the legal personality of this new institution in the law of the sea--by the new approach according to which the principle of sovereignty and the principle of freedom are both valid within the same maritime space, their respective applications being distributed in relation to different purposes; and this approach is reflected in the provisions ensuring that the coastal state's exercise of its sovereign rights for economic purposes, with attribution, in this respect, of the residual rights, as well as of its specialized jurisdiction (over installations, scientific research, and preservation of the marine environment) shall be coordinated with the exercise by all states of the freedoms of navigation, overflight, and laying of submarine cables and pipelines, with attribution, in turn, of the corresponding residual rights.

Precisely because of the coastal state's functional sovereignty in economic matters and the exclusive nature of its specialized jurisdiction over the Exclusive Economic Zone, the EEZ may be considered, from this point of view, as a zone of national jurisdiction. The qualifying adjective "exclusive" is in itself indicative of such a character.

This institution, in its essential characteristic (as just indicated, with the further inclusion of the 200-mile limit), formulated in the 1982 Convention on the Law of the Sea, and reflecting as it does a consensus that is constituted by common elements a generalized practice among states, is now a customary rule of international law.

NOTES

1. Alfonso Arias Schreiber: "La zona económica de 200 millas y los intereses marítimos del Perú." Revista de la Comisión Permanente del Pacífico Sur, 1978.
2. See the document prepared by the Department of Legal Affairs of the General Secretariat of the OAS. OAS/Ser O.II.4 CJI-7. December 1971.
3. The main provision in the Ecuadorian legislation is contained in decree 1542 of 10 November 1966, which amends paragraph 1 of Article 628 of the Civil Code to read: "The adjacent sea, to a distance of 200 nautical miles...comprises the territorial sea and is of national domain."
4. Article 2 of Law 17094 repeats the claim to the sea bed already set forth in Decree 14708 of 11 October 1946, Article 1 of which declared sovereignty over the epicotinental sea and Argentine continental shelf. The expression "epicontinental sea" refers to waters overlying the continental shelf. However, the 1966 law makes reference not to the continental shelf but to "the seabed and subsoil beneath waters adjacent to the territory, to a depth of 200 metres or to such depth as permits exploitation of the natural resources of said zone." Thus, the Argentine legislation adopted the formula contained in the 1958 Geneva Convention on the Continental Shelf, which Argentina signed but did not ratify.

5. National sovereignty was also extended to the continental shelf for purposes of exploration and exploitation of natural resources. In the decree of 3 December 1969 and in the law of 29 December 1969, the continental shelf is defined in the same terms used in the 1958 Geneva Convention on the Continental Shelf, which Uruguay signed but did not ratify.

6. For more complete information on the Uruguayan regime and those of other countries of the Americas up to 1970, and on regional Latin American agreements and conferences, see "América Latina y la extensión del Mar Territorial: Régimen jurídico." Office of the President of Uruguay, Montevideo, 1971.

7. The Montevideo meeting adopted several resolutions that formed the basis of responses to the United Nations secretary general's survey concerning the convening of a conference on the law of the sea and to initiatives of the United States and the Soviet Union in this same period. Measures were also taken to share experiences and coordinate the efforts of participating states in order to increase their knowledge of marine resources, improve utilization of these resources, and promote joint action among Latin American and other states, especially developing countries, in all areas relating to the law of the sea.

8. The countries participating in this meeting were Argentina, Barbados, Bolivia, Brazil, Colombia, Chile, the Dominican Republic, Ecuador, El Salvador, Guatemala, Honduras, Jamaica, Mexico, Nicaragua, Panama, Paraguay, Peru, Trinidad and Tobago, Uruguay, and Venezuela. Also attending as obersers were representatives of the governments of Canada, Costa Rica, Iceland, India, Senegal, South Korea, the United Arab Republic, and Yugoslavia. In addition, there were accredited observers from the United Nations and the Organization of American States. For more information regarding the Montevideo and Lima meetings, see "América Latina y la extensión del Mar Territorial: Régimen jurídico," op.cit., pp. 145-189.

9. In addition, six resolutions were adopted dealing with the following areas: the sea bed and ocean floor beyond the limits of national jurisdiction; convening of a new international conference on the law of the sea; the problem of pollution of the marine environment; the ban on nuclear and other arms on the sea bed and in its subsoil; legal aspects of scientific research on the sea; and formation of a Latin American ad hoc committee on questions of the sea.

10. This idea is already contained in the "Principles of Mexico concerning the legal regime of the sea." Resolution XIII of the Inter-American Council of Jurists, 1956.

11. Javier Illanes Fernández: El Derecho del Mar y sus problemas actuales. Editorial Universitaria, Buenos

Aires, 1974, pp. 32-33.

12. Edmundo Vargas Carreño: Preliminary Report on the Law of the Sea: The Territorial Sea and the Patrimonial Sea. Inter-American Juridical Committee, Rio de Janeiro, 1971.

13. Luis Valencia Rodríguez: "El Ecuador y las 200 millas." Quito, Ecuador, 1977, p. 191.

14. Vargas Carreño, op.cit., pp. 27-28.

15. With respect to the limits of the continental shelf, the report proposes that it should be 200 nautical miles for a state whose continental shelf is very small or nonexistent, while a state possessing a wide continental shelf would have the right to choose between the 200-mile limit and the definition given in the 1958 Geneva Convention on the Continental Shelf.

16. Vargas Carreño, op. cit., p. 30.

17. The first country to incorporate the patrimonial sea in its national legislation was Costa Rica in 1972.

18. The participating countries in the Santo Domingo Conference were Barbados, Colombia, Costa Rica, the Dominican Republic, El Salvador, Guatemala, Guyana, Haiti, Honduras, Jamaica, Mexico, Nicaragua, Panama, Trinidad and Tobago and Venezuela.

19. Jorge Castañeda: México y el régimen del mar. Ministry of External Relations, Mexico City, 1974, pp. 159-160.

20. Valencia Rodríguez, op. cit., p. 54.

21. Inter-American Juridical Committee, Doc.A/Conf.13-19, p. 572.

22. Winston Conrad Extavour: The Exclusive Economic Zone, Institut Universitaire des Hautes Etudes Internationales, Geneva, 1979, pp. 155 et seq.

23. Ibid., p. 160. Recommendation II invited the African states to extend their sovereignty over all resources of the high seas contiguous to their territorial waters within the economic zone to be established, which was to include, at least, the continental shelf. In Recommendation III it is explained that the term resources is understood to include both living and nonliving resources, the latter including petroleum, natural gas, and other mineral resources.

24. In the section on scientific research, the declaration adds that scientific research in territorial waters or in the Exclusive Economic Zone shall be conducted only with the consent of the coastal state. The inclusion of jurisdiction over scientific research in the list of rights of the coastal state represents an innovation in relation to Kenya's proposal. Regarding the preservation of the marine environment, the declaration recognizes the right of every state to manage its resources in conformity with its environmental policies and with its obligation to

prevent and control pollution of the marine environment.

25. Extavour, op. cit., p. 161.

26. Doc. A/AC.138/SC.II/L.21, presented in April 1973. Other drafts relating to the Exclusive Economic Zone or including articles referring to it, although less specific, were submitted by Australia and Norway (Doc.A/AC.138/SC.II/L.36); Argentina (Doc.A/AC.138/SC.II/L.37 and Corr.1), which did not use either the denomination Exclusive Economic Zone or the term "patrimonial sea"; and Algeria, Cameroun, Ghana, Ivory Coast, Kenya, Liberia, Madagascar, Mauritius, Senegal, Sierra Leone, Somalia-Sudan, Tunisia, and the United Republic of Tanzania (Doc.A/AC.138/SC.II/L.40 and Corr.1-3). The draft on regional or subregional zones was presented by Uganda and Zambia (Doc.A/AC.138/SC.II/L.41). There are other drafts submitted to the committee on the sea bed that contain some references to the Exclusive Economic Zone. Furthermore, several Latin American countries presented drafts on territorial waters or zones of sovereignty up to the 200-mile limit, cases in point being Uruguay (Doc.A/AC.138/SC.II/L.24), proposing plurality of regimes in the territorial sea, which, as has been shown, was an embryonic formula for the Exclusive Economic Zone; Brazil (Doc.A/AC.138/SC.II/L.25); Ecuador, Panama, and Peru (Doc.A/AC.138/SC.II/L.27 and Corr. 1 and 2) as part of a more comprehensive set of draft articles for a convention on the law of the sea.

27. According to Article 70 of the convention, "states with special geographical characteristics" means coastal states whose geographical situation makes them dependent upon the exploitation of the living resources of the exclusive economic zones of other states in the region for adequate supplies of fish to feed their populations and coastal states that can claim no economic zones of their own.

28. Arias Schreiber, op.cit., p. 144.

29. The final version of the Uruguayan draft to replace Article 44 of the revised text reads as follows:

> 1. The coastal State shall have, in a zone situated outside its territorial sea and contiguous thereto, termed an Exclusive Economic Zone:
> (a) Sovereign rights for the purpose of exploring and exploiting, conserving, and managing natural resources, both renewable and nonrenewable, of the sea, its sea bed and subsoil and with regard to other activities for the economic exploration and exploitation of the zone, such as the production of energy from water, currents and winds:
> (b) Jurisdiction, in conformity with the

provisions of the present convention, in respect of:
    (i) the establishment and use of artificial islands, installations, structures and devices;
    (ii) regulation, authorization and control of scientific research;
    (iii) preservation and protection of the marine environment, including control and reduction of pollution;
(c) Other rights and duties compatible with the present Convention.
2. Same as the revised text.

30. The provision contained in this article is known as the Castañeda formula, owing to its having been proposed by the distinguished Mexican jurist, head of that country's delegation; and if it is not exempt from technical defects, this is attributable to the difficulties of acommodating different views. It had at the time the political merit of surmounting a major obstacle to the attainment of a compromise solution.

31. Early in 1976, the United States established a fishery conservation and management zone of 200 miles as from 1 March 1977 (Fishery Conservation and Management Act of 1976). As Ambassador Hugo Caminos remarks in "El régimen de pesca y conservación de los recursos vivos en la zona económica exclusiva: Implicaciones jurídicas y económicas" (The regime of fishing and conservation of living resources in the exclusive economic zone: legal and economic implications) (Seminario sobre economía de los Océanos, Vol.I, E/CEPAL/L.156/Rev.2, pp. 111 et seq; published jointly with the Institute of International Studies of the University of Chile), the passage of the United States law, like the Truman proclamations in 1945, triggered off an expansion and acceleration of the movement to create 200-mile zones, even among the leading users of the seas. Some of these maritime powers have adopted temporary measures for the conservation of living resources in 200-mile areas, as, for instance, the Soviet Union has done by a decree dated 10 December 1976 and Japan by Law 31 of 2 May 1977, which came into force 1 July 1977. Other developed countries have established 200-mile fishing zones, like Canada, which passed a law on 1 November 1976 that began to be applied on 1 January 1977. In its turn the Council of Ministers of the European Communities adopted a resolution on 3 November 1976, implemented on 1 January 1977, that likewise created a fishing zone of the same extent. Other developed countries have established 200-mile economic zone, e.g., France, by Act 76-655 of 16 July 1976, and Norway, by an act dated 17 December 1976 that has been in force since 1 January 1977. Lastly, others have

established exclusive economic zones, such as New Zealand, by Act 28/977 of 26 September 1977, Portugal, by Act.33 of 28 May 1977, and Spain, by Act 15/978 of 20 February 1978.

Of course there are countless developing countries that have instituted exclusive economic zones. According to an FAO table, in December 1980, eighty-six states had adopted the 200-mile limit, establishing either a territorial sea or a zone of sovereignty and jurisdiction (fourteen), an Exclusive Economic Zone (forty-eight) or again a fishing zone (twenty-four). Other states have been unable for geographical reasons to reach the 200-mile limit but have established zones beyond the 12 miles corresponding to the territorial sea.

32. Eduardo Jiménez de Aréchaga: *El Derecho Internacional Contemporáneo*, Ed. Tecnos, Madrid 1980, pp. 15-16.

33. Ibid., pp. 25-26.

34. Carl August Fleischer: "The right to a 200-mile exclusive economic zone or a special fishery zone." *San Diego Law Review*, vol. 14, no. 3, 1977, p. 580. Fleischer considers that the negotiating texts of the conference had a twofold importance, both directly, as evidence of a consensus or a growing consensus among the states, and indirectly inasmuch as they serve as a guide to the states' practice, which contributes to the formation of customary law.

35. A similar opinion is expressed by Eduardo Jiménez de Aréchaga, who asserts that the positions manifested by the states at successive sessions of the United Nations Conference on the Law of the Sea and the practice they have followed in conformity with those positions have already given rise to certain customary norms that have radically modified the law of the sea as it existed prior to the conference (Jiménez de Aréchaga, op. cit., p. 19).

36. See José Luis Meseguer: "Temas de la II Conferencia sobre Derecho del Mar: la Zona Económica Exclusiva." ICE, no. 1517, 29 April 1976, p. 1264. Furthermore, in the Statement of Motives for the Proposal of a Decree appended to Article 27 of the Political Constitution of the Mexican States with a view to the establishment of an Exclusive Economic Zone, in referring to the conference negotiations and the convergent proposals presented by several states. Meseguer gives a reminder that there is no rule of general international law to the effect that a treaty signed and ratified constitutes the sole valid expression of agreements among states and that the existence of international legal rules based on agreements can also be demonstrated by other means, especially when, as in this case, there are reliable proofs of the will of the states; and later he adds

that the Exclusive Economic Zone of a coastal state can unquestionably be said to exist today as a legal institution backed by the general consensus of the community of nations. See Fernando Zegers, in Mesa Redonda sobre Derecho del Mar: La zona económica. Instituto Latinoamericano, Rome, 12-15 May 1975, pp. 152 et seq.

37. See Extavour, op.cit., pp. 57 et seq. See also the publications periodically issued by FAO, "Limits and Status of the Territorial Sea, Exclusive Fishing Zones, Fishery Conservation Zones and the Continental Shelf."

38. The Panama Declaration, adopted on 3 October 1939 by the Consultative Meeting of Ministers of Foreign Affairs of the American Republics, laid it down that the American republics, as long as they maintained their neutrality, had the right to keep free from any hostile act on the part of any non-American belligerent nation those waters contiguous to the American continent that they regards as of primordial interest and direct usefulness for their relations. A description is also given in the declaration of the sea area to which it applies, which comprises a belt of about 300 miles along the coasts of the American continent, with the exception of the territorial waters of Canada and undisputed possessions of European countries. It is the direct antecedent of the safety zone established in Article 4 of the Inter-American Treaty of Reciprocal Assistance, although the latter is of wider scope than the former since it surrounds the entire continent, including Canada, Greenland and the Arctic and Antarctic zones. See Extavour, op. cit., pp.61 et seq., on the scope of the Panama Declaration, the degree to which it is internationally accepted, and its relation to subsequent Latin American claims in respect of maritime jurisdiction.

39. See Jean Pierre Quénedec: "Un Problème en suspens: La Nature de la zone économique." Revue Iranienne des Relations Internationales, nos. 5-6, 1975-76, pp. 44-45. See also Mario Scerni, in Mesa Redonda sobre Derecho del Mar: La zona económica, Instituto Italo-Latinoamericano, Rome, 12-15 May 1975, pp. 109 et seq.

40. Jean Pierre Quénedec states in his article "Les Problèmes de l'exploitation des resources biologiques de la mer," in Institut des Hautes Etudes Internationales, Paris, Droit de la Mer, ed. A. Pedone, 1976-1977, pp. 172-173, that the tenor of the negotiating texts of the conference implies the express exclusion from the high seas of maritime spaces incorporated in the exclusive economic Zones and, therefore, the rights of the coastal states over biological resources in these zones can be described as sovereign and not merely exclusive, as in the context

of a reserved fishing zone. An he adds that as soon as recognition is thus accorded to the permanent sovereign right of the states with regard to the resources of their economic zones, it becomes evident that his right covers not only the exploitation of such resources but also their exploration, conservation, and management. In other words, the rights of the state over living resources are greater in an Exclusive Economic Zone than in a fishing zone. In the latter, indeed, exploration activities could hardly be reserved to the coastal state. There, accordingly, the principle of freedom of scientific research is applied. On the contrary, in the Exclusive Economic Zone, research, prospecting and evaluation activities concerned with living resources will henceforward fall within the competence of the coastal state.

41. The delegations of Peru and Uruguay to the conference submitted, first to the territorialist group and later to Andrés Aguilar in his capacity as chairman of the Second Committee during the sixth session (1977), a proposal for the reorganization of the articles of Part VII on the high seas, dividing them into three sections: provisions applicable only to the high seas (at present articles 86, 87, 89, and 112 to 120); provisions applicable to the Exclusive Economic Zone and to the high seas (at present articles 88, 90, 97 and 99 to 111); and general provisions relating to vessels (articles 91 to 96 and 98). Subsequently the delegation of Peru submitted it as part of the informal suggestion C.2/Informal Meeting/9, 27 April 1978.

42. The convention also makes provision for a right of passage via such archipelagic sea lanes and air routes as the archipelagic state may designate through or over its archipelagic waters and the adjacent territorial sea, a right that consists in the exercise of the rights of navigation and overflight in the normal made solely for the purpose of continuous expeditions and unobstructed transit between one part of the high seas or an Exclusive Economic Zone and another part of the high seas or an Exclusive Economic Zone (Article 53). This "archipelagic sea lanes passage" is very similar to the transit passage through straits used for international navigation, since although with respect to the former no reference is made to the freedoms of navigation and overflight, neither does it simply constitute a right of innocent passage but is rather a right of deeper significance assimilable in its exercise to the freedoms of navigation and overflight that are enjoyed in maritime spaces subject to the sovereignty of a state without in other respects affecting the legal status of the waters concerned , or their bed, subsoil, and superjacent airspace (Article 49).

43. Arias Schreiber, op.cit., p. 146.

44. E. Jiménez de Aréchaga: *Curso de Derecho Internacional Público*. Centro de Derecho, Montevideo 1961, p. 643.
45. Extavour, op.cit., p. 270.
46. Eduardo Ferrero Costa: "El nuevo Derecho del Mar: Naturaleza jurídica de la zona económica exclusiva." *Revista de la Comisión Permanente del Pacífico Sur*, special Issue on *El Nuevo Derecho del Mar*, vol. 8, 1978, p. 63.
47. Ibid., pp. 67-68.
48. Benedetto Conforti, "Does freedom of the seas still exist?" *Italian Yearbook of International Law*, vol. I, 1975, p. 12.
49. Meseguer, op.cit, p. 1204.
50. Revised Single Negotiating Text, emanating from the fourth session, held in New York from 15 March to 7 May 1976. In this inaugural address to the Academica de Ciencias y Políticas Sociales of Venezuela, Andrés Aguilar reiterates and enlarges upon his opinion to the effect that the Exclusive Economic Zone is a maritime space sui generis, entirely distinct from the territorial sea and from the high seas (pp. 48 et seq).
51. Jorge Castañeda, *Mesa Redonda sobre Derecho del Mar: La Zona Económica*, Instituto Italo-Latinoamericano, Rome, 12-15 May 1975, p. 174.
52. See, for instance, Carl August Fleischer, who states that obviously the Exclusive Economic Zone is not a zone of the high sas, in which all states are at liberty to fish. Neither is it a part of the territorial waters. The point of departure is that the Exclusive Economic Zone is a creation sui generis (Fleischer, op.cit., p. 568). Meseguer asserts that this new maritime space, sui generis or special in its nature, will have a legal status different from that of the territorial sea or the high seas, although, up to a point, it will share in the regimes applicable to the two traditional maritime spaces (Meseguer, op.cit., p. 1265). Ferrero Costa, on his part, after analyzing the fundamental differences between the high seas and the Exclusive Economic Zone, concludes that the Exclusive Economic Zone must be regarded as a zone of maritime space that is neither the high seas nor the territorial sea but a distinct and special zone sui generis, which has come into being in consequence of the evolution of the law and, what is more, a product of the law of the sea (*El nuevo Derecho del Mar: El Perú y las 200 millas*. Pontificia Universidad Católica of Peru, Lima, 1979, p. 168).
53. Valencia Rodríguez, op.cit., pp. 195-196.

Alfonso Arias Schreiber

7. The Exclusive Economic Zone: Its Legal Nature and the Problem of Military Uses

This chapter focuses on two questions that have been the center of fierce controversies in regard to the Exclusive Economic Zone (EEZ): first, that of its legal nature, and second, that of military uses. In connection with these two aspects, we shall discuss the regime applicable to other activities in the zone, in accordance with the convention that has been the outcome of the Third United Nations Conference on the Law of the Sea.

THE LEGAL NATURE OF THE EXCLUSIVE ECONOMIC ZONE

Why has the EEZ been and why does it continue to be so debated? Is it only an academic issue? Upon what principles is the EEZ based according to the different approaches to the subject?
The EEZ is a relatively new institution that has caused a revolution in the law of the sea and in the traditional dichotomy of territorial sea, a domain of the coastal state--and high seas--a field of nobody's or of everybody's domain, or of common use. It is therefore understandable that the first question is, To whom does the zone belong? This question has given rise to opposing interpretations both within the conference and among scholars of law. It is not merely an academic question because any answer given involves very important practical implications for the conduct of the states in that maritime space. The most evident of such consequences is that of determining to whom the so-called residual rights belong, that is, rights that are not expressly conferred either on the coastal state or on other states. This issue has special

---

This chapter is based on a presentation made by the author before the Argentine Council for International Relations on 9 September 1981.

significance for military activities and can have even more significance in the future with regard to new uses of the sea resulting from technological and scientific advances.

There are three basic theses that define the legal nature of the EEZ:

>1. that it is part of the high seas, with certain rights delegated to the coastal state for economic purposes together with jurisdiction for related purposes; and that other states retain the traditional freedoms of the high seas;
>2. that it is a zone sui generis, different from the territorial sea and the high seas, where the rights and duties of the coastal state and other states are subject to a specific legal regime established by the convention; and
>3. that, although it is a sui generis zone, it is of national jurisdiction, because of the nature and scope of the rights of the coastal state recognized in it without prejudice to the freedoms of international communication.

The basic arguments in favor of each position follow.

First Thesis: The Exclusive Economic Zone is Part of the High Seas

Those who maintain this conservative position start from the historic fact that before the advent of the Exclusive Economic Zone as a new institution of the law of the sea, the space that it now includes was considered the high seas. In this view, the fact of attributing to the coastal state special rights or jurisdiction for certain purposes in a space measured from the baselines of the territorial sea to a maximum distance of 200 miles does not change the legal nature of the space that continues to be high seas, just as certain competences for certain purposes were also recognized as belonging to the coastal state in the contiguous zone without modifying that zone's status as high seas.

In this connection, it is proper to observe that in the same way that the classic notion of the high seas was taken up in the Geneva convention of 1958 by agreement among the participating states (which were then 86), the legal status of the Exclusive Economic Zone must be defined, in its turn, by agreement among the states participating in the Third United Nations Conference on the Law of the Sea (UNCLOS III) (more than 160); and if the new convention establishes that the EEZ has a specific legal regime, different and separate from that of the territorial sea and the high seas, nobody can validly attribute to it the status of the high seas.

On the other hand, as we shall see below, the nature and extension of the rights accorded to the coastal state in the Exclusive Economic Zone are essentially contrary to the rights enjoyed equally by all states on the high seas, and it is inappropriate to compare these latter rights with the competences established in the contiguous zone, from the definition of which has now been deleted the reference to it as part of the high seas.

Furthermore, the sponsors of this thesis cannot agree to a definition of the legal nature of the high seas, that is, whether it is <u>res nullius</u>, <u>res communis</u>, or <u>res communitatis usus</u>; nor, consequently, can they explain which of these three interpretations would be applicable to the EEZ. Some have held the opinion that the holder of the right in the high seas--and hence in the Exclusive Economic Zone--is the international community, which would have the authority to delegate determinate competences to the coastal state. This theory was upheld during the preparatory work of the Third Conference on the Law of the Sea under the notion of the "international mandate," by which the coastal state should operate as a trustee of the international community; the exercise of the powers that would be entrusted to it would be subject to the control of other states.

However, this idea was rejected, perhaps because in the opinion of some it was based on the fiction of the international community as the holder of a right that it cannot possess and therefore can hardly delegate, since the community itself does not even have legal personality (<u>nemo plus juris tranfere potest quod non habet</u>) or perhaps because the idea stood in contradiction to the "economic sovereignty" thesis supported by the majority of developing coastal countries as a basis for the establishment of a zone under the jurisdiction of the coastal state.

It is important to remember this background because if the notion of the international mandate had been accepted, there would be a basis to maintain that the zone in which the powers delegated to the coastal state could be applicable is part of the high seas and is not a zone of national jurisdiction. In fact, the contrary may be true: the rejection of the former thesis confirms the validity of the latter.

In spite of these clear considerations, Jean Pierre Quéneudec has brought up the following arguments to uphold on interpretative bases the idea that the EEZ must be qualified as high seas:[1]

Argument 1. The coastal state does not exercise territorial sovereignty in the EEZ. Answer: The EEZ is not subject to the same regime of full sovereignty that applies in the territorial sea and that differentiates the zone from the latter institution. Rather, in the EEZ, the coastal state exercises a functional sovereignty of an economic nature, which is only possible in a zone of national jurisdiction and which is ruled out in the high seas.

Argument 2. Freedoms of international communication that are characteristic of the high seas exist in the Exclusive Economic Zone. Answer: Even though these freedoms do exist, they are subject to certain restrictions not occurring in the high seas. In the EEZ the exercise of freedoms must be compatible with the rights of the coastal state and with the provisions of its laws and regulations (Article 58, paragraphs 2 and 3). For example, the coastal state may detain a vessel and institute proceedings against it if it causes damage or threatens major damage from pollution (Article 220, paragraphs 3, 5, and 6). Also, the delineation of the course for the laying of submarine pipelines is subject to the consent of the coastal state (Article 79, paragraph 3 on the continental shelf, applying to the sea bed and subsoil of the EEZ up to 200 miles). Therefore, the exercise of freedoms is not the same in the EEZ as in the high seas.

Argument 3. The law of the flag state of a vessel is applied in the EEZ, or rather, a vessel is subject to the exclusive jurisdiction of the state of which it is a national. Answer: In regard to this point, there are very important exceptions to the general rule that is applicable in the EEZ. One of them is the case of pollution, which we have just mentioned. Another is the case of fishing, in which the coastal state may also detain a vessel and institute proceedings for violations of its laws and regulations (Article 73). None of these exceptions is possible in the high seas, where only the law of the flag state is applied (Article 92).

Argument 4. Warships and other government owned vessels have immunity in the EEZ. Answer: This rule applies equally in the territorial sea, where warships and other public vessels maintain their immunity, with the sole exception that the coastal state may prevent noninnocent passage and may demand that such vessels leave the area in such cases (Articles 25 and 30).

Argument 5. The right of hot pursuit is not interrupted when the vessels pursued enters or traverses the EEZ of another state. Answer: This is true, but another fact is much more important: the right of hot pursuit is _also_ applied to violations committed in the EEZ, no longer only to those occurring in the territorial sea (Article 111, paragraph 2). This is an essential innovation that certainly does not apply in the high seas.

As we can see, none of the invoked arguments is sufficient to support assimilating the Exclusive Economic Zone into the high seas. Rather, the arguments allow one to infer that this is a question of two distinct spaces. Further, there are other basic considerations assisting this last interpretation:

1. In the high sas all states have the same rights and no one may exercise any kind of sovereignty or special jurisdiction, whereas in the EEZ the coastal state exercises sovereign rights with regard to the resources and other economic activities and jurisdiction as regards installations, scientific research, and preservation of the marine environment.

2. In the high seas the exercise of the freedoms of international communication (that is, navigation, overflight, and laying of submarine cables and pipelines) must take into account equally the interests of all states, while in the EEZ exercise of these freedoms must take into account the special rights of the coastal state and the provisions established in its laws and regulations.

3. In the high seas freedoms of establishing installations, fishing, and carrying on scientific research govern, while in the EEZ those activities are subject to the authorization and exclusive control of the coastal state.

As is clear from the preceding considerations, the essential elements typifying the high seas are opposed to and incompatible with those typifying the Exclusive Economic Zone. The logical consequence of this examination is that it is not possible to ascribe the same legal nature to both spaces.

Second Thesis: The Exclusive Economic Zone is a Zone Sui Generis

During the debates at the Third Conference on the Law of the Sea, when the legal status of the EEZ was discussed, many delegations maintained that it was a new institution with special characteristics that identify it as a sui generis zone, different from the territorial sea and the high seas. This concept was taken up by Andrés Aguilar, chairman of the Second Committee, in the reports he submitted in 1976 when putting forward the revisions of the Single Negotiating Text.

In support of this thesis, the EEZ is alleged to contain some elements of the notion of high seas, specifically the freedoms of international communication, and at the same time certain elements of the territorial sea, particularly rights regarding resources and other economic activities, installations, scientific research, and preservation of the marine environment, although these elements are subject to certain conditions. However, these two sets of elements are not juxtaposed in a sort of hybrid or bivalent institution. Rather, they have been reformulated and adapted within a unitary regime distinct from the other unitary regimes of the territorial sea and the high seas.

Of course we agree that the EEZ is a special institution different from the two classic institutions already mentioned. It is a *tertium genus*, to repeat the term used by the International Court of Justice in the case of fisheries zones; with greater reason it is possible to apply this term to the Exclusive Economic Zone. Notwithstanding this, in our opinion the label of sui generis zone is an incomplete truth, not solving the problem of identity, affiliation, or ownership of the zone.

Certainly this last problem is also a subject of controversy. Some think that the human mind necessarily associates the concepts of *res* and *dominium* and demands that everything must have an owner, whether public or private, individual or collective. Others argue about the projection of this requirement onto international law, since even though there is no objection to the notion that the territorial sea belongs to the coastal state, as we already have seen there is some disagreement about whether the high seas is the domain of nobody, the domain of everybody, or a domain of common use.

We understand that the application of the ownership concept to the high seas may be questioned, because one of the essential characteristics of the high seas is precisely that it does not belong to any state; but we think that in the case of the Exclusive Economic Zone there is certainly a holder of the right that cannot be other than the coastal state, for reasons that will be explained below. We must admit that the convention does not so define it expressly, since it has left without solution the question of residual powers. Consequently the matter has been left to interpretation.

As far as I know, the supporters of the concept of the sui generis Exclusive Economic Zone have refrained from determining to whom this maritime space belongs. From their point of view, it could be supposed that it would be a condominium zone having rights distributed between the coastal state, for economic and related purposes, and other states, for international communication purposes. This description does not suffice, however because "condominium" implies a common property right in an indivisible thing with regard to which the coowners exercise of equal rights and a shared jurisdiction. Both of these elements are incompatible with the legal regime of the EEZ.

Unless further explanation is obtained from the supporters of the second thesis, its principal merit is that it rules out the concept of the EEZ as part of the high seas. Article 75 of the Single Negotiating Text had the advantage of expressly defining the high seas as a space that does not include the Exclusive Economic Zone. Article 86 of the convention is, on the other hand, ambiguous in establishing that the provisions of the high seas are not applicable to the Exclusive Economic Zone. This must be understood in general terms since, in its turn, Article 58, paragraph 2, applies to the EEZ several provisions of Section 1 on the high seas, albeit subject to the criterion of compatibility.

However, it would be wrong to infer that this modification of the text has had the purpose or the effect of assimilating the Exclusive Economic Zone into the high seas. This is true, first, because the change was accompanied by a new provision (Article 55), according to which the EEZ is subject to a specific legal regime. If that zone were to be considered part of the high seas, the provisions regarding it would appear in a section of the provisions on the latter institution and would not be presented independently. Second, in reporting on these changes, the president of the conference gave evidence that these provisions maintained the essential characteristics of the specific legal regime of the EEZ without upsetting the implicit balance in the Single Negotiating Text between the rights and duties of the coastal and those of other states. Since the chairman of the Second Committee had declared in his previous reports that it was not possible to assimilate the Exclusive Economic Zone into either the territorial sea or the high seas, it is obvious that in deciding to include the new articles, he did so with the understanding that they preserved the legal nature of the EEZ, defined by himself as a sui generis zone.

In this connection, we must take into account that the chairmen acted neither in their personal capacities nor as delegates of their respective countries but as authorities elected by the conference, entrusted with the fulfillment of a mandate prescribed by it. Therefore their reports are of signigficant value in the interpretation of the provisions of the convention.

Having established that the EEZ is distinct from the high seas and the territorial sea, one may wonder whether the concept of a sui generis zone rules out the possibility that it be a zone of national jurisdiction. In our opinion, the notions are compatible, because even though no one argues with the proposition that the EEZ is distinct from the territorial sea, it is also true that the territorial sea is not the only zone of national jurisdiction. As we shall see below there are other spaces falling within this same class, such as the continental shelf. The convention recognizes this in Article 1, which defines "the Area" (that is, the international sea bed) as beyond the limits of national jurisdiction, in this context meaning beyond the continental shelf. On the other hand, Article 76 establishes that the continental shelf extends to 200 miles where the outer edge of the continental margin does not extend to that distance. Also, Article 56 recognizes the sovereign right of the coastal state over the sea bed and subsoil of the EEZ with regard to the disposition of resources existing there.

Consequently, if the sea bed and subsoil of the Exclusive Economic Zone cannot be distinguished from the continental shelf when the latter does not surpass 200 miles, and if the continental shelf is considered a zone of national jurisdiction, it is clear as a conclusion of the syllogism that the sea bed and subsoil of the EEZ fall likewise within the category of a zone of national jurisdiction. Due to the character and the range of the rights exercised by the coastal state, not only on the sea bed and subsoil of the EEZ but also in the superjacent waters, in accordance with Article 56 of the convention, both sectors of the EEZ are integrated into a unitary regime as an indivisible zone of national jurisdiction.

It might be said that the supporters of the second thesis have stopped halfway in their interpretation, perhaps for strategic reasons in the management of negotiations or perhaps because they judge that in the present circumstances there would be no agreement to go any further. A proof of this incomplete interpretation is what happened when the problem of the residual rights was discussed. This problem has remained unresolved in the convention, since the formula of Article 59 limits itself to provide that where the convention does not attribute rights or jurisdiction to the coastal state or to other states within the EEZ, when a conflict of interests arises between them, it should be resolved on the basis of equity and in the light of all the relevant circumstances, taking into account the respective importance that the interests have to the parties as well as to the international community as a whole.

This formula put an end to an unproductive debate at the conference, due to the fact that the positions of states were irreconcilable. However, technical faults aside, the formula was abridged too much to allow for the determination of the limits between the preservation of the freedoms of international communication on the one hand and the protection of other interests of the coastal state on the other, in a zone within which the latter should be increasing its domain for reasons of necessity, as will be explained later.

Third Thesis: The Exclusive Economic Zone is a Zone of National Jurisdiction

Perhaps the most simple way of introducing the third interpretation of the legal nature of the EEZ is to establish ab initio what is meant by a zone of national jurisdiction. As the convention does not contain a definition of the matter, we shall have to determine the intent on our own. Personally, I consider that all those zones in which the coastal state exercises full sovereignty, rights of sovereignty (in the Spanish text) or sovereign rights (in the other languages), and jurisdiction with a view to make use of the resources in its adjacent seas for the benefit of its national development and to protect the interests of its people, fall within the class of zones of national jurisdiction.

In accordance with that definition, and taking into account the relevant provision of the convention, it is possible to consider as zones of national jurisdiction the following:

1. the internal waters and the territorial sea up to a distance of twelve miles, where the coastal state exercises sovereignty without exception other than the right of innocent passage accorded to other states;
2. the archipelagic waters, composed of the waters within the baselines joining the outermost points of the outermost islands and drying reefs of an archipelago, under certain conditions, in which the archipelagic state exercises sovereignty without exception other than the right of innocent passage or the right of passage through determined sea lanes;
3. the Exclusive Economic Zone up to a maximum distance of 200 miles, in which the coastal state exercises sovereign rights with regard to resources and other economic activities and jurisdiction in regard to installations, scientific research, and preservation of the marine environment, also under certain conditions and without prejudice to the freedoms of international communication. Today the contiguous zone is included within the Exclusive Economic Zone up to a maximum distance of 24 miles; and
4. the continental shelf up to 200 miles or up to the outer edge of the continental margin, where the coastal state exercises, mutatis mutandis, the same sovereign rights and jurisdiction as in the

Exclusive Economic Zone.

On the other hand, the following are not zones of national jurisdiction:

1. the high seas, where all states exercise equal rights under the umbrella of freedoms of international communication, fishing, and scientific research; and
2. the international sea bed area, which has been declared the common heritage of mankind, and where activities will be subject to the management and control of an international authority opened to the participation of all states.

The inference that the Exclusive Economic Zone is a zone of national jurisdiction in the framework of the provisions of the convention is based, on the one hand, on the nature of the concepts used to characterize the powers of the coastal state, and, on the other hand, on the scope of the rights ascribed to it in that maritime space.

From the conceptual point of view, although the term "rights of sovereignty" or "sovereign rights" does not involve sovereignty in its integral sense as supreme authority of a state within a determined space, it certainly carries a functional application of sovereignty for certain purposes in relation to which the state to which said rights are attributed is sovereign and is not subject to the superior authority of any other state.

As for the term "jurisdiction", etymologically meaning "to say (or to declare) the right," it denotes the authority of a state to issue applicable rules, putting into practice the competences attributed to it, and to assure the enforcement of those rules vis-à-vis other states.

The mere utilization of these two concepts, conferred by the convention solely on the coastal state in the Exclusive Economic Zone, would be enough to conclude that the zone is an area of national jurisdiction. However, there are considerations of equal or more significance, as a consequence of the scope of the rights attributed to the coastal state, applicable to the main uses of the zone in question: exploration and exploitation, conservation and management of the natural resources, both living and nonliving, of the sea bed, subsoil, and superjacent waters; other economic activities such as the production of energy derived from water, currents, and winds; establishment and utilization of artificial islands, installations, and structures; marine scientific research; protection and preservation of the marine environment; and so on. Reading such an enumeration, one may wonder what is left to other states. Really all that is left are the freedoms of international communication, the exercise of which is not without restrictions since it must take into account the rights and duties of the coastal state as well as the right of landlocked states and states with special geographical characteristics to participate in the exploitation of the surplus of living resources, a right also subject to restrictive conditions in the convention.

Therefore, in balancing the rights and jurisdiction of the coastal state against the freedoms and rights of other states in the EEZ, from both a qualitative and a quantitative viewpoint, one must admit that the scale tilts a great deal in favor of the coastal state. If one adds to this the power accorded to the latter to ensure compliance with its laws and regulations in cases expressly provided for, including the visit, inspection, and seizure of vessels and the institution of proceedings against vessels, it is not logical to question that the coastal state exercises in the zone the characteristic attributes of national jurisdiction.

These considerations were aired both in the Second Committe debates and in the informal negotiation groups of the conference, where the supporters of the high seas thesis only proffered fragmentary arguments in support of their viewpoint (mainly the absence of sovereignty and the application of freedoms of international communication) or limited themselves to repeating the assertion that the characterization of the EEZ as an area of national jurisdiction was tantamount to "territorializing" that zone. The group of landlocked states and geographically disadvantaged states put forward a proposal on the Exclusive Economic Zone expressly defining it as a part of the high seas, but the proposal was not welcomed. Even though there is no record of this event because the meetings and proposals were informal, those who participated in the conference remember well what happened there.

Furthermore, the Exclusive Economic Zone must be analyzed in its historic perspective for a better understanding of its scope. The most remote antecedent of this new institution is the 200-mile maritime zone established in 1947, first by Chile and later by Peru, to protect and make use of the resources therein for the benefit of their coastal populations without affecting the right of free navigation. Since then, similar zones have been established for essentially economic aims with characteristics of national sovereignty and jurisdiction. The Santiago Declaration in 1952, signed by Chile, Ecuador, and Peru, expressly provided for these same attributes. In the decades from 1950s through the 1970s, other Latin American states extended their domain up to 200 miles, some of them claiming the area as territorial sea. In 1972, the countries of the Caribbean region, assembled at the Conference of Santo Domingo, adopted the institution of the patrimonial sea as an adjacent zone of the territorial sea, also up to 200 miles, adding to the competences for economic aims those related to scientific research and pollution. In the same year at the Seminar of Yaoundé, the African states approved a recommendation recognizing their right to establish beyond the territorial sea an economic zone in which they would exercise exclusive jurisdiction to exploit marine living resources for the benefit of their peoples as well as to prevent and control pollution.

When the preparatory work of the Third Conference on the Law of the Sea had started, the concept of the Exclusive Economic Zone was making its way as a compromise solution between the position of the maritime powers, which were only prepared to recognize a territorial sea up to the 12-mile limit and preferential rights of the coastal state to exploit certain species in adjacent areas considered within the high seas, and the position of the countries that had established 200-mile territorial seas.

This brief survey of the genesis of the institution reveals that from the beginning it was conceived with the characteristics of a zone of national jurisdiction. At present, the majority of coastal states has established maritime zones up to the 200-mile limit. According to a chart published by FAO in December 1980, eighty-six countries have adopted that limit: fourteen as territorial sea or zone of sovereignty and jurisdiction, forty-eight as Exclusive Economic Zone, and twenty four as fisheries zone. Another twelve states have established zones beyond 12 miles--to 15, 24, 50, or 100 miles--or, in the case of enclosed or semienclosed seas where it is not possible to extend such zones up to the maximum distance of 200 miles, have established median lines beyond 12 miles.

Altogether, almost a hundred countries have extended beyond the twelve mile limit by establishing zones of differing natures. Among them, those who consider those zones to be a part of the high seas do not number more than ten. Consequently, the general practice of the states that have so behaved by virtue of unilateral acts, without awaiting the conclusion of the conference negotiations, proves the thesis that the great majority of coastal countries consider these areas zones of national jurisdiction, in relation to which they feel empowered to legislate.

This conclusion is also assisted by the prevailing doctrine today. As is commonly known, the starting point in justifying the enlargement of traditional limits is the existence of a natural relationship between the sea and its resources and between the coast and its inhabitants, relationships that are independent from and existed prior to the will of any state. It would exceed the framework of this chapter to analyze the different theories that have been unfolded on this matter, such as the doctrine of contiguity or proximity, that of ecological unity or ecosystem, that of dependency or vital interest, that of permanent sovereignty over natural resources, that of the right to develop, and that of self-protection of the coastal state. The fact is that the prevailing opinion today is that due to geographical, economic, and social considerations and, I would add, those of security, the coastal state has a right superior to that of any other state to dispose of the resources of its adjacent seas and to protect other interests of its population within a zone not exceeding 200 miles.

In referring to this new institution, confirmed in the convention, an increasing number of authors, including those of developed countries, qualify the EEZ as a zone of national jurisdiction. Likewise, the Fisheries Committee of FAO, among other bodies, alludes to the establishment of that zone as an enlargement of the national jurisdiction of a state, emphasizes the economic and social benefits that it will bring to coastal states, and points out the measures to be adopted by them for the observation, control, and monitoring of fisheries in zones subject to their jurisdiction.

On its part, the International Court of Justice, in its opinion of 1974 on an affair between the United Kingdom and Iceland, had referred to the fisheries zone as a <u>tertium genus</u> between the territorial sea and the high seas. This concept was applied to a zone other than the EEZ because the latter was not under discussion in the court. It is, however enough to compare the characteristics of both kinds of zones in order to understand that if the court had judged relevant the concept of the "third genre" in the case of the fisheries zone, that idea would be even more appropriate in the case of the EEZ.

For all the reasons stated, we must conclude that the Exclusive Economic Zone is an area of national jurisdiction inasmuch as only the coastal state exercises in it sovereign rights and jurisdiction to regulate the most important activities, with a view to promote its economic development and protect other interests of its population. None of the freedoms or rights accorded to other states in the EEZ has the same character. The uses of third states are marginal with respect to this zone, in which they do not exercise any special competence but only jurisdiction over their own vessels. Even that jurisdiction is nott absolute since, as was already said, the coastal state may detain and institute proceedings against vessels that violate its laws and regulations in matters of fishing and pollution.

The rights attributed to the coastal state in the Exclusive Economic Zone to achieve the aims provided for in the convention are of such nature and scope that their exercise may be assured only by the subjection of that maritime space to the authority of the coastal state as the owner of the zone concerned, without prejudice to the jus communicationis, which is of interest to all states.

If this is already a valid concept, with more reason it will be so in the future to the extent that scientific and technological advances, the new uses of the sea, the increase in the capacity of the developing countries to benefit from their coastal zones, and the possible conflicts resulting from this increase with regard to the activities of other nations demand that the coastal states exercise competences very similar in practice to those corresponding to the territorial sea, with the exception of those regarding innocent passage. It is possible to anticipate some contingencies today with regard to the uses of the sea.

1. The establishment of artificial islands for different purposes (ports, aeronautical bases, weather stations, research and training centers, factories, depots, dwellings, etc.), as well as other installations and structures, will entail an increasing exercise of competences to assure the order, monitoring, and management of the activities concerned.

2. Pollution dangers resulting from these and other activities, as exemplified by the consequences of the serious accidents occurring in the recent past owing to traffic of tankers and to operations on the continental shelf, will demand the adoption of further measures by the coastal state to protect its adjacent sea, its living resources, and other interests of its populations.

3. The intensification of smuggling, stupefacients and weapons traffic, fiscal fraud, nonauthorized radio and TV transmissions, clandestine migrations, and other unlawful activities, in some countries more than in others, will also demand broader and more systematic control by coastal services in the Exclusive Economic Zone.

It may be said that at the time of negotiations, the representatives of the maritime powers had reason to be afraid that the acceptance of our viewpoints would lead to what they called "creeping jurisdiction," that is, the surreptitious advance of the domain of the coastal state. This was admittedly a well-founded fear, not with respect to the freedom of navigation but to other uses in the Exclusive Economic Zone, and I maintain that this possibility is unavoidable. Nobody is ignorant of the fact that the convention has been the result of political compromises more than the work of illustrious jurists and that many of its provisions have not taken into account the foreseeable evolution of the conduct of states but their immediate interests, so often contradictory.

However, even if the authors of the text had been able to correct its defects, its gaps, and its lack of foresight, we would be unrealistic to think that they would have solved definitively the problems concerning the utilization of ocean space. Although the new convention has been elaborated with the hope that it will be governing for the longest possible time, this attempt at permanence can only be relative with respect to a discipline like the law of the sea, which regulates individuals, situations, and activities that are continually changing. The evolution that has occurred since the middle of this century is only too illustrative of this point to allow one to develop false expectations that a similar process, if not perhaps a more radical one, will not occur in the next decades.

We believe that the growing uses of the sea and political, economic, and social factors will lead states to reinforce their domain in zones of national jurisdiction, without interpreting that irreversible process as a manifestation of an abusive intention of the coastal state. Rather, such reinforcement is a requirement resulting from the coastal states' development needs and from their duty to protect their interests against threats emanating from or damaging to the sea.

This requirement is recognized by Gilbert Apollis in L'emprise maritime de l'État Cotier, a book that gives a very objective description of the foundations of coastal states' extension of their maritime domain, the role played by unilateral practices in the development of the law of the sea, the justification of exercise of national powers of the coastal state in its adjacent sea, and the causes and conditions of this strengthening of coastal protection.[2] Three paragraphs of the book very eloquently support the ideas mentioned above. In a chapter on "the political-juridical bases of nationalization of coastal resources," after an analysis of the economic value of not only the mineral, animal, and vegetable resources existing in the continental shelf and in the Exclusive Economic Zone but also of abandoned objects on the sea bed, the water, the energy, and the space itself (the uttilization possibilities of which are increased with advances in marine technology), Apollis says:

> The only purpose of this inventory is to demonstrate the gradual transformation of

sovereignty applied over specific resources into a form of sovereignty applied globally over maritime areas considered in a broader dimension, as constituting a whole containing economic wealth. This transformation of economic sovereignty into political or territorial sovereignty is the result of the increasing need of protection experienced by the coastal state. This protection is related both to the dangers encountered by the national interest in the maritime areas and to the advantages that are found in such areas. Protection has given place to nationalization and all of it results is a form of reinforced protection.

Further on, after referring to the protection of coastal state security, of its national juridical order, of its adjacent sea, and of its living resources, he writes:

The maritime interest of the coastal state tends to become at the end of this evolution an area of national sovereignty where diversified powers are exercised in a closely linked manner, whose characteristics will depend on the specific needs of each type of state. Because these needs are legitimate, the lawfulness of the national powers which are required for their satisfaction will follow.

Finally, in formulating his general conclusions, the Professor Apollis admits with honesty and a certain bitterness:

The impression prevailing after reading the draft Convention published on 27 August 1980 is that there has been a complete victory of the views of the most militant coastal states, who also consider that some of the principles of such draft are already a part of customary international law. Whether it is the exclusive character of the economic zone and its withdrawal from the high seas, the extension of rights over the continental shelf beyond the two hundred-mile limit and its encroachment upon the common heritage of mankind, or the concept of the archipelagic state resulting in a territorialization of vast ocean areas, the claims which were until recently deemed scandalous have now become a part of public international law.

This conclusion is perhaps exaggerated, since we are not fully satisfied with the provisions of the convention although we certainly believe that state practice will undertake to make up for its gaps and shortcomings, as happened after the convention of 1958.

MILITARY USES IN THE EXCLUSIVE ECONOMIC ZONE

Besides the general considerations expounded at the Caracas session in 1974 and the discussions in informal meetings of the Second Committee throughout several sessions, the subject of military uses in the Exclusive Economic Zone and the sea in general was introduced by the representatives of some developing countries in the plenary session of the conference. These delegates recalled that the subject was included in the list of issues under the heading "Peaceful Uses of the Ocean Space, Peace and Security Zones."

At the request of those delegations, the president of the conference at that time Ambassador H. S. Amerasinghe, convened the plenary session in April 1976 to examine this subject, although he stated then that it must be linked to the international negotiations initiated in the disarmament sphere and to other measures adopted by the United Nations regarding the denuclearization and demilitarization of the sea bed and the creation of zones of peace, all of which in his opinion imposed certain limitations on its treatment by the Conference on the Law of the Sea.

Only seventeen delegations took part in the debate. The majority of the developing countries' representatives who spoke held that the conference should establish definite provisions directed to secure the pacific conduct of states in both the international and national zones of ocean space, since the convention would be incomplete if it did not add to the objectives of justice, development, and welfare those of peace and security. They repeated the proposals that had been put forward regarding the Exclusive Economic Zone, which I shall refer to presently, and stated that it was necessary to define what was meant by "peaceful uses" in order to avoid arbitrary interpretations.

The delegates of the Soviet Union, Bulgaria, Cuba, and the United States aduced that even though they were supporters of the peaceful uses of ocean space, as it was established in articles of the Single Negotiating Text, their support must be considered within the framework of the forums in which negotiations were conducted for the maintenance of international peace and security, the promotion of cessation of the arms race, and general and complete disarmament, not within the framework of the law of the sea conference. The debate within the law of the sea conference finished without the president's recommending any procedure for considering the inclusion of further provisions in the Revised Single Negotiating Text.

Something similar transpired in the Second Committee, where the delegates of some developing countries put forward several proposals for the protection of the national security of the coastal state in its Exclusive Economic Zone against the military uses of other states. Without claiming the establishment in said zone of the regime of innocent passage applicable to the territorial sea, they suggested that at least the obligation of all states to observe peaceful conduct in the EEZ by refraining from military activities that could endanger the security of the coastal state, such as naval maneuvers with firearms exercises, should be provided. They also proposed that the article regarding the deployment of installations and structures in the zone should be modified so that the authorization of the coastal state would be required in all cases.

These proposals were objected to by the maritime power representatives under the familiar pretext that they tended to "territorialize" the Exclusive Economic Zone and that carrying out military activities with peaceful purposes is in accordance with the charter of the United Nations and with principles of international law. The lack of sufficient support for the proposals in question resulted in their being excluded by the Presidential Collegium from the revised negotiating texts. The majority of delegations remained silent, apparently indicating that any initiative along these lines would be destined to fail in view of the categorical opposition of the maritime powers.

Instead, after long negotiations, the inclusion of Article 301 among the general provisions was obtained in 1979. This article provides that "in exercising their rights and performing their duties in accordance with the provisions of this Convention, all States' Parties shall refrain from any threat or use of force against the territorial integrity or political independence of any State, or in any other manner inconsistent with the principles of international law embodied in the Charter of the United Nations."

Moreover, the convention contains other provisions that can be invoked by the coastal state to protect itself against activities detrimental to the interests of its own security. The first is contained in Article 58, paragraph 3, which provides that "in exercising their rights and performing their duties under this Convention in the exclusive economic zone, States shall have due regard to the rights and duties of the coastal State and shall comply with the laws and regulations adopted by the coastal State in accordance with the provisions of this Convention and other rules of international law insofar as they are not incompatible with this Part."

Consequently, for example, if the warships or the

military aircraft of a state carried out munitions testing in the Exclusive Economic Zone of another state, causing damage to the living resources or the marine environment or endangering installations of the coastal state, the security of navigation, the conduct of scientific research, or other related interests, then the coastal state should have the right to demand the suspension of such activities and to require the fulfillment of its laws and regulations that had been adopted on the matter.

In the second place, by effect of the cross reference provided in Article 58, paragraph 2, the provision of Article 88 of the convention, according to which "the high seas shall be reserved for peaceful purposes," is also applicable to the Exlcusive Economic Zone, giving a firm basis to the coastal state for opposition to any nonpeaceful use of its sea.

On the other hand, in accordance with Article 301 of the general provisions, the coastal state could object to military activities undertaken in its EEZ by another state, not only when such activities threatened its territorial integrity or its political independence, but also when it considered them contrary to the principles of international law embodied in the charter of the United Nations, among which those of international peace and security appear prominently.

As for the establishment by a state of installations, structures, and devices for military purposes in the Exclusive Economic Zone of another state, the silence of the convention on this subject has given occasion for different interpretations. Some authors, probably starting from the principle of "that which is not forbidden is permitted," consider that such deployment would be lawful. Others admit that while the establishment of monitoring devices may serve as an instrument of international peace and security, the deployment of arms would be at least a potential threat to the coastal state.

In any event, according to Article 60, paragraph 1(c), the coastal state has the authority to object to the establishment of installations and structures of any kind if they interfere with the exercise of its rights in the EEZ. Likewise, as an extension of what is provided in Article 81 regarding the continental shelf, the coastal state may oppose the deployment of installations and structures for any purposes (including military ones) when this deployment entails drilling in the sea bed and subsoil. Finally, from what is provided in Article 246, paragraph 5(b), regardinng marine scientific research projects, it is proper to infer that the coastal state would also be empowered to object to the deployment of installations, structures, or devices involving the utilization of explosives or the introduction into the marine environment of noxious substances.

Whatever the case may be, the permissibility of utilizing the EEZ for purposes neither forbidden nor authorized in the convention--as in the case of military uses--must be determined by balancing the effects that such use would have on the interests of the coastal state, the user state, and the international community as a whole, in accordance with Article 59 of the convention, which is intended to solve the problem of residual rights.

Notwithstanding this, Article 59 does not envisage who has the burden of proving which of these interests are superior. In the case with which we are dealing, it is not spelled out whether the coastal state must demonstrate that military activities threaten its security or the exercise of its rights in the EEZ, or whether the foreign state must prove that such activities are essential for its own security or for the benefit of the international community as a whole. On the other hand, according to Article 298, paragraph 1(b), any state may declare that it does not accept the procedures of the convention for the settlement of disputes concerning military activities. In such a case, Article 59 on residual rights does not apply.

Clearly, the convention is not without deficiencies and gaps that, in my opinion, should have been rectified in order to avoid possible conflicts later. We know well that corrections would not have been easy to make, in view of the attitude adopted by some states that tried to amend substantive provisions of other parts of the text already negotiated at the risk of destroying all that had already been done. In any case, now that the convention has been adopted, experience will demonstrate to what extent the articles on the Exclusive Economic Zone agree, satisfactorily or not, with the objectives for which they were conceived.

NOTES

1. Jean Pierre Quéneudec, "Un Problème en suspens: La Nature de la zone économique", Revue Iranienne des Relations Internationales, nos. 5-6, 1975-1976.

2. Gilbert Apollis, L'Emprise maritime de l'État Cotier. Revue Générale de Droit International Publique, Paris, 1981.

Hugo Caminos

8. The Regime of Fisheries in the Exclusive Economic Zone

INTRODUCTION

This article analyzes the rules relating to fisheries contained in Part V of the 1982 Convention on the Law of the Sea.[1] The provisions that refer specifically to the fishing regime did not undergo any major changes from their form in the negotiating texts put forward during previous sessions of that important international forum.

The right of coastal states to exercise sovereignty over the living resources in waters within a maximum limit of 200 nautical miles from the baselines used to measure the width of their territorial seas, the essential element of the juridical concept of the Exclusive Economic Zone, had been gaining ground not only within the conference but also in the practice of such states. Since 1975, about a hundred coastal countries had promulgated laws in this area, the common denominator of which was precisely the establishment of an exclusive fishing zone up to 200 nautical miles wide.

In addition to this abundance of new legislation, several hundred bilateral fisheries agreements have been entered into in recent years that either openly or implicitly express the growing acceptance of the new concept within the international community. Countries traditionally opposed to this new movement, which began in Latin America over thirty years ago, were busily incorporating it--in one way or another--into their national legislation, and the argument that exclusive fisheries zones were contrary to international law was no longer being put forward at the United Nations conference. Against the background of this irreversible trend, the Fisheries Committee of the FAO approved a global program of assistance to developing coastal states for the creation and management of fisheries within their exclusive economic zones. This program was adopted by the conference of that specialized agency in November 1979.

From the economic standpoint, the most significant factor in this development is that 99 percent of the living resources subject to commercial fishing are found within the 200-mile limit. The most important exceptions are the various species of tuna, approximately 40 percent of which are taken outside this limit.[2]

All indications are that notwithstanding the adoption and entering into force of the Convention on the Law of the Sea, the 200-mile fishing zone--which forms a part of the broader concept of the Exclusive Economic Zone--possesses the distinctive features of international custom. However, the customary regime that is arising from the practice of the states is not identical to that of the convention, since the latter includes the compromises arrived at during the process of negotiation at the conference. For example, it is doubtful that the right of noncoastal states and states with special geographical characterisitics to participate in the exploitation of living resources in the exclusive economic zones of coastal states within the same region or subregion, which is contained in the convention, would be recognized in a fisheries regime established by means of customary norms.

BASIC RULES OF THE REGIME ON FISHERIES IN THE EXCLUSIVE ECONOMIC ZONE

Most of the rules of Part V of the convention, which deals with the Exclusive Economic Zone (articles 55-75), refer to fisheries questions. The reason for this is clear: the exercise of the coastal states' rights to sovereignty over the natural resources of the sea bed and subsoil in the zone is regulated by the provisions concerning the continental shelf in Part VI of the convention. These resources include minerals and hydrocarbons, and also sedentary species such as corals, shellfish, mollusks, and sponges. Thus, the latter species are excluded from the fisheries regime that is characteristic of the Exclusive Economic Zone and to which we are referring here.

The principle on which regulation of the fisheries in the Exclusive Economic Zone is based is that the coastal state enjoys rights of sovereignty for the purposes of exploration and exploitation, conservation, and management of the living resources within this zone.[3] From these rights are derived the basic rules of the system:

> 1. The coastal state shall determine the allowable catch within its zone and shall ensure that preservation of the living resources is not

endangered by overfishing.
2. The coastal state shall determine its own capacity for harvesting the living resources within its exclusive economic zone.
3. The coastal state shall promote optimum utilization of the living resources of its zone.
4. When the coastal state does not have the necessary capacity to take all its allowable catch, it shall allow other states to harvest the surplus.[4]

Limiting allowable catch is intended to maintain or reestablish the various stocks of fish being taken at levels that will produce the maximum sustainable yield. Such limitation is not to be determined solely according to the laws of biology, but should also be based on economic and environmental factors such as "the economic needs of coastal fishing communities and the special requirements of developing States, and taking into account fishing patterns, the interdependence of stocks and any generally recommended international minimum standards, whether subregional, regional or global." In other words, each coastal state should take conservation and administrative measures in line with its fisheries policy, according to its own evaluation of the appropriate scientific, economic, and social factors.

The right of the coastal state to assess its own capability for harvesting the living resources of its Exclusive Economic Zone is of fundamental importance, for it is this assessment that determines whether a surplus exists and, therefore, whether other states may be granted access to it. It is likely that the capacity of developing countries will increase until they are able to take all of their allowable catch, at which point third countries would not be permitted to fish in their zones. With this possibility in mind, the convention includes a provision to safeguard the participation of developing countries (both noncoastal states and states with special geographical characteristics), to which we will refer below.

The third basic rule of the fisheries regime in the Exclusive Economic Zone is that the coastal state is obliged to promote optimum utilization of its living resources. This concept "requires the adjustment of the conservation regulations, seeking the average maximum sustainable yield, so as to take into account environmental and economic factors as well as special requirements of developing countries (social considerations). In a practical sense, this results in reducing total fishing effort on a particular stock of fish and maintaining, on the average, a higher level of stock size with a reduced average annual yield from the fishery."[5]

Optimum utilization aims at a more rational management, thus ensuring conservation and improving yield, particularly for stocks that have been subjected to constant overfishing by large fleets from countries located far from the zone in question.

The fourth basic rule has its origin in the recognition of the coastal state's preferential fishing rights within the waters adjacent to its territorial sea. This rule was incorporated into the regime applicable to the Exclusive Economic Zone as a compromise solution worked out between supporters of the territorialist thesis and those who favored freedom of fishing. According to this rule, whenever the coastal state lacks the necessary capacity to take all of the allowable catch within its Exclusive Economic Zone, it will allow other states to harvest the surplus through agreements and other arrangements in accordance with the methods and conditions set forth in the laws and regulations of the coastal state. Thus, the participation of third states in harvesting this surplus is not automatic.

In granting access to its surplus, the coastal state exercises a high degree of autonomy consistent with its "sovereign rights" over the resources of its Exclusive Economic Zone. Among other factors, therefore, the coastal state must bear in mind the significance of the living resources of the area to its economy and other national interests. Clearly, these are judgments in which the state enjoys the widest possible discretion. By way of example, the convention states that the requirements of certain countries should be borne in mind when the coastal state is entering into agreements allowing others to fish its surplus. They include landlocked states and those with special geographical characteristics--particularly developing states--within the subregion or region. The convention also refers to the need to minimize economic dislocation in states whose nationals habitually fish in the zone (the traditional fishery) or have made substantial efforts in research and identification of stocks within the zone.

Third countries that fish within the zone must take the conservation measures and satisfy the conditions set forth in the laws and regulations of the coastal state. The convention offers the following partial list of questions to which such laws and regulations may relate: granting of licenses, including the payment of fees and other forms of remuneration that "in the case of developing coastal states, may consist of adequate compensation in the field of financing, equipment and technology relating to the fishing industry"; determination of the species that can be fished and fixing of the respective quotas; fishing seasons and areas as well as the type, size, and amount of gear and the type, size, and number of fishing vessels that may be used; the age and size of fish that may be harvested; the information that must be provided by fishing vessels; requirements regarding the conduct of fisheries research programs; placement of nationals of the coastal state aboard vessels as observers or for training purposes; landing of all or a part of the catch in ports of the coastal state; conditions for joint ventures or other cooperative arrangements; personnel training and transfer of fisheries technology; and enforcement procedures.

For cases in which the distribution of fish stocks extends beyond the limits of the Exclusive Economic Zone, the convention indicates how states may achieve cooperation and coordination. Two situations are dealt with:

    1. If the same stocks' or species are located within the exclusive economic zones of two or more coastal states, these states shall endeavor, either by direct negotiations or through the appropriate subregional or regional organizations, to reach the necessary agreement to coordinate their efforts and ensure conservation and development of the stocks.[6]

    2. If the same stocks or species are found both within the Exclusive Economic Zone of a coastal state and in the high seas adjacent to this zone, the same principle of cooperation is established between the coastal state, on the one hand, and the states that fish these stocks in the adjacent high seas, on the other hand, but only with respect to the conservation of these stocks within the adjacent area.[7]

One final observation is due on this subject: although at first glance the basic rules of the fisheries regime appear to consist of a series of rights and obligations on the part of the coastal state, in fact, as one author has pointed out, a closer examination of the system reveals that the state enjoys broad discretionary powers in the conservation and management of the living resources of its Exclusive Economic Zone.[8] In my opinion, this is consistent with the juridical nature of the zone and is confirmed by the procedure for settling disputes involving the interpretation or application of the provisions of the convention relating to fishing within this zone. The method for settling disputes, which was worked out by the conference after extensive negotiations, does not play down the powers conferred on the coastal state. In effect, disputes involving the sovereign rights of the coastal states with respect to the living resources of the Exclusive Economic Zone or the exercise of these rights, including its discretionary powers in determining allowable catch, its harvesting capacity, the allocation of surpluses to other states, and the terms and conditions established under its laws and regulations concerning conservation and management of resources, are excluded from the mandatory procedure that results in binding decisions.[9] The coastal state is not required to submit these disputes to any compulsory procedure. Instead, such disputes are subject to a conciliation method set out in Annex V of the convention, in cases where it is alleged that

> 1. the coastal state has manifestly failed to comply with its obligation to ensure, through proper conservation and management measures, that the maintenance of the living resources of the zone is not seriously endangered;
> 2. the coastal state has arbitrarily refused to determine, in compliance with another state's request, the allowable catch and its capacity to harvest living resources with respect to stocks that the other state is interested in fishing; or
> 3. the coastal state has arbitrarily refused to allocate to any state, in accordance with the appropriate articles of the convention and under the conditions established by the coastal state consistent with the convention, all or part of the surplus that it has declared to exist.[10]

Finally, it is specifically stated that "in no case shall the conciliation commission substitute its discretion for that of the coastal State."[11]

SPECIAL FISHING REGIMES IN THE EXCLUSIVE ECONOMIC ZONE

In addition to setting forth the principles for a general fisheries regime, the convention also contains provisions regarding the conservation and utilization of certain species whose biological characteristics or migratory habits require special consideration. These provisions are supplementary to those discussed above and constitute a separate regime applicable to particular species. The text divides these into five categories: (1) highly migratory species, (2) marine mammals, and (3) anadromous, (4) catadromous, and (5) sedentary species.

Highly Migratory Species

Highly migratory species are listed in Annex I of the convention. The most important of these, from a commercial standpoint, are the various types of tuna, around two million tons of which are taken annually. In the conference negotiations, the countries of Latin America--particularly those of the Pacific coast, where tuna are most abundant--maintained that on the basis of the coastal state's rights over the living resources of its Exclusive Economic Zone, the rules regarding this species should be no different from those of the general regime. Therefore, while not denying the competence of subregional or regional intergovernmental organizations to adopt resolutions, such as declarations that a resource has been sufficiently exploited or formulations of conservation and utilization methods, an approach supported by the powers that fish these highly migratory species in areas far removed from their own shores and that maintain their supremacy in the tuna fishery, the countries of Latin America nevertheless opposed having these resolutions apply within the Exclusive Economic Zone of a state without its express consent. They also proposed that the state itself should be the sole authority responsible for carrying out such resolutions together with its own laws and regulations.

The text in the convention[12] is vague and general. Its first paragraph simply states that the coastal state and those other states whose nationals fish for those species in the region "shall cooperate directly or through appropriate international organizations with a view to ensuring conservation and promoting the objective of optimum utilization of such species throughout the region, both within and beyond the exclusive economic zone." In the case of regions in which there is no appropriate international organization, such states shall "cooperate to establish such an organization and participate in its work." In other words, the provision does not create a specific regime for highly migratory species. Rather, it proposes a very broadly worded commitment to cooperation among the states directly involved.

Finally, paragraph 2 states that "the provisions of paragraph 1 apply in addition to the other provisions in this part." This means that the concept of the coastal state's rights of sovereignty over the living resources of the Exclusive Economic Zone and the general rules for their conservation and utilization shall also apply to highly migratory species.

Marine Mammals

Some marine mammals are listed with the highly migratory species in Annex I of the convention and are thus subject to the special regime for such species. This is the case with the cetaceans (porpoises and whales). However, the United States delegation, responding to pressure from conservationists in their country bent on protecting the whale, insisted on including and giving greater emphasis to a passage that would provide the basis for achieving this goal. The current provision[13] satisfies the conservationists by safeguarding the right of a coastal state "to prohibit, limit or regulate the exploitation of marine mammals more strictly" than by the regulations in the part relating to the Exclusive Economic Zone or to do so through the competence of an international organization. Finally, the article indicates that states shall cooperate in the conservation of these species, and "in the case of cetaceans shall in particular work through the appropriate international organizations for their conservation, management and study."

Anadromous Species

These are species such as salmon that begin life in rivers, migrate to the sea where they live for several years, and then ascend the same rivers to spawn. A provision contained in the convention[14] recognizes that the state in whose rivers such species originate has the primary interest in and responsibility for such stocks and that this state must take all necessary steps not only to guarantee their conservation but also to ensure that their peculiar biological cycle is not interrupted. Account must also be taken of the interests of states that fish for such species, both within exclusive economic zones and on the high seas.

The text states that anadromous species must be fished only in waters landward of the outer limits of the Exclusive Economic Zone, except where this provision might cause economic dislocation for a state other than the state of origin. With regard to fishing outside the Exclusive Economic Zone, the states concerned shall consult to draw up appropriate agreements. The state of origin shall also cooperate in minimizing economic dislocations that may arise. In cases where the anadromous species migrate into or through waters landward of the outer limits of the exclusive economic zones of states other than the state of origin, such other states shall cooperate with the latter to ensure conservation and management of such stocks. Where appropriate, these special rules shall be implemented up through regional organizations.

Catadromous Species

Catadromous species such as eels spend most of their lives in rivers but return to the sea to spawn. The general rule established in the provision of the convention regarding these species[15] is that the coastal state in whose waters such species spend the greater part of their life cycle "shall have responsibility for the management of these species and shall ensure the ingress and egress of migrating fish." These species may only be harvested in waters landward of the outer limits of exclusive economic zones. When catadromous species migrate through the Exclusive Economic Zone of another state--whether as juvenile or as maturing fish--the management of such species shall be governed under an agreement between this other state and the coastal state in whose waters the species concerned spend most of their lives.

Sedentary Species

As indicated above, sedentary species are subject to the regime of the continental shelf, together with the other natural resources of the sea bed and subsoil within the Exclusive Economic Zone--i.e., minerals and other nonliving resources.[16] The inclusion of these species in the rules governing the exploration and utilization of the resources of the continental shelf is taken from the 1958 Geneva convention. This regime confers upon the coastal state exclusive sovereignty for purposes of exploitation of such resources. The convention also defines sedentary species as those that "at the harvestable stage either are immobile on or under the sea bed or are unable to move except in constant physical contact with the sea bed or the subsoil."[17]

Therefore, these species are not subject to the basic rules of the fisheries regime within the Exclusive Economic Zone, including the rules on conservation, utilization, and the rights of landlocked states and states with special geographical characteristics.

RIGHTS OF LANDLOCKED STATES AND STATES WITH SPECIAL GEOGRAPHICAL CHARACTERISTICS

The question of the rights of landlocked states and states with special geographical characteristics to participate in exploitation of the living resources of the exclusive economic zones of coastal states within the same region or subregion gave rise to some of the most arduous negotiations of the conference.

The regime set forth in the convention was the result of the work carried out by Negotiating Group 4, chaired by Ambassador Nandan of Fiji, during the 1978 Geneva meeting. This group was established by the plenary session along with six other negotiating groups to deal with the most difficult questions facing the conference. In turn, the work of the group was based in good part on texts prepared by the so-called Group of 21 at the fifth session in 1976. This latter group was made up of ten representatives from coastal states and another ten from landlocked and geographically disadvantaged states, plus Ambassador Nandan as chairman.

The regime is contained primarily in two articles, one relating to landlocked states and the other concerning states with special geographical characteristics.[18] Both provisions are directly linked with the rules concerning conservation and utilization of the living resources within the Exclusive Economic Zone. Article 69, which deals with the situation of landlocked states, sets forth the following rules:

1. Landlocked states shall have the right to participate, on an equitable basis, in the exploitation of an appropriate part of the surplus of the living resources of the exclusive economic zones of the coastal states within the same subregion or region, taking into account the relevant economic and geographical circumstances of all states concerned.

2. The states concerned shall establish the terms and modalities of their participation through bilateral, subregional, or regional agreements.

3. Among other things, such agreements shall take account of (1) the need to avoid effects detrimental to the fishing communities or fishing industries of the coastal state; (2) the extent to which the landlocked state, under this regime, is participating or is entitled to participate in the exploitation of the living resources of the exclusive economic zones of other states; (3) the extent to which other landlocked states and states with special geographical characteristics are participating in the exploitation of the living resources of the coastal state's Exclusive Economic Zone, bearing in mind the need to avoid placing a special burden on any one coastal state or part thereof; and (4) the nutritional needs of the populations of the respective states.

4. The regime shall be applied without prejudice to existing arrangements in subregions or regions in which landlocked states are given equal or preferential rights to the exploitation of the fisheries resources of exclusive economic zones. (This rule was included at the request of the group of landlocked and geographically disadvantaged states to take account of certain principles declared by African countries).

Article 70 deals with states with special geographical characteristics, which are divided into two types of coastal states: (1) those whose geographical situation is such that obtaining adequate supplies of fish for the nutritional purposes of their population depends upon exploiting the living resources of the exclusive economic zones of other states within the subregion or region, including states bordering enclosed or semienclosed seas; and (2) coastal states that cannot claim an Exclusive Economic Zone of their own. The conditions by which these states can exercise their right to participation are identical to those established for landlocked states.

The essential points of the regime set forth in the convention are as follows.

1. The access of landlocked states and states with special geographical characteristics to exclusive economic zones is classified as a "right." Coastal states argued that the fact that they enjoy sovereignty over the resources of the Exclusive Economic Zone meant that any recognition of rights of third countries over those resources would be inconsistent with the very concept of the Exclusive Economic Zone. The solution to this problem in the convention, as explained by Ambassador Nandan, is based on the idea that there is no incongruity between these concepts and that the important thing is the content of the rights and the context in which these are recognized. In this sense, the rights accorded to landlocked states and states with special geographical characteristics are subject to the coastal state's competence in determining both the allowable catch within its Exclusive Economic Zone and its own fishing capacity, as well as depending on the goal of ensuring optimum utilization of the living resources in its zone.

2. The right of landlocked states and states with special geographical characteristics to participate in this fishery is not automatic and applies only to the surplus of living resources within the exclusive economic zones. In other words, it is only after the coastal state has determined the total allowable catch within its zone, and provided it does not have the necessary capacity to harvest all of this allowable catch, that it must grant access to third states to fish these surplus stocks. The terms and modalities under which such access is granted must be established through bilateral agreements within the subregion or region. In order to avoid, as far as possible, situations in which no surplus exists, the text contains a compromise formula that specifies that when the coastal state is approaching a point that would enable it to harvest all of its allowable catch, the state shall cooperate with other states concerned in the establishment of equitable arrangements to permit the participation of developing landlocked states or developing states with special geographical characteristics in exploiting the living resources of the zone "as may be appropriate in the circumstances and on terms satisfactory to all parties." As may be seen, this safeguard, which deals only with developing countries, is based on the concept of cooperation.

3. In principle, the right to participate in fisheries activities is conferred on all landlocked states and states with special geographical characteristics, whether or not they are developing countries. However, the method of dealing with the two

groups of countries is different. The group of fifty-four landlocked and geographically disadvantaged countries that participated in the conference included highly developed states, such as Switzerland and the Federal Republic of Germany, along with some of the least developed countries in the world, such as Afghanistan and Cameroun.

The convention has taken account of these differences. It states that developed countries, whether they are landlocked or have special geographical characteristics, shall only have the right to participate in the exploitation of resources within the exclusive economic zones of developed coastal states in the same subregion or region. In other words, these countries cannot exercise their rights within the exclusive economic zones of developing coastal states.

Also, in assigning the surpluses of the allowable catch within the Exclusive Economic Zone to third states, a coastal state must take special account of those landlocked states and states with special geographical characteristics that are developing countries. As Ambassador Nandan pointed out, this solution avoids the use of the words "priority" and "preference" (which were questioned by coastal states) while, at the same time, establishing the need to give particular consideration to landlocked states and those with special geographical characteristics that are also developing countries.

4. A point--but one with political and legal overtones--is the use of the expression "states with special geographical characteristics" in place of "geographically disadvantaged states."[19]

The latter term was coined at the conference by the special interest group made up of the states in question and the landlocked states. The members of this group favored the use of the term "geographically disadvantaged states," because they identified themselves in that way. Nevertheless, this nomenclature was not used in any of the texts drafted by the Second Committee of the conference. As indicated by Ambassador Nandan, the coastal states objected to it because of difficulties in arriving at a precise definition and therefore in determining which countries would fit into this category. Subsequent negotiating texts simply listed the requirements that must be met in order for certain developing coastal states to obtain the right to participate in exploitation of the resources within the exclusive economic zones of a subregion or region.

5. As mentioned above, the convention is without prejudice to arrangements made within subregions or regions under which landlocked states or states with special geographical characteristics are granted equal

or preferential rights for the exploitation of the living resources in exclusive economic zones. The text does not define the scope of the terms "region" and "subregion," and some delegations, such as those of Rumania and Yugoslavia, had proposed that these be replaced by broader concepts, including having these clauses apply without any geographical limitation.

6. Fisheries disputes will be settled in accordance with Part XV of the convention, which deals with the procedures of the settlements of disputes. With regard to the settlement of disputes relating to the coastal states' rights of sovereignty over the living resources of its Exclusive Economic Zone, or the exercise of these rights, the convention provides that the state in question shall not be obliged to submit such disputes to the compulsory procedures entailing binding decisions established in Section 2 of Part XV. This exception includes the state's discretionary powers for determining the allowable catch, its harvesting capacity, the allocation of surpluses to other states, and the terms and conditions established under its laws and regulations concerning conservation and management of resources.[20] Any dispute involving these matters may only be submitted to compulsory settlement by an agreement between both parties.

Where no such agreement exists, the dispute shall be submitted to a conciliation procedure, at the request of either party, when it is alleged that:

> 1. a coastal state has manifestly failed to comply with its obligations to ensure though proper conservation and management measures that the maintenance of the living resources in the Exclusive Economic Zone is not seriously endangered;
> 2. a coastal state has arbitrarily refused to determine, at the request of another state, the allowable catch and its own capacity to harvest living resources with respect to stocks that the other state is interested in fishing; or
> 3. a state has arbitrarily refused to allocate to any state, in accordance with conditions for participation of other states in the exploitation of the living resources of its Exclusive Economic Zone as set forth in the convention, all or part of the surplus it has declared to exist.

APPLICATION OF THE COASTAL STATE'S LAWS AND REGULATIONS IN THE EXCLUSIVE ECONOMIC ZONE: CONTROLS AND SUPERVISION

As indicated above, the regime established by the convention for the Exclusive Economic Zone gives to the coastal state "sovereign rights for the purposes of exploring and exploiting, conserving and managing the natural resources, whether living or non-living." Therefore, the coastal state has the right to utilize fish stocks within its Exclusive Economic Zone and, at the same time, to take appropriate conservation and management measures to ensure that the living resources within the zone are not endangered by overfishing.

The convention includes in this regard a provision[21] that authorizes the coastal state, in exercising the above-mentioned rights of sovereignty, to "take such measures, including boarding, inspection, arrest and judicial proceedings, as may be necessary to ensure compliance with the laws and regulations adopted by it in conformity with this Convention." This provision is followed by sections dealing with the posting of a bond or security to release the vessel, a prohibition against imprisonment or any form of corporal punishment for violation of fishing laws and regulations within the Exclusive Economic Zone, and notification of the flag state in case of arrest or detention of foreign vessels.

Extension of national jurisdiction over fisheries resources in waters within 200 nautical miles of a state's coasts requires the adoption of a policy regarding management of its living resources and creation of appropriate mechanisms for enforcing this policy.

In fact, this extension of the coastal state's jurisdiction has given many countries the opportunity, for the first time, to determine a clear fisheries policy and create a specific mechanism for enforcing such a policy.[22] Both of these aspects are important. The adoption of a coordinated policy regarding the living resources of the sea is a complex task in which many different disciplines must be taken into account and various governmental agencies must be brought together in consultation. Even so, a coordinated policy may yet prove inoperable if the state fails to adopt an adequate system for enforcing and monitoring its regulations.

The purpose of a monitoring system is both to prevent fishing by unauthorized vessels and to enforce compliance with the laws and regulations of the coastal state and with the conditions applicable to domestic and foreign vessels licensed to fish in the exclusive economic zone.

A recent report mentions in this regard that whichever organization the government chooses to make responsible for the entire task of monitoring, controlling, and carrying out its fisheries policy, it is imperative that proper procedures be established for consultation, information gathering, and decision making in this area, and that each of the government departments that may affect or be affected by these decisions take part in such procedures.[23] No doubt these procedures will have to be duly coordinated to ensure that instructions given to officials responsible for monitoring operations are consistent.

An example of the type of organization that may be established, and that is characteristic of a developed country, is that adopted by the United Kingdom, described in the report just mentioned.[24] In this case, enforcement of the regulations at sea and reconnaissance in the air are primarily the responsibility of the Navy and the Air Force. This task is assigned to specific units, and the costs for these services are borne by the Department of Fisheries, not the Department of Defense. In one region, the Department of Fisheries also operates its own vessels with civilian crews. The activities of this branch are coordinated with those of the Navy and Air Force. Onshore operations are carried out by marine fisheries inspectors of the Department of Fisheries. These inspectors are also responsible for training officials engaged in monitoring and enforcement tasks. The Navy and Air Force carry out these latter tasks under the corresponding directives and instructions and maintain the necessary controls. Details of the fishing activities observed and the inspections carried out are fed into computers, and this information is then used to plan monitoring tasks and to assess penalties against violators.

Other countries use different systems, such as making a single government agency responsible for the entire area. In any event, it is essential that those who carry out the tasks of controling, monitoring , and applying the regulations governing fisheries activities receive proper training in technical and legal aspects, fishing agreements, licensing laws, and other matters.

The fisheries regime in the Exclusive Economic Zone offers new opportunities for developing coastal states, but at the same time it also makes them responsible for rational management of a large part of the living resources of the sea. This responsibility requires formulation of a maritime policy together with effective application of the policy through the adoption of proper mechanisms. And this need, in turn, presents many scientific, technical, and economic difficulties. The United Nations can contribute to the solution of these difficulties by providing information, consultation, and assistance to developing countries.

NOTES

1. Adopted on 30 April 1982 at the eleventh session of the Third United Nations Conference on the Law of the Sea. See also the two following articles by this author: "La explotación de los recursos vivos del mar: Los problemas involucrados en las negociaciones de Naciones Unidas y otros foros" and "El régimen de la pesca y conservación de los recursos vivos en la zona económica exclusiva: implicaciones jurídicas y económicas," United Nations CEPAL.E/CEPAL/L.156, Rev.2 of 28 April 1978 (published jointly with the Institute of International Studies of the University of Chile).

2. Jean Carroz, "Les problèmes de la peche a la Conférence sur le droit de la mer et dans la practique des États," Revue Générale de Droit International Publique, 1980, no. 3, pp. 705-751.

3. Article 56, paragraph 1(a).
4. Articles 61 and 62.
5. Donald L. McKernan, "Fisheries and the Law of the Sea," Marine Technology Society Journal, vol. 2, no. 2 (May 1977), p. 20.
6. Article 63, paragraph 1.
7. Article 63, paragraph 2.
8. Jean Carroz, op. cit., p. 714.
9. Article 297, paragraph 3(a). See also Chapter 9 in this volume.
10. Article 297, paragraph 3(b).
11. Article 297, paragraph 3(c).
12. Article 64.
13. Article 65.
14. Article 66.
15. Article 67.
16. Article 68.
17. Article 77, paragraph 4.
18. Articles 69 and 70, respectively.
19. In its last plenary meeting on September 24, 1982 the conference decided by consensus to replace the expression "states with special geographical characteristics" with the expression "geographically disadvantaged states" in Article 70 of the Convention. Since the term "geographically disadvantaged states" also appears in other parts of the Convention it was agreed that the characterization of these states contained in paragraph 2 of Article 70 would only apply for the purposes of Part V.
20. Article 297, paragraph 3(a).
21. Article 73.
22. FAO Committee on Fisheries Fourteenth Session (Rome, 26-30 May 1981), Doc. COFI/81, p. 2.
23. M. C. Jennings, "The Enforcement of Fisheries Regulations." CECAF/TECT/80/22 (Eng.) FAO-UNDP Dakar, July 1980.
24. Ibid., p. 13.

Maria Teresa Infante

9. The Settlement of Disputes Regarding the Law of the Sea and Its Bearing on the Legal Nature of the Exclusive Economic Zone

GENERAL CONSIDERATIONS

Without underestimating the input that can be obtained from international practice, particularly on a bilateral level, it can be asserted that the most revealing source regarding the problems arising in this area is the convention adopted as a result of the Third United Nations Conference on the Law of the Sea[1] and its antecedent texts.

Given the nature of the negotiations and the broad range of interests represented at the conference, an examination of the conflict-resolution mechanisms established in Part XV of the Convention provides a perspective that sheds light on the concept of the Exclusive Economic Zone (EEZ).

According to the convention, this concept is derived from Article 56, which expands upon Article 55 and which describes the "rights, jurisdiction and duties" of the coastal state in the Exclusive Economic Zone, stating that they are to be exercised with "due regard to the rights and duties of other States." The specific regime of this maritime space is, moreover, a compromise among different positions that also acted as a balancing factor within the overall negotiations of the conference.

The mechanisms for the settlement of disputes regarding the Exclusive Economic Zone also contain other points of interest, since some aspects of the convention's overall approach have a bearing on concrete applications of that space; these are connected with the recognition of "sovereign rights" or the "jurisdiction" of the coastal state and with the exclusive nature of these powers, primarily with regard to fisheries and scientific research within the Exclusive Economic Zone.

As it is set forth in the convention, the Exclusive Economic Zone has some specific characteristics. These include: (1) the absence of a general definition and its replacement by a description and enumeration of rights, jurisdiction, and uses associated with the coastal state (articles 55 and 56, paragraph 1); (2) the recognition of rights and duties of other states (Article 56, paragraph 2), which implies possible concurrent jurisdictions; and (3) the existence of so-called residual rights (Article 58) which introduces the existence of a hierarchy between the rights of coastal states and legal uses by other states.

This last characteristic offers another standpoint from which the nature of the Exclusive Economic Zone can be examined; to a certain extent, it is complementary to the study of conflict-resolution mechanisms. Thus Article 59 embodies the assumption of the existence of conflicts of interest regarding which the convention does not confer rights or jurisdiction to the coastal state or to other states. In such cases, the settlement should be sought "on the basis of equity and in the light of all the relevant circumstances..."; although these criteria accommodate various alternatives with respect to the nature of the Exclusive Economic Zone, they do not provide concrete elements for a precise interpretation of the concept. The problem can be looked at from two different points of view: either it concerns a zone of the high seas where special functional jurisdictions are exercised by the coastal state in all matters related to economic uses[2] or it concerns an area that is more closely linked to the coastal state but in which some important freedoms of the high seas persist, although these are necessarily coordinated with the purposes of the Exclusive Economic Zone itself. These positions can be more clearly identified with reference to the exclusive nature of the Exclusive Economic Zone and, in particular, with regard to the terms "sovereign rights" and "jurisdiction."

It is therefore not surprising that the various problems connected with the quality and quantity of the rights possessed by states are open to a variety of interpretations in which the jurisdictions of coastal state over legal uses by other states play a major role.[3]

This situation must also be understood within the setting of negotiations, in which the mechanisms accepted by coastal states for settling disputes were seen as a concession to other interest groups; hence, in this respect, the system for conflict resolution does not reflect a unified concept of the Exclusive Economic Zone. The original proposal of the group of coastal countries was to confer exclusive jurisdictions on the internal agencies of the states with respect to disputes arising within areas subject to exclusive jurisdiction, including the EEZ.[4]

The basic approaches noted above should therefore be taken into account in the examination of the content and scope of the current provisions in this area, particularly those contained in Section 3 of Part XV regarding the settlement of disputes.

THE GENERAL SYSTEM OF DISPUTE SETTLEMENT AND ITS EXCEPTIONS

The Convention on the Law of the Sea establishes an overall system based on the primacy of procedures leading to a compulsory or binding settlement issued by an international tribunal. Part XV, sections 1 and 2, lays down the general principles in this area, coordinating diplomatic means with jurisdictional methods freely chosen by the parties to a dispute,[5] and also incorporating some functional processes for specific cases.

The treaty in question contains detailed regulations regarding the procedures as well as the jurisdiction conferred upon the entities called upon to play a role in the various processes. It differs from the alternatives used in other multilateral conventions, which include an arbitration clause or which relegate the settlement of disputes to an optional protocol. Since this chapter is incorporated in the body of the convention, its impact on the nature of the Exclusive Economic Zone exhibits some novel aspects in regard to both the negotiation of key provisions and their interpretation and application.

The issue of conflict resolution was a subject of critical importance at the Third Conference, since it necessarily reflects the rights and interests involved in the substantive negotiations concerning the Exclusive Economic Zone. Thus, for example, procedures initiated by unilateral action and leading to binding adjudication were defended by countries that considered it necessary to ensure that reasonable interpretations were given to the substantive definitions in order to safeguard them from eventual interference by the coastal state's discretionary powers. This was stated to be an indispensable condition for gaining consent to a convention, and it sustained the negotiations in their initial stage.[6]

The general rule with regard to conflict resolution is contained in Article 286, according to which all disputes related to the interpretation or application of the convention that are not resolved through an application of Section 1 shall, upon the request of any of the parties to the dispute, be submitted to the competent court or tribunal in accordance with the provisions of this section.[7] The tribunals may be of different origins and compositions, but the underlying principle remains the same in all cases.

Section 3 of Part XV establishes the exceptions to the general principle; this section includes Article 297, which concerns disputes over the coastal state's exercise of its sovereign rights or jurisdiction, these terms being reserved for the Exclusive Economic Zone (or the continental shelf).

This focus represents a departure from the approach originally worked out at the conference, where the position espoused by countries carrying out distant water fishing, maritime powers, and the group of landlocked countries and nations having special geographical characteristics met with greater acceptance.[8]

The earlier approach was based on a three-dimensional focus that centered on the following elements: (1) compulsory settlement as a general rule, (2) cases in which the state could limit the application of the general rule, and (3) cases in which the coastal state could declare that it did not accept an established procedure (or all of them) related to, inter alia, the exercise of discretionary rights, except in cases in which an abuse of power was involved. This system's relevance to the Exclusive Economic Zone was based on the way the terms "exclusive jurisdiction" and "discretionary rights" were interpreted in cases where the convention had not defined them clearly. A disagreement as to whether a matter fell within the areas not exempt from the general rule[9] should be resolved by a tribunal as a preliminary question. In the case of discretionary rights, exemption from compulsory settlement could practically be neutralized by a rigorous application of the abuse-of-power concept. In turn, the coastal state could exempt itself in specific cases by asserting that local remedies had not been exhausted; this allegation in itself, however, would not justify bringing international jurisdiction to a standstill. Consequently, what is involved is a group of principles intended to strengthen international procedures, including international jurisdiction, with the possibility of limiting them in certain cases related to the EEZ that involved the exercise of the "exclusive jurisdiction" or "discretionary rights" of the coastal state.

THE 1982 CONVENTION

The final text of Article 297, which heads Section 3 of Part XV, incorporates the negotiations that dealt with two basic elements: (1) the nature of the disputes submitted to procedures in which third parties play a role, and (2) the procedures themselves, in respect to whether they lead to binding adjudication. In the former case, the identification of the substantive matters subject to a regime replaces the unprecise criteria used in previous drafts, which were based on the state's exclusive jurisdiction and discretionary rights, and opts for a phased settlement centering on issues related to the EEZ itself, the result being a mitigated general rule.

Article 297 being understood as a limitation of the general rule (Article 286), disputes with regard to the exercise by a coastal state of its sovereign rights or jurisdiction shall be submitted to a procedure leading to binding adjudication in certain specific cases: (1) when it is alleged that a coastal state has acted in contravention of international lawful uses of the sea by other states (Article 58) in regard to, inter alia, the freedoms and rights of navigation, overflight, or the laying of submarine cables and pipelines; (2) when it is alleged that a state, in exercising these freedoms, rights, or uses, has acted in contravention of the provisions of the convention or of laws or regulations established by the coastal state in conformity with the convention or other rules of international law not incompatible with it; and (3) when it is alleged that a coastal state has acted in contravention of international rules for the protection and preservation of the marine environment that are established by the convention or by the processes specified.

These provisions, which reinforce the jurisdictional approach, allow the interpretation that the coastal has jurisdictions even in the case of the rights, freedoms, and lawful uses associated with other states, but that these jurisdictions are subject to regulation. Events occurring in the EEZ that involve the exercise of these jurisdictions are nevertheless subject to the local courts and agencies of the coastal state to the extent that the rule regarding the exhaustion of local remedies pursuant to international law is applicable. This may be of special importance in regard to the protection of the marine environment.

With regard to problems stemming from military activities, the situation is not unrelated to the application of paragraph 1. Nevertheless, in Article 298, paragraph 1(b), the convention accepts the concept that disputes regarding such activities may be excepted from compulsory settlement by means of a unilateral declaration in accordance with the optional exceptions provided for in that article. The other state party to the dispute is bound by that declaration. It should be noted, however, that the scope of the optional exception for military activities is not confined to activities taking place within the 200-mile limit of the EEZ.

There is a counterpart to this optional exception that favors the coastal state. It provides that the coastal state may exclude disputes from application of the general rule embodied in Section 2 of Part XV when they concern activities aimed at enforcing the rules governing the exercise of sovereign rights or jurisdictions that are, in turn, excepted from the jurisdiction of a court or tribunal under Article 297, paragraphs 2 and 3. It is actually a question of unilaterally exempting from the jurisdiction of a tribunal necessary enforcement measures that arise from the exercise of those rights and jurisdictions.

RESOLUTION OF CONFLICTS REGARDING FISHERIES AND THE CASE OF SCIENTIFIC RESEARCH

These activities provide the most illustrative elements for an examination of the nature of the EEZ.

Until the seventh session, negotiations at the Third Conference had not resulted in a satisfactory agreement as to conflict resolution with the involvement of third parties in regard to fisheries and scientific research. The protection and preservation of the marine environment were not covered in this discussion. The unofficial texts prepared by the conference did not originally contain provisions in this area, and the settlement presented in the first Informal Composite Negotiating Text (1977)[10] dealt with situations in which the exercise of the sovereign rights or jurisdiction of the coastal state could validly be submitted to the consideration of a court or tribunal, particularly with respect to living resources.[11]

Safeguards for the coastal state's normal exercise of its sovereign rights and jurisdiction were established through the conditions placed on the admissibility of complaints against it. As the president of the conference explained at one point, the corresponding article (then 296) provided guarantees regarding the abuse of power by a coastal state while at the same time avoiding the abuse of procedural recourses against it.[12]

Negotiating Group 5, established in 1978[13] in order to seek an agreement among countries directly concerned with the issue of the settlement of disputes regarding the exercise of sovereign rights by coastal states in the Exclusive Economic Zone, served as a leading forum for this purpose. The creation of that group, which acted under the direction of the Greek Ambassador C. Stavropoulos, implied recognition of the fact that it was a "difficult issue."

A compromise was reached with respect to sovereign

rights over living resources in the EEZ or their exercise, including the coastal state's discretionary powers for determining the allowable catch, harvesting capacity, allocation of surplus to other states when its harvesting capacity is insufficient, and terms and conditions established in its conservation and management regulations. It is worth noting that the core of the EEZ (articles 56, 58, 61 and 62 of the convention) is not submitted to compulsory international settlement, a point that reaffirms the nature of this zone.

Part of the compromise reached was the acceptance by the coastal states of compulsory recourse to conciliation in three instances: if it is alleged (1) that the state has manifestly failed to comply with its obligations to ensure through proper conservation and management measures that the maintenance of the living resources in the EEZ is not seriously endangered; (2) that the state has arbitrarily refused to determine, upon the request of another state, the allowable catch and its capacity to harvest the living resources with respect to stocks that the other state is interested in fishing; or (3) that the state has arbitrarily refused to allocate to any other state, under the provisions of articles 62, 69, and 70 and under the terms and conditions established by the coastal state consistent with the convention, all or part of the surplus it has declared to exist. The conciliation procedure is described in Annex V, Section 2, of the convention.

An interpretation of this formula, which reaffirms the sovereignty of rights related to fisheries, should take into account the provisions of articles 62 (the use of living resources), 69 (the rights of landlocked states), and 70 (the rights of states with special geographical characteristics), which make the activities of other countries in the EEZ contingent upon prior agreement based on a right to participate in the harvesting of the surplus, subject to certain conditions, and not on a right on the part of those countries to the living resources.

The convention indicates that agreements reached pursuant to articles 69 and 70 (on landlocked nations and on geographically disadvantaged countries, respectively) shall include clauses on procedures to be employed to resolve the disagreement which may arise. In all cases it is understood that, unless the parties agree otherwise, a coastal state may not be obliged to include an arbitration clause in that arrangement, since the exception from compulsory settlement is in full effect.

This framework, which uses conciliation as a balancing factor, indirectly defines the nature of the coastal state's rights and discretionary powers with regard to living resources. The fact that the excepted cases to be submitted to conciliation under Article 297, paragraph 3, are described in such a restrictive manner--as indicated by the terms "manifestly" and "arbitrarily"--makes it unlikely that the full force of the principle stated at the beginning of paragraph 3 could be sustained, to wit, that "disputes relating to the interpretation or application of the provisions of this Convention with regard to fisheries shall be settled in accordance with section 2" (i.e., by a court or tribunal). As Rosenne indicates, the exceptions to this principle may be greater in number than the cases guided by the principle itself.[14]

During the negotiations within Group 5, the spokesmen of the landlocked countries Austria and Switzerland defended the proposition that a dispute over the actual existence of a sovereign right or its scope, rather than about its exercise, could be heard by a competent tribunal.[15] There is no doubt that the purpose of the text of paragraph 3 of Article 297 is not to promote such an interpretation, since it states that no "dispute relating to its sovereign rights with respect to the living resources in the Exclusive Economic Zone or their exercise" shall be submitted to binding settlement without the consent of the coastal state.

A problem of interpretation could arise with respect to species having a life cycle extending beyond the EEZ that fall within special categories (articles 64, 65, 66, and 67, on highly migratory species, marine mammals, and anadromous and catadromous species, respectively). An examinatton of Article 297 reveals that it applies to living resources in the EEZ; it would thus seem relevant to bring this article and Article 286 into line with each other insofar as the living resources mentioned, as well as with the respective substantive articles which establish some measures of cooperation among interested states, particularly in regard to activities that states may undertake beyond the outer limit of the EEZ. The obligation to cooperate in the pursuance of certain purposes in certain cases is in itself a substantive element of the regime that is applicable to those living resources. The convention is clearly intended to strengthen the fundamental responsibilities of the coastal state, even beyond the outer limit of the EEZ.

Living resources pose yet another problem that is manifested in all the texts prepared at the Third Conference: the force or applicability of the principle of the abuse of power. This problem was expressly included in previous drafts. It is not merely a theoretical, although the term has been eliminated in Part XV of the convention and included as a general principle (Article 300)[16] in response to a proposal made by Mexico and amended by the United States.[17]

The originating interest in the inclusion of a provision on the abuse of power in the rules on sovereign rights and jurisdictions over fisheries was to establish a guarantee for the states that wished to weaken the concept of the EEZ; at the same time, however, an attempt was made to balance this factor with a formula to prevent the abuse of procedural means open to other parties.

In the settlement offered by the convention, the general principle could be applied to any subject area whatsoever. Nevertheless, it should be pointed out that certain types of conflicts over EEZ fisheries that have to do with the exercise of discretionary powers arising out of the sovereign rights and jurisdiction of a coastal state are covered by exceptional and restrictive conciliation procedures. Therefore, the course open to other parties in such cases is the conciliation procedure under Article 297, paragraph 3(b); in no case may such parties take a jurisdictional route. A similar form of settlement exists for disputes related to scientific research, which are subject to a conciliation regime. In both cases, the principle that the conciliation commission may in no case substitute its discretion for that of the coastal state is fully in force (Article 297, paragraph 3(c)).

The settlement arrived at in the convention in this regard is that, by means of a procedure prior to the preliminary proceedings, the tribunal shall determine if the action undertaken "constitutes an abuse of legal process" or if it is established prima facie "to be well founded" (Article 294, paragraph 1). The court or tribunal takes no further action if it determines, at the request of a party or on its own initiative, that such an abuse exists. Under such circumstances, this procedure refers only to the prima facie admissibility of the claim, in regard to either its foundations or the abuse of legal process; it does not prevent preliminary objections from being raised in accordance with the applicable rules of procedure. This procedure is not limited to claims against a coastal state, and it lays the burden of proof on the plaintiff.[18]

With regard to marine research, which is also covered by Article 297, Section 2 of Part XV on procedures leading to binding adjudication is applicable, if paragraph 2 is followed to the letter. Nevertheless, the principle does not hold in the case of the exercise of a discretionary power or right of the coastal in accordance with Article 246 to withold consent or to order suspension or cessation of a research project in accordance with Article 253.

These rules give rise to the same types of doubts as arise in the case of interpreting the provisions on living resources, that is, whether or not a question can be brought before an international tribunal or court that does not regard the exercise of discretionary powers and rights but rather determines whether the requirements for the exercise of such powers are actually present.

This supposition arises particularly in those cases in which scientific research has a bearing on the freedoms or rights of navigation, overflight, the laying of submarine cables and pipelines or on the other uses of the sea to which Article 58 refers.[19] An international tribunal, according to this suggestion, could verify whether the necessary conditions for the exercise of those rights are present.

The provisions by which conciliation is applicable when it is alleged that the coastal state is not exercising its rights under articles 246 and 253 in a manner compatible with the convention provide adequate criteria to clarify this hypothesis.

The instances in which the coastal state exercises discretionary powers that cannot be questioned by the conciliation commission involve the withholding of consent for specific projects in accordance with paragraph 5 of Article 246 (living resources, drilling, artificial installations, inexact information, or pending obligations on the part of the researcher). The instances also include the designation of specific zones beyond the 200-mile limit in areas of an extensive continental shelf where activities of exploration or exploitation are to be carried out.

These principles operate in such a way in the convention that, once it has been established that a conflict deals with the exercise of discretionary powers or rights regulated by paragraphs 5 and 6 of Article 246, there is no basis upon which the conciliation commission may review the decision taken by the coastal state under those provisions. In the case of other matters also subject to discretionary powers (articles 246 and 253), the conciliation commission may only state that, with regard to a specific project, rights are not being exercised in a manner that is compatible with the convention; it may not substitute its discretionary powers for those of the coastal state. The same situation holds true in the case of living resources.

SUMMARY

An examination of conflict-resolution mechanisms contributes to an approximate, although not exhaustive, interpretation of the nature of the EEZ. This is true with regard to sovereign rights and discretionary powers, but less so in some other areas, such as the protection of the marine environment or some of the uses of artificial islands, installations, and structures.

This situation arises from the fact that the convention makes distinctions on a <u>ratione materiae</u> basis, according to which functional jurisdictions are introduced in order to establish a hierarchy among the various procedures. On such subject as the freedoms that other states may exercise within the EEZ, the settlement proposed by Article 297, paragraph 1(a) and the alternative provisions on military activities contained in Article 298, paragraph 1(b), which except such activities from compulsory international settlement, are important elements in determining the meaning and nature of the coastal state's jurisdictions in the EEZ; these settlements do not, however suffice to clarify it fully. This last point must be understood in the context of the provisions of articles 58, paragraph 3, and 59, which are an attempt to balance the relations between the coastal state and other states that make lawful use of the EEZ. Article 59 leaves uncertainty about determining the uses of the EEZ about which the convention does not attribute jurisdiction or rights either to the coastal state or to others. This uncertainty is not directly resolved by the mechanisms of conflict resolution; it can be considered to be a formula that accommodates the widest range of theses regarding residual rights and that allows the interplay of the parties' interests "on the basis of equity and in the light of all the relevant circumstances."

Article 297 reflects a compromise between what are in a certain sense the opposing positions of the countries adopting a maximalist posture on the resolution of disputes, which generally support procedures leading to a binding adjudication, and those that could be called minimalist, being in favor of reducing the jurisdiction of international tribunals. This article also reflects a compromise between countries that support the concept of the EEZ as a territorial sea in which the coastal state's sovereignty has full play and countries that consider it a zone of the high seas that is subject to certain rights and jurisdictions of the coastal state in specific matters.

These characteristics have formed the texts included in the convention, and entail a recognition of the fact that the positions favoring a jurisdictional settlement are not necessarily consistent with those that seek to reinforce the freedoms of the seas within the EEZ. Lastly, recourse to conciliation that leads to a nonbinding opinion tends to balance those positions, reinforcing the elements linked to the exclusive jurisdictions of the coastal state but not assuring it total discretion with regard to all manifestations of the EEZ.

NOTES

1. Doc.A/CNF.62/L.78, 28 August 1981.
2. This position is supported in Doc.A/CNF.62/C.2/C.38, 5 August 1974, sponsored by Byelorussia, the German Democratic Republic, Poland, the Ukraine, and the Soviet Union, and Doc.A/CNF.62/C.2/C.47, 8 August 1974, of the United States.
3. See B. H. Oxman, "The Third United Nations Conference on the Law of the Sea: the 1977 New York Session," *American Journal of International Law*, 72, 1978, 1, p. 69. Also, F. Orrego Vicuña, "Incidente en la Zona Económica," *El Mercurio*, 27 August 1981, p. A3.
4. Doc.A/AC.8/SC.II/L.38, Art. 13, sponsored by Canada, India, Kenya, Madagascar, Senegal, and Sri Lanka; Doc.A/AC.138/SC.II/L.54, Art. F, sponsored by Ecuador, Panama, and Peru.
5. An analysis of the principal provisions is presented in J. C. Lupinacci, "El Sistema de Solución de Controversias: Antecedentes y Trabajos de la Tercera Conferencia de las Naciones Unidas sobre el Derecho del Mar," *Economía de los Océanos*, vol. II, Santiago, Instituto de Estudios Internacionales, CEPAL, 1978, pp. 329-369.
6. See J. R. Stevenson and B. H. Oxman, "The Third United Nations Conference on the Law of the Sea: the 1975 Geneva Session," *American Journal of International Law*, 69, 1975, 4, p. 796.
7. The International Tribunal of the Law of the Sea, established in accordance with Annex VI, which may operate through chambers; the International Court of Justice; a chamber for disputes regarding the sea bed of the International Tribunal of the Law of the Sea and its ad hoc chamber of the chamber for disputes regarding the sea bed; an arbitral tribunal established in accordance with Annex VII, a special arbitral tribunal established pursuant to Annex VIII for a specific category of disputes; and a commercial court of arbitration for a specific category of disputes relating to the sea bed and ocean floor.
8. See UN Doc.S.D.Gp/2nd Sess./No.1/Rev.5, 1 May 1975. The document was prepared by an informal working group and originated in an initiative of the United States. In that document, the delegate from Peru, Andrés Aramburu, advanced the territorialist thesis on disputes in the Exclusive Economic Zone; this proposition was not accepted.
9. See, op. cit., Note 8, supra. Article 17, paragraph 1, made reference to the following cases: (1) disputes with respect to freedoms of navigation,

overflight, the laying of submarine cables and pipelines, or related rights and duties of other states; (2) contravention or lack of consideration for the rights and duties of other states in accordance with the convention; (3) nonapplication of international standards or of criteria established by the convention or in accordance with them; and (4) abuse of rights conferred by the convention to the detriment of other contracting parties.

10. Doc.A/CNF.62/WP.10, 15 July 1977.
11. With respect to the history of these provisions on conflict resolution, useful comments are to be found in A. O. Adede, "Settlement of Disputes arising under the Law of the Sea Convention," *American Journal of International Law*, 69, 1975, 4, pp. 798-818; "Law of the Sea: the Scope of the Third Party, Compulsory Procedures for Settlement of Disputes," Ibid., 71, 1977, 2, pp. 305-311; "Law of the Sea--The Integration of the System of Settlement of Disputes under the Draft Convention as a Whole," Ibid., 72, 1978, 1, pp. 84-95.
12. 8 Off. Rec., Doc.A/CNF.62/WP.10, Add. 1, 1977, pp. 65 and 70.
13. Doc.A/CNF.62/62, 13 April 1978.
14. S. Rosenne, "Settlement of Fisheries Disputes in the Exclusive Economic Zone," *American Journal of International Law*, 73, 1979, 1, p. 98.
15. Proposal of Switzerland in NG.5/1.
16. Article 300 of the convention reads as follows: "The States Parties to this Convention undertake to discharge in good faith the obligations entered into in conformity with this Convention, and to exercise the rights, jurisdictions and freedoms recognized in this Convention in a manner which would not constitute an abuse of rights."
17. Doc.GP/2, Rev. 1, 1980.
18. Regarding unofficial proposals previous to Article 294, see NG.5/7, NG.5/8, and NG.5/12.
19. See T. Treves, "Principes du Consentement et Recherche Scientifique dans le Nouveau Droit de la Mer," *Revue Générale de Droit International Publique*, 84, 1980, 1, p. 265.

Contributors

Alfonso Arias Schreiber. Ambassador of Peru to France and former Head of the Peruvian Delegation to the Law of the Sea Conference.

Pilar Armanet. Director of the Institute of International Studies of the University of Chile.

Hugo Caminos. Ambassador of Argentina to Brazil and former Director of the Office for the Law of the Sea Conference of the United Nations Secretariat.

Reynaldo Galindo Pohl. Former Head of the Delegation of El Salvador to the Law of the Sea Conference and Chairman of the Second Committee.

F.V. García-Amador. Professor of Law at the University of Miami and former Head of the Cuban Delegation to the First and Second United Nations Conferences on the Law of the Sea.

María Teresa Infante. Professor of International Law at the Institute of International Studies of the University of Chile and at the Law School of the University of Chile. Former member of the Chilean Delegation to the Law of the Sea Conference.

Julio César Lupinacci. Ambassador of Uruguay to Chile and former Head of the Uruguayan Delegation to the Law of the Sea Conference.

Vicente Marotta Rangel. Dean of the Law School of the University of Sao Paulo, Brazil, and former member of the Brazilian Delegation to the Law of the Sea Conference.

Francisco Orrego Vicuña. Professor of International Law at the Institute of International Studies of the University of Chile and the Law School of the University of Chile. Former Vice-chairman and Head of the Delegation of Chile to the Law of the Sea Conference. Currently ambassador of Chile to Great Britain.

Index

Accommodation process. See Negotiations
Addis Ababa Declaration, 89-90
Adjacent zone, 11, 137, 138
Afghanistan, 154
Africa, 68, 82, 88-90, 92, 111, 134. See also Addis Ababa Declaration; Afro-Asian Legal Consultative Committee; Mogadishu Declaration; Organization for African Unity; Regional Seminar of African States on the Law of the Sea; individual countries
Afro-Asian Legal Consultative Committee, 37, 88, 90
Aguilar, Andrés, 94, 110, 120(n41), 121(n50), 127
Airspace. See Overflight
Algeria, 116(n26)
Amadeo, Mario, 63
Amerasinghe, H. S., 67, 139
Andromous species, 50, 150, 166. See also Fishing rights; Living resources
Anglo-Norwegian Fisheries case (1951), 44
Anglo-Venezuelan Treaty, 16
Angola, 69
Antarctic zone, 119(n38)
Apollis, Gilbert, 137, 138
Arbitration. See Dispute settlement; International tribunal
Archipelagic states, 42-43, 51, 69, 105, 106, 120(n42), 131, 138

Arctic zone, 119(n38)
Arechaga, Eduardo Jimenez, 96, 118(n35) (two accents)
Argentina, 17-18, 18-19, 37, 77, 80, 113(n4), 114(n8), 116(n26)
Artificial islands. See Installations
Asia, 68, 88, 92
Australia, 37, 116(n26)
Austria, 166

Bahamas, 18
Barbados, 114(n8), 115(n18)
Bardina, Juan, 29
Belgian Congo, 64
Benin, 69
Bering Sea, 7, 8-9
Biological resources, 62, 68, 70, 82-83, 119(n40). See also Fishing rights; Living resources; Resource conservation; Resource exploitation
Bobino's Tratado sobre la República, 45
Bolivia, 114(n8)
Brazil, 18, 69, 78-79, 80, 114(n8), 116(n26). See also Santo Domingo Declaration
Bulgaria, 139
Buzan, Barry, 67, 72 (N5)

Cameroun, 116(n26), 154
Caminos, Hugo, 117(n31)
Canada, 37, 112, 114(n8), 117(n31), 119(n38)
Cape Verde, 69
Carreño, Edmundo Vargas, 84, 85, 88

175

Caribbean states, 86. See also Santo Domingo Declaration; Specialized Conference of Caribbean Countries on Problems of the Sea; individual countries
Castañeda, Jorge, 86-87, 110, 117(n30)
Catadromous species, 150-151, 166
Central America, 86. See also Latin America; Santo Domingo Declaration; individual countries
Cetaceans, 149-150
Ceylon, 15
Chile, 2, 3, 27, 28-30, 37, 75, 111, 114(n8)
  and the Santiago Declaration, 21-24, 75, 76, 133
  and 200-mile zone, 20, 29-30, 75, 77, 79, 80, 133
  See also Lima Declaration
Coastal states,
  abuse of power, 164, 167
  and adjacent zone, 11
  and continental shelf, 17-18
  discretionary powers, 161, 162, 163, 165, 167, 168
  economic interests, 84, 85, 88, 95, 108
  and fishing rights, 3, 8, 15, 27, 40, 47, 53, 80, 96, 126, 127, 136, 143, 144-148, 155-157, 164-166
  jurisdiction, 4, 34, 45-47, 48, 52, 95, 96, 97, 109, 111-112, 131-139, 163, 169. See also High seas, and legal nature of EEZ; Living resources; National jurisdiction; Negotiating Group 5
  vs. landlocked states, 68-69, 153
  and marine conservation, 11, 83, 85, 144, 145, 146, 148, 156, 163, 165. See also Fishery regimes; Fishery management; Optimum utilization; Resource conservation
  and optimum utilization. See Optimum utilization; Resource conservation
  policing rights, 103-104, 126, 133, 136, 156
  and residual rights, 98, 99
  right to detain vessels, 126, 133, 136, 156
  right to exploit resources, 88, 110, 111, 116(n27), 133
  rights to submarine areas, 15-16, 39
  and sui generis status of EEZ, 106
  security interests, 135, 138, 139-142
  sovereign rights. See Dispute settlement; National jurisdiction; Reasonable criteria; Sovereign rights
  See also Preferentialists; Resource conservation, and coastal states; Territorialists; Territorial sea
Codification Conference (1930), 11-12, 38
Codification process, 70
Colombia, 81, 86, 91, 111, 114(n8), 115(n18)
Commercial fishing, 144. See also Fishery regimes; Fishing rights; Tuna fishing; Whaling industry
Commercial shipping, 40. See also Navigation; Transport
Commission on the South Pacific (1952), 35
Committee on the Peaceful Uses of the Sea Bed and the Ocean Floor Beyond the Limits of National Jurisdiction, 34, 79, 91
Common heritage of humanity, 42, 43, 54, 58, 68, 132, 138. See also International jurisdiction
Communications. See International communications
Competences, 52, 125
  of developing countries, 83, 84
  and international custom, 57. See also Customary international law
  See also Customs; Emigration; Fishing rights; Health; Immigration; National

Competences (continued)
    jurisdiction; Sovereign
    rights; State's rights;
    Taxation
Conciliation. See Dispute
    settlement, conciliation
    procedure
Condominium zone, 128-129
Conference on the Exploitation
    and Conservation of the
    Maritime Resources of the
    South Pacific. See Santiago
    Declaration
Conference on the Law of the
    Sea. See United Nations
    Conference on the Law of
    the Sea, First, Second,
    Third
Conflict resolution. See
    Dispute settlement
Conforti, Benedetto, 109
Congo, 69
Consensus, 63-67, 72(n5),
    72(n6), 74(n15). See also
    Negotiations, consensus in
Contact group, 71
Contiguous zone, 11, 43, 75, 99,
    131
  and high seas, 99-100, 108,
    124
  jurisdictions over, 52, 75,
    77, 80
Continental shelf, 16, 43, 58,
    81, 86, 141
  claims to, 16, 17-19, 30, 33,
    46, 80, 92, 101, 138
  demarcation of, 43, 58, 69,
    89, 115(n15), 130, 131
  as precedent to EEZ, 54, 101,
    114(n5)
  See also Convention on the
    Continental Shelf;
    International sea bed
    areas; Patrimonial sea;
    Submarine areas;
    Territorial sea
Convention on Policing of
    Fisheries of the North Sea
    (1882), 10
Convention on the Continental
    Shelf (1958), 34, 44, 58,
    77, 114(n5)
Convention on the High Seas
    (1958), 41, 51, 52, 55

Convention on the Law of the Sea,
    7, 49, 50, 95, 132, 137, 138,
    159-160
  Article 56. See Dispute
    settlement
  Article 58, 102, 103, 140, 141.
    See also Coastal states,
    jurisdiction
  Article 60, 141. See also
    Installations
  Article 286. See International
    tribunal
  Article 301. See Military
    activities
  Castañeda formula (Article 59),
    117(n30), 159, 160
  and dispute settlement, 161,
    162-164. See also Dispute
    settlement
  and fishing regime, 144, 149.
    See also Coastal states, and
    fishing rights; Fishing
    regimes
  Informal Composite Negotiating
    Text, 95, 164
  Part V. See Exclusive Economic
    Zone
  Part VI. See Coastal states,
    sovereign rights
  Part XV. See Dispute settlement
  See also Exclusive Economic
    Zone; High seas; Law of the
    sea; Territorial seas
Corals, 144
Cornwall Submarine Mines Act
    (1958), 16
Costa, Eduardo Ferrero, 108,
    121(n52)
Costa Rica, 20, 86, 114(n8),
    115(n17), 115(n18). See also
    Lima Declaration; Santo
    Domingo Declaration
Council of Ministers of the
    European Community, 117(n31)
Council of the Sea Bed Authority,
    67. See also International
    seabed areas
Creeping jurisdiction, 47, 99,
    112, 136. See also National
    jurisdiction; Territorial sea
Cuba, 15, 139
Customary international law,
    95-98, 113, 118(n35), 118(n36),
    134, 138. See also International

Customary international law
  (continued)
  custom
Customs, 43

Declaration of Latin American
  States on the Law of the
  Sea. See Lima Declaration
Declaration of Principles
  Regarding the International
  Sea Bed Area, 66. See also
  International seabed areas
Declaration of the Organization
  for African Unity on
  Questions of the Law of
  the Sea. See Addis Ababa
  Declaration
Defense zones, 99. See also
  National security; Security
  interests
Democratic Yemen, 69
Developing countries, 82, 88,
  96, 118(n31), 136
  coastal, 92, 125, 154
  and fishing regime, 143-144,
  145, 146, 154
  and military use of EEZ, 139,
  140
  See also individual countries
Development, law of, 50
Dispute settlement, 4, 55, 63,
  69, 103, 106, 130, 147-148,
  155, 159-170
  conciliation procedure, 165,
  167, 168, 169
  jurisdictional approach, 163
  See also Fishery resources;
  Fishery management; International tribunal; Negotiating Groups 4; Nego-
  tiating Group 5; Principle
  of cooperation; Scientific
  research, disputes over
Domain of common use, 128. See
  also Common heritage of
  humanity; International
  jurisdiction
Dominican Republic, 15, 18,
  81, 86, 114(n8), 115(n18).
  See also Lima Declaration;
  Montevideo Declaration;
  Santo Domingo Declaration

Eastern Europe, 68

East-West relations, 65
Ecology. See Biological resources;
  Optimum utilization; Resource
  conservation
Economic exploitation. See
  Resource exploitation
Economic jurisdiction, 87.
  See also Coastal states,
  economic interests; Economic
  sovereignty; National
  jurisdiction; Sovereign
  rights
Economic sovereignty, 45-46,
  48-49, 76, 125, 138. See
  also Coastal states,
  economic interests; Economic
  jurisdiction; National
  jurisdiction; Sovereign
  rights
Economic zone. See Exclusive
  Economic Zone
Ecuador, 3, 37, 69
  and the Lima Declaration, 114(n8)
  and the Santiago Declaration,
  21-24, 75, 116(n26), 133
  and 200-mile zone, 77, 79, 80,
  113
Eels, 150-151
EEZ. See Exclusive Economic Zone
El Salvador, 20-21, 69, 77, 80,
  114(n8), 115(n18)
Emigration, 43
Emprise maritime de l'État
  Cotier, L' (Apollius), 137
Energy production, 132
England. See United Kingdom
English Channel, 44
Engo, Ambassador, 71
Epicontinental sea, 18-19, 113(n4)
Equatorial Guinea, 69
Equidistance, principle of,
  43-44, 69
Equity, principle of, 69, 107, 109
Espinosa, Augusto, 37
Eudis, R., 61
Europe. See Council of Ministers
  of the European Community;
  Eastern Europe; Western Europe
Evensen Group, 41, 69-70, 91
Exclusive Economic Zone (EEZ),
  competences in, 8, 45-47
  and Convention on the Law of the
  Sea. See Convention on the
  Law of the Sea; United Nations

EEZ (continued)
    Conference on the Law of
      the Sea, Third
    delimitation of, 38, 39,
      43-44, 51-53, 90, 91, 92,
      94, 95, 98-99
    exclusivity of, 48-49, 108,
      119(n40), 138
    legal status, 2, 3, 94, 95-98,
      98-99, 104, 107-110, 111,
      112-113, 121(n52), 123-124,
      127-128. See also High seas;
      Sui generis zone; Territorial
      sea
    military uses of, 39, 40,
      54-55, 169. See also
      Military activities
    negotiations. See Negotiations,
      and EEZ
    origins of, 1, 2, 7-24, 25(n30),
      27, 32-38, 40-41, 75-80,
      88-91, 133
    ownership of, 128, 136
    and UNCLOS III, 33. See also
      United Nations Conference
      on the Law of the Sea, Third
    See also National jurisdiction;
      Negotiations; Resource
      conservation; Resource
      exploitation; Resource
      exploration; Sovereign
      rights
Exclusive fishing zone. See
    Fishing zones
Extavour, Winston Conrad, 89, 107

Federal Republic of Germany,
    57, 67, 111, 154
Fernández, Illanes, 83, 85
Fiji, 69
Fisher, Jerman, 29
Fisheries Committee (FAO), 143
Fishery conservation claims,
    11-15. See also Fishery
    management; Fishery
    regimes; Fishing rights;
    Living resources; Resource
    conservation
Fishery management, 76,
    143-144, 147-148,
    155-157, 164-166. See also
    Coastal states, and fish-
    ing rights; Fishery con-
    servation claims; Fishery
    regimes; National jurisdiction;
    Optimum utilization
Fishery regimes, 3, 143-158. See
    also Coastal states,
    sovereign rights; Fishery
    conservation claims; Fishery
    management; Fishing rights;
    Fishing zones; Negotiations,
    and fishing regimes
Fishery resources. See Living
    resources
Fishing rights, 48, 52, 100, 102,
    108, 121(n52), 132, 146,
    164-168
    and Addis Ababa Declaration, 89
    and coastal states, 40, 47, 96,
      126, 127
    and EEZ origins, 28, 33, 35-36,
      40
    and surplus, 165
    See also Andromous species;
      Catadromous species; Coastal
      states, and fishing rights;
      Marine mammals; Migratory
      species; Sedentary fisheries;
      States with special geo-
      graphical considerations
Fishing zones, 99, 102, 111,
    117-118(n31), 120(n40), 128,
    134, 143, 144. See also
    Biological resources;
    Fishery regimes; Fishing
    rights; Living resources
Fleischer, Carl August, 121(n52)
France, 44, 117(n31)
Freedom of passage. See Innocent
    passage; Navigation, freedom
    of
Freedom of the seas. See High
    seas, freedom of; Innocent
    passage
Functional rights, 109, 113, 126,
    132, 169. See also National
    jurisdiction; Navigation,
    freedom of; Overflight;
    Resource conservation;
    Resource exploitation;
    Sovereign rights
Functional sovereignty. See
    Functional rights

Gabon, 69
Gentlemen's Agreement, 66. See
    also Negotiations

Geographically disadvantaged states. See Landlocked states; States with special geographical considerations
Germany. See Federal Republic of Germany
Ghana, 15, 116(n26)
Gidel, Gilbert, 38
Global package, 63, 66
Good faith. See Negotiations, good faith in
Great Britain. See United Kingdom
Greece, 52
Greenland, 119(n38)
Grotius, 84
Group of 21, 151. See also Interest groups; Negotiations
Group of 77, 41. See also Interest groups; Negotiations
Guarello, Fernando, 28, 29, 30
Guatemala, 18, 81, 86, 114(n8), 115(n18). See also Lima Declaration; Montevideo Declaration; Santo Domingo Declaration
Guernsey, 44
Guinea-Bissau, 69
Guyana, 115(n18)

Haiti, 86, 115(n18)
Health, 43
Heinzen, Helmut, 28
Helsinki Conference on Security and Cooperation in Europe (1973), 63
Highly migratory species. See Migratory species
High seas, 35, 41, 80, 107, 128
  compared with EEZ, 45, 51-53, 87, 99-105, 106-107, 125
  defined, 106, 120(n41)
  and EEZ negotiations, 42, 106, 134
  fishing rights in, 50. See also Fishing rights
  freedom of, 54, 55, 100. See also Contiguous zone; Innocent passage; Navigation, freedom of; Principle of freedom
  and legal nature of EEZ 124-127, 120, 132, 133, 138, 169
  military uses of, 39, 141
  See also Common heritage of humanity; Patrimonial sea
Honduras, 21, 81, 86, 114(n8), 115(n18). See also Lima Declaration; Montevideo Declaration; Santo Domingo Declaration
Hsu, 43

Iceland, 14-15, 57, 97, 111, 112, 114(n8), 135
Immigration, 43
India, 15, 112, 114(n8)
Indonesia, 69, 112
INDUS. See Industrial Company of Valparaíso
Industrial Company of Valparaíso (INDUS), 28, 29, 30
Industrialized countries, 62. See also individual countries
Informal Composite Negotiating Text, 95, 164
Informal negotiations. See Negotiations, informal
Innocent passage, 136, 140. See also High seas, freedom of; Navigation, freedom of
Installations, 86, 89, 90, 91, 94, 95, 96, 103, 113, 126, 127, 131, 132, 136, 141, 168, 169. See also Submarine areas, right to lay cables and pipes in
Inter-American Council of Jurists, 76, 84
Inter-American Juridical Committee, Resolution on the Law of the Sea, 87
Inter-American Treaty of Reciprocal Assistance, 119(n38)
Interdependence. See International cooperation
Interest groups, 68-69
International communications, 45, 62, 83, 84, 88, 91, 97, 101, 102, 106, 108, 109, 110, 127, 130, 131, 132, 133. See also Installations; Navigation; Overflight
International cooperation, 49, 50, 107-108, 147, 153

International Court of
 Justice, 43, 44, 57,
 96, 97, 111, 128, 135
International custom, 57-58.
 See also Customary
 international law
Internationalists, 94
International jurisdiction, 162.
 See Common heritage of
 humanity; Dispute settlement
International Law Association's
 International Committee
 on the EEZ, 1
International Law Commission,
 46, 47, 54
International mandate, 125
International sea bed areas,
 54, 58, 80, 86, 87, 90,
 101, 130, 132
 Declaration of Principles
 regarding, 66
 and EEZ negotiations, 38, 43
 See also Continental shelf;
 Submarine areas
International straits, 41-42,
 105, 120(n42), 131. See
 also Navigation
International tribunal, 161-162,
 164, 166, 167, 168. See
 also Law of the Sea Tribunal
Interpretive declarations, 56.
 See also Reservations
Iran, 17
Ireland, 55
Islands, 43-44, 89. See also
 Archipelagic states
Ivory Coast, 116(n26)

Jackling, Sir Roger, 42
Jamaica, 18, 114(n8), 115(n18).
 See also Lima Declaration;
 Santo Domingo Declaration
Japan, 52, 62, 69
Jersey, 44
Jurisdiction. See Coastal
 states, jurisdiction;
 National jurisdiction
Jurisdictional waters. See
 200-mile maritime zone
Jus Communicationis, 85, 104,
 136

Kenya, 37, 88, 90, 91,
 115(n24), 116(n26)

Koh, Ambassador, 71

Landlocked states,
 competences of, 45
 and EEZ negotiations, 36, 51,
 68-69, 92-93, 133, 151, 162
 See also Living resources,
 landlocked states rights to;
 Resource exploitation, landlocked states rights to;
 States with special geo-
 graphical considerations
Latin America, 4, 66, 76
 and fishing zone, 143, 148, 149
 as interest group, 68
 and patrimonial sea, 85
 position of, 4, 79, 80, 81, 82,
 92, 133-134. See also Lima
 Declaration; Montevideo
 Declaration
 unilateral declarations, 77
 See also Panama; individual
 countries
Law of the Sea, 61-62, 68-69,
 123-124, 137. See also
 Convention on the Continental
 Shelf; Convention on the High
 Seas; United Nations Conference
 on the Law of the Sea, First,
 Second, Third
Law of the Sea Tribunal, 67. See
 also International tribunal
Legal custom. See Customary
 international law
Legal relations, 62
Lege ferenda, 97
Lever Brothers Corporation, 28
Liberia, 52, 116(n26)
Libya, 69
Lima Declaration (1970), 36, 38,
 79, 80-84, 85, 88, 89,
 114(n8), 114(n9), 115(n15),
 115(n23)
Living resources, 8, 33, 36, 39,
 48, 53, 62, 80, 117(n31),
 144, 146
 coastal states rights to, 8,
 89, 90, 93, 108, 133, 134,
 143, 145, 148, 168
 conservation of, 11-14, 80, 141,
 138, 144, 152, 164. See also
 Optimum utilization;
 Resource conservation
 developing countries rights to,

Living resources (continued)
146, 153-154
  landlocked states rights to,
    3, 89, 90, 91, 93, 107,
    108, 133, 144-146, 151-155
  sovereign rights to, 7, 78,
    91, 153, 164-165, 166, 169
  See also Fishery conservation
    claims; Fishery regimes;
    Optimum utilization;
    Overfishing

Madagascar, 69, 116(n26)
Magalhaes, Barbosa de, 11
Mare Clausum, 84
Mare Liberum, 84
Marine environment, protection
  of. See Living resources,
  conservation of; Resource
  conservation
Marine mammals, 149-150, 166
Marine parks, 53
Marine resources. See Living
  resources; Mineral resources
Maritime powers. See Naval powers
Maritime routes. See International straits; Navigation
Maritime space. See Exclusive
  Economic Zone; High seas;
  Territorial sea
Maritime zone. See 200-mile
  maritime zone
Mauritania, 69
Mauritius, 69, 112, 115(n26)
Maximum food yield. See Living
  resources; Optimum utilization
Maximum sustainable yield, 53,
  145. See also Optimum
  utilization
Menchaca, Andrés Aramburu, 47
Meseguer, José Luis, 98, 109,
  118(n36)
Mexico, 14, 19, 38, 81, 86,
  91, 111, 112, 114(n8),
  115(n18). See also Lima
  Declaration; Montevideo
  Declaration; Political
  Constitution of the
  Mexican States; Principles
  of Mexico Concerning the
  Law of the Sea; Santo
  Domingo Declaration

Migratory species, 50, 148-150,
  166. See also Fishing rights;
  Tuna fishing; Whaling Industry
Military activities, 46, 54-55,
  62, 68, 124, 139-142, 163-164,
  169. See also Munitions testing; Naval powers; Warships
Mineral resources, 62, 68, 90,
  115(n23), 144. See also Oil;
  Resource conservation;
  Resource exploitation;
  Resource exploration
Ministers of Foreign Affairs of
  the American Republics,
  Consultative Meeting, 119(n38)
Mogadishu Declaration (1974), 111
Mollusks, 144
Montevideo Declaration (1970),
  36, 38, 79, 80-84, 88, 89,
  114(n7)
Moray Firth, 7, 10
Mortensen v. Peters, 10
Mozambique, 69
Munitions testing, 141. See also
  Military activities

Nandan, Ambassador, 151, 153, 154
National Fisheries Zone. See
  Fishing zones
National jurisdiction, 1, 2, 9,
  34, 75-80, 92, 95, 113
  and legal nature of EEZ, 124,
    125, 126, 129-130, 131-139
  reasonable criteria for, 81
  and resources, 81, 156
  over seabed areas, 90, 114(n5).
    See also International sea
    bed areas
  See also Coastal states,
    jurisdiction; Sovereign rights
National security, 89, 139, 140.
  See also Coastal states,
  security interests; Defense
  zones; Naval powers, security
  interests; Security interests
Natural resources. See Living
  resources; Mineral resources;
  Resource conservation;
  Resource exploitation
Naval powers,
  in EEZ negotiations, 92, 96,
    117(n31), 134, 162
  security interests, 40, 41, 85,
    99, 140

Navigation, 40, 45, 52
  freedom of, 23-24, 36, 40, 47,
    68, 75, 76, 77, 78, 79, 80,
    81, 83, 84, 85, 86, 87, 89,
    90, 91, 94, 95, 96, 99,
    101, 102, 103, 105, 113,
    120(n42), 127, 133, 136,
    141, 163, 168. See also
    High seas; Innocent passage;
    Principle of freedom
  military, 40, 41, 55. See also
    Military activities; Naval
    powers
  See also Innocent passage;
    International straits
Negotiating Group 4, 151
Negotiating Group 5, 164, 165
Negotiations, 36, 38-43, 130
  ambiguity in, 38-39, 51, 83
  consensus in, 62-65, 118(n34),
    119(n36). See also Consensus;
    Customary international law
  and dispute settlement, 159,
    160. See also Dispute
    settlement
  economics in, 62, 68, 82, 85,
    88, 128
  and EEZ, 38-43, 51-52, 56,
    58, 61-63, 65, 66, 69-71,
    90-95, 95-98. See also
    Convention on the Law of
    the Sea; United Nations
    Conference on the Law of
    the Sea, Third
  equidistance issue in, 43-44,
    69
  exclusivity in, 48-49,
    119(n49)
  and fishing regimes, 144, 147.
    See also Fishery regimes
  good faith in, 49, 50
  informal, 61-63, 69-71, 96,
    133. See also Informal
    Composite Negotiating Text
  security as issue in, 40-41,
    140. See also Security
    interests
  See also Consensus; Contact
    group; Convention on the
    Law of the Sea; Creeping
    jurisdiction; Gentlemen's
    Agreement; Group of 21;
    Group of 77; Interest
    groups; Landlocked states,
    and EEZ negotiations;
    Negotiating Group 4;
    Negotiating Group 5;
    Pactum de Contrahendo; Veto
New International Economic Order
  (NIEO), 62
New Zealand, 37, 112, 118(n31)
Nicaragua, 18, 77, 79, 80, 86,
  114(n8), 115(n18). See also
  Lima Declaration; Santo
  Domingo Declaration
NIEO. See New International
  Economic Order
1982 Convention on the Law of the
  Sea. See Convention on the
  Law of the Sea; United
  Nations Conference on the Law
  of the Sea, Third
Nonliving resources. See Mineral
  resources; Oil; Resource
  conservation; Resource
  exploitation; Resource
  exploration
Nonreciprocity, principle of, 59
North Sea shelf, 43, 57
North-South relations, 62, 65
Norway, 37, 112, 116(n26),
  117(n26)
Nuclear deterrents, 84
Nutritional needs, 152. See also
  Living resources; Optimum
  utilization

OAU. See Organization for African
  Unity
Oceanography. See Scientific
  investigation
Oil, 62, 115
100-mile fisheries zones. See
  Fishing zones
Open seas, 44. See also High seas
Optimum utilization, 48, 50, 53,
  80, 95, 108, 145, 146, 149,
  150, 153. See also Coastal
  states, and optimum utiliza-
  tion; Living resources;
  Resource conservation;
  Resource exploitation;
Ordenación, 53
Organization for African Unity
  (OAU), 37, 89
Outer Space Committee, 64
Overfishing, 61, 83, 146. See
  also Fishery management;

Overfishing (continued)
  Living resources;
  Resource conservation
Overflight, 77, 78, 79, 85,
  86, 88, 90, 91, 94, 95,
  96, 99, 103, 105, 113,
  120(n42), 127, 163, 168

Pactum de Contrahendo, 49-50
Pakistan, 15
Panama, 29, 31, 69, 77-78,
  80, 114(n8), 115(n18),
  116(n26), 119(n38). See
  also Lima Declaration;
  Santo Domingo Declaration
Paraguay, 114(n8)
Patrimonialists, 48, 87, 88,
  92, 93, 111, 112. See also
  Negotiations; Patrimonial
  sea
Patrimonial sea, 36-37, 84-88,
  91-92, 115(n17), 116(n26),
  134
  defined, 85, 86
  See also Patrimonialists;
    Territorialists;
    Territorial sea
"Peaceful Uses of the Ocean
  Space, Peace and Security
  Zones," 139
Permanent Commission for the
  Conservation and Exploita-
  tion of the Marine Resources
  of the South Pacific, 3,
  76. See also Santiago
  Declaration
Peru, 3, 20-24, 27, 37, 75,
  76, 77, 78, 79, 80, 114(n8),
  116(n26), 120(n41), 133.
  See also Afro-Asian Legal
  Consultative Committee; Lima
  Declaration; Santiago
  Declaration
Petroleum. See Oil
Philippines, 18, 69
Piracy, 102-103
Pohl, Galindo, 66
Political Constitution of the
  Mexican States, 118(n36).
  See also Mexico
Pollution, 61, 81, 83, 86, 90,
  99
  control, as state competence,
    45, 91, 104, 116(n24), 126,
    134, 136
Porpoises, 149-150
Portugal, 67, 118(n31)
Pourparlers, 63
Prebisch, Raul, 64
Preferentialists, 48, 93, 112.
  See also Negotiations;
  Preferential rights
Preferential rights, 134, 146,
  152, 155
President Truman's fisheries
  proclamation. See Truman's
  Fisheries Proclamation
Principe, 69
Principle of cooperation. See
  International cooperation
Principle of freedom, 98, 99,
  101, 105-110, 112. See also
  High seas, freedom of;
  Navigation, freedom of
Principle of sovereignty, 98, 99,
  101, 102, 105, 108-110, 112.
  See Mare Clausum; Mare Liberum;
  National jurisdiction;
  Sovereign rights
Principles of Mexico Concerning
  the Law of the Sea. See
  Inter-American Council of
  Jurists

Quéneudec, Jean Pierre, 107, 125

Reasonable criteria, 81
Regional Seminar of African States
  on the Law of the Sea, 88-89
Res communis, 107, 125
Res communitatis usus, 125
Res dominium, 128
Research. See Scientific research
Reservations, 55-56
Residual rights, 46, 48, 92, 95,
  98, 99, 108-109, 110, 113,
  128, 130, 142, 160, 169
  defined, 123
Res nullius, 107, 125
Resolution of Ciudad Trujillo, 76
Resource conservation, 7, 33, 50,
  68, 75, 76, 77, 79, 80, 81,
  83, 85, 155, 168
  and Brazil, 79
  and coastal states, 53, 81, 85,
    91, 92, 93, 95, 102, 106, 108,
    120(n40), 128, 131, 136, 144,
    145, 164, 166

Resource conservation (cont)
and Codification Conference, 11
and fishing, 117(n31), 149, 150, 151
precedent of Bering Sea Seals, 8-9
See also Living resources; Optimum utilization; Overfishing; Patrimonial sea; Pollution; Resolution of Ciudad Trujillo
Resource development. See Resource exploitation
Resource exploitation, 7, 8, 33, 36, 75, 76, 77, 79, 100
coastal states rights, 39, 45, 47-48, 85, 88, 91, 120(n40), 128, 132, 144. See also Living resources, coastal states rights to; Optimum utilization
landlocked states rights to, 90, 91, 93, 152
and navigation, 52. See also Navigation
obligation to develop, 48, 107. See also Living resources; Optimum utilization
and superpowers, 61. See also Soviet Union; United States
See also Functional rights; Optimum utilization; Patrimonial sea; Resource conservation; Resource exploration
Resource exploration, 7, 8, 69, 85
sovereign rights to, 47-48, 51, 91, 144
See also Mineral resources; Optimum utilization; Patrimonial sea
Right of hot pursuit, 126
Rights. See Coastal states, right to detain vessels, right to exploit resources, rights to submarine areas, Competences; Fishing rights; National jurisdiction; Navigation, freedom of; Sovereign rights
Rivero, Bustamante y, 27

Rodriquez, Luis Valencia, 84, 87, 111
Rolin, Henri, 11
Rosenne, S., 166
Rumania, 155
Russia. See Soviet Union

Safety zone, 119(n38)
Salmon, 150
Sanctions, 76
Santiago Declaration, 20, 21-24, 27, 29-30, 75, 76, 133
Protocol of Accession, 76
See also Permanent Commission for the Conservation and Exploitation of the Marine Resources of the South Pacific; Territorial sea
Santo Domingo Declaration (1972), 36, 38, 84, 86-87, 88, 91-92, 111, 115(n18), 134. See also Patrimonialists; Patrimonial sea; Territorialists; Territorial sea
Sao Tomé, 69
Saudi Arabia, 17
Sayan, Enrique Garcia, 27
Schreiber, Alfonso Arias, 76, 94
Schuecking, 11
Scientific investigation. See Scientific research
Scientific research, 68, 86, 90, 93, 100, 103, 106, 108, 112, 115(n24), 120(n40), 127, 128, 131, 132, 141
as coastal state competence, 45, 81, 83, 91, 92, 95, 102, 159
disputes over, 164-168
Seabeds. See International sea bed areas
Sea lanes. See International straits; Navigation
Sea law. See Law of the Sea
Seals, in the Bering Sea, 8-9
Security interests, 139. See Coastal states, security interests; Defense zones; National security; Naval powers, security interests
Sedentary fisheries, 7-8
Seldon, 84
Semana Internacional, 29
Senegal, 69, 114(n8), 116(n26)

Seychelles, 69
Shellfish, 144
Shipping. See Transport
Sierra Leone, 69, 116(n26)
Single Negotiating Text (1975). See United Nations Conference on the Law of the Sea, Third, Single Negotiating Text
Somalia, 69, 116(n26)
South Korea, 114(n8)
Sovereign rights, 4, 46, 51, 54, 76
  of coastal states, 47-48, 49, 69, 79, 80-81, 83, 90, 91, 92, 95, 98, 100-101, 102, 107-108, 125, 127, 132, 138, 144-148, 159, 160, 168
  limits to 107-108, 111-112
  See also Mare Clausum; Mare Liberum; National jurisdiction; Resource conservation; Resource exploitation; Resource exploration
Sovereignty-freedom equation, 84, 100-111
Soviet Union, 9-10, 52, 62, 64, 80, 114(n6), 117(n31), 139. See also Naval powers; Superpowers
Spain, 118(n31)
Specialized Conference of Caribbean Countries on Problems of the Sea (1972), 84, 86. See also Santo Domingo Declaration
Specialized Inter-American Conference on Conservation of Natural Resources: Underwater Shelf and Marine Waters, 76
Special jurisdictions, 113, 127
  on high seas, 52, 160. See also Exclusive Economic Zone
  and Santiago Declaration, 22-23
  See also Fishing rights; International communication; Navigation; Resource conservation; Resource exploitation; Resource exploration

Sponges, 144
Sport fishing, 53. See also Fishing rights
Sri Lanka, 67
States with special geographical considerations, 36, 45, 51, 58-59, 90, 91, 92-93, 107, 108, 133, 151, 152, 153-154, 162, 165. See also Landlocked states
State's rights. See Coastal states; Competences; Exclusive Economic Zone; Fishing rights; Landlocked states; Living resources; National jurisdiction; Sovereign rights
Statute of freedom. See Principle of freedom
Statute of sovereignty. See Principle of sovereignty
Stavropoulos, C., 164
Submarine areas, 15-16, 68
  coastal states claims to, 15-16
  right to lay cables and pipes in, 86, 89, 90, 91, 94, 95, 96, 103, 113, 126, 127, 163, 168
  See also Continental shelf; International sea bed areas
Submarines, 84
Sui generis zone, 37, 40, 41, 47, 51, 104, 105-111, 112-113, 121(n50), 121(n52), 127
Superpowers, 64, 84, 85. See also Soviet Union; United States
Switzerland, 154, 166

Tanzania, 116(n26)
Taxation, 43
Technological advances, 61, 98, 124, 136
Territorialists, 48, 56, 69, 87, 88, 92, 93, 94, 112, 120(n41), 146. See also Patrimonialists; Territorial sea; Zonists
Territorial sea, 42, 131, 134
  and Addis Ababa Declaration, 89
  compared to EEZ, 45, 46, 47, 51, 52, 69, 106-107, 125, 169
  limits, 80, 83, 84, 88
  and right of innocent passage, 136
  and 200-mile limit, 75-80, 93

Territorial sea (continued)
See also Patrimonial sea;
Santiago Declaration;
Santo Domingo Declaration; Territorialists;
Twelve mile limit
Territorial sovereignty. See
National jurisdiction;
Sovereign rights
Tertium genus, 111, 128, 135
Thibaut, Francoise, 62
Third Conference on the Law of
the Sea. See United
Nations Conference on
the Law of the Sea, Third
Third Meeting of the Inter-
American Council of Jurists.
See Inter-American
Council of Jurists
Three-mile zone, 8-9, 11, 38
Tobago, 69, 86, 114(n8),
115(n115)
Togo, 69
Tonga, 69
Tourism, 53
Transport, 45, 62, 68, 109
Tratado sobre la República
(Bobino's), 45
Trinidad, 69, 86, 114(n8),
115(n18)
Truman's Fisheries Proclamation
(1945), 11, 12-14, 17, 34,
101, 117(n31)
Tuna fishing, 28, 50, 144,
148-149
Tuna war, 35
Tunisia, 116(n26)
Twelve-mile limit, 35, 78, 131,
134. See also Territorial
sea
200-Mile Club, 36, 38, 80.
See also 200-mile maritime
zone
200-mile maritime zone, 29-30,
69, 75-80, 92, 117(n31),
133, 134
and Santiago Declaration,
19-24, 75-76
and Santo Domingo Declaration, 85
and sea bed committees, 36
See also Exclusive Economic
Zone; Patrimonial sea;
Territorial Sea

Uganda, 116(n26)
UNCLOS. See United Nations
Conference on the Law of the
Sea, First, Second, Third
UNCTAD. See United Nations
Conference on Trade and
Development
Unilateral claims, 34, 90, 96, 134
United Arab Emirates, 94
United Arab Republic, 114(n8)
United Kingdom, 16, 44, 55, 57,
111, 135, 157
United Nations, 57, 63, 65, 139,
157
 Charter, 44, 54, 63, 65, 140,
 141
 General Assembly, 63, 64, 65,
 66, 79, 80, 91. See also
 Committee on the Peaceful
 Uses of the Sea Bed and the
 Ocean Floor beyond the Limits
 of National Jurisdiction
 See also United Nations
 Conference on the Law of the
 Sea, First, Second, Third;
 United Nations Conference on
 Trade and Development
United Nations Conference on the
 Law of the Sea, First (1958),
 33, 34, 35, 46, 47, 51, 54,
 55, 86, 97, 129, 138, 139.
 See also Contiguous zone;
 Convention on the Continental
 Shelf; Convention on the High
 Seas
United Nations Conference on the
 Law of the Sea, Second, 33, 97
United Nations Conference on the
 Law of the Sea, Third, 1, 13,
 35, 37, 38, 44, 71, 72(n5),
 74(n15), 88
 conflict over high seas in, 51-52
 and contiguous zone, 100
 and customary law, 57-58, 97-98
 draft treaties, 91-92, 94, 95
 and fishery regimes. See
 Fishery regimes
 List of Topics and Questions, 66
 and military use, 54-55, 139.
 See also Military activities
 negotiations. See Negotiations,
 and EEZ
 and NIEO, 58-59

United Nations Conference on the Law of the Sea (continued)
"Peaceful Uses of the Ocean Space, Peace and Security Zones," 139
Rules of Procedure, 74
Single Negotiating Text (1975), 40, 51, 98, 106, 121(n50), 127, 129, 139, 140
and 200-mile limit, 78. See also 200-mile maritime zone
See also Convention on the Law of the Sea; Dispute settlement; Negotiations; United Nations Conference on the Law of the Sea, First, Second
United Nations Conference on Trade and Development (UNCTAD), 64, 65
United States, 8-9, 11-14, 17, 62, 117(n31), 139
and EEZ negotiations, 51, 66, 80, 114(n7)
Executive Order 9634, 13
See also Naval powers; Superpowers; Truman's Fisheries Proclamation
Unlawful activities, 136

Uruguay, 69, 78, 79, 80, 94, 114(n6), 114(n8), 116(n29), 120(n41)

Vann, Prince, 43
de Vattel, Emerich, 8
Venezuela, 15, 16, 86, 111, 114(n8), 115(n18)
Veto, 63, 65. See also Negotiations
Videla, Gabriel González, 27, 29, 30

Warships, 126, 140-141
Western Europe, 62, 68. See also Council of Ministers of the European Community; individual countries
Whaling industry, 28, 29-30, 149-150

Yepes, José María, 34
Yugoslavia, 114(n8), 155

Zaire. See Belgian Congo
Zambia, 116(n26)
Zonists, 92, 93, 112. See also Territorialists

About the Book and Editor

The Exclusive Economic Zone: A Latin American Perspective
edited by Francisco Orrego Vicuña

Developed and implemented over a period of three decades through legislation and practice in the countries of Latin America, the concept of the Exclusive Economic Zone (EEZ) is the most recent of those incorporated into the body of international law resulting from the Third United Nations Law of the Sea Conference. A distinguished group of Latin American jurists and diplomats--most of whom were participants in Law of the Sea negotiations--present in this book their views on various aspects of the EEZ. This first systematic analysis of the EEZ concept grew out of a conference sponsored by the Institute of International Studies at the University of Chile.

Francisco Orrego Vicuña is currently ambassador of Chile to Great Britain. He is also professor of International Law at the Institute of International Studies of the University of Chile and the Law School of the University of Chile. He is the former vice-chairman and head of the Delegation of Chile to the Law of the Sea Conference.